Honda Civic Owners Workshop Manual

by J H Haynes
Associate Member of the Guild of Motoring Writers
and Adrian Sharp

Models covered

Honda Civic 1169 cc (71.4 cu in)
Honda Civic 1237 cc (75.5 cu in)

ISBN 0 85696 160 4

Printed in England   *(160 - 9A1)*

**J H HAYNES AND COMPANY LIMITED
SPARKFORD YEOVIL SOMERSET ENGLAND**
distributed in the USA by
**HAYNES PUBLICATIONS INC.
9421 WINNETKA AVENUE
CHATSWORTH LOS ANGELES
CALIFORNIA 91311 USA**

Acknowledgements

Thanks are due to the Honda Motor Company Limited for their assistance with technical information and the supply of certain illustrations. Castrol Limited supplied information on lubrication.

Car mechanics magazine kindly provided many of the photographs used in the bodywork repair Section of Chapter 11.

Burnham-on-Sea Motors Limited supplied the Honda Civic used in our workshop to obtain the photographs which illustrate this manual.

Lastly, we are grateful to all of those people at Sparkford who helped in the production of this manual. Particularly, Brian Horsfall and Les Brazier, who carried out the mechanical work and took the photographs, respectively; Rod Grainger who edited the text and Stanley Randolph who planned the layout of each page.

About this manual

The aim of this manual is to help Honda Civic owners who wish to carry out their own maintenance and repair work, efficiently and effectively.

The step-by-step photographs show how to deal with major repair tasks, and should with the text and 'exploded' illustrations, make all the work quite clear - even to the novice who has never attempted the more complex job.

It is the practice of J. H. Haynes and Company Ltd., to procure an example of the car with which the projected manual will deal. The car is dismantled in their workshop by a mechanic, a photographer and the author.

They examine all the facets of the tasks which the reader might expect to do, and photographs are taken to help illustrate essential points from the text.

From practical experience therefore, we have found that the Honda Civic is not a particularly difficult car to maintain, and fortunately for you, the owner of a Civic, we found that few special tools were required to complete all the repair and maintenance tasks covered in this book.

We hope you will find that the Civic deserves the various awards it has received internationally.

Using the manual

The manual is divided into eleven Chapters, each covering a logical sub-division of the vehicle. The Chapters are each divided into numbered Sections, and the Sections into paragraphs (or sub-Sections). The paragraphs have decimal numbers following on from the Section number (eg; 5.3 is the third paragraph in Section 5).

The manual is freely illustrated, especially in those parts where there is a detailed sequence of operations to be carried out. There are two forms of illustration; figures and photographs. The figures are numbered in sequence with decimal numbers, according to their position in the Chapter (eg; Fig 6.4 is the fourth illustration in Chapter 6). Photographs have numbers which relate to the Section and paragraph of the text where the operation they show is described (eg; photo 6.31 relates to paragraph 31 of Section 6, in the same Chapter as the photo appears).

There is an alphabetical index at the back of this manual as well as a contents list at the front and on the first page of every Chapter.

Reference to the 'left' and 'right' of the vehicle is in the sense of a person in a seat facing forwards, towards the front of the car.

Where appropriate, fault diagnosis instructions are given at the end of Chapters. Accurate diagnosis of faults depends on a careful, and above all, systematic approach, so avoid the attitude: 'If all else fails, read the book'. It is better, and almost always quicker, to say: 'This could be one of several things, so let's have a look at the *Haynes* manual before trying anything'.

Every care has been taken to assure the accuracy of this manual but no liability can be accepted by the authors' or publisher's for any loss, damage or injury caused by any errors in, or omissions from, the information given.

Contents

4

Honda Civic 1200 - UK

Honda Civic 1200 with Hatchback option - UK

Honda Civic 1200 - US

Engine compartment -
Honda Civic 1200

As this book has been written in England, it uses the appropriate English component names, phrases, and spelling. Some of these differ from those used in America. Normally, these cause no difficulty, but to make sure, a glossary is printed below. In ordering spare parts remember the parts list will probably use these words:

Glossary

English	American	English	American
Accelerator	Gas pedal	Roof rack	Car-top carrier
Alternator	Generator (AC)	Saloon	Sedan
Anti-roll bar	Stabiliser or sway bar	Seized	Frozen
Choke/venturi	Barrel	Side indicator lights	Side marker lights
Battery	Energizer	Side light	Parking light
Bonnet (engine cover)	Hood	Silencer	Muffler
Boot lid	Trunk lid	Spanner	Wrench
Boot (luggage compartment)	Trunk	Sill panel (beneath doors)	Rocker panel
Bottom gear	1st gear	Split cotter (for valve spring cap)	Lock (for valve spring retainer)
Bulkhead	Firewall	Split pin	Cotter pin
Camfollower or tappet	Valve lifter or tappet	Steering arm	Spindle arm
Carburettor	Carburetor	Sump	Oil pan
Catch	Latch	Tab washer	Tang; lock
Circlip	Snap ring	Tailgate	Liftgate
Clearance	Lash	Tappet	Valve lifter
Crownwheel	Ring gear (of differential)	Thrust bearing	Throw-out bearing
Disc (brake)	Rotor/disk	Top gear	High
Driveshaft	Propellor shaft	Trackrod (of steering)	Tie-rod (or connecting rod)
Drop arm	Pitman arm	Trailing shoe (of brake)	Secondary shoe
Drop head coupe	Convertible	Transmission	Whole drive line
Dynamo	Generator (DC)	Tyre	Tire
Earth (electrical)	Ground	Van	Panel wagon/van
Engineer's blue	Prussion blue	Vice	Vise
Estate car	Station wagon	Wheel nut	Lug nut
Exhaust manifold	Header	Windscreen	Windshield
Fast back (Coupe)	Hard top	Wing/mudguard	Fender
Fault finding/diagnosis	Trouble shooting		
Float chamber	Float bowl		
Free-play	Lash		
Freewheel	Coast		
Gudgeon pin	Piston pin or wrist pin		
Gearchange	Shift		
Gearbox	Transmission		
Halfshaft	Axle-shaft		
Handbrake	Parking brake		
Hood	Soft top		
Hot spot	Heat riser		
Indicator	Turn signal		
Interior light	Dome lamp		
Layshaft (of gearbox)	Counter shaft		
Leading shoe (of brake)	Primary shoe		
Locks	Latches		
Motorway	Freeway, turnpike etc.		
Number plate	Licence plate		
Paraffin	Kerosene		
Petrol	Gasoline		
Petrol tank	Gas tank		
'Pinking'	'Pinging'		
Quarter light	Quarter window		
Retread	Recap		
Reverse	Back-up		
Rocker cover	Valve cover		

Miscellaneous points

An "Oil seal" is fitted to components lubricated by grease!

A "Damper" is a "Shock absorber" it damps out bouncing, and absorbs shocks of bump impact. Both names are correct, and both are used haphazardly.

Note that British drum brakes are different from the Bendix type that is common in America, so different descriptive names result. The shoe end furthest from the hydraulic wheel cylinder is on a pivot; interconnection between the shoes as on Bendix brakes is most uncommon. Therefore the phrase "Primary" or "Secondary" shoe does not apply. A shoe is said to be Leading or Trailing. A "Leading" shoe is one on which a point on the drum, as it rotates forward, reaches the shoe at the end worked by the hydraulic cylinder before the anchor end. The opposite is a trailing shoe, and this one has no self servo from the wrapping effect of the rotating drum.

Routine maintenance

Diligent inspection and maintenance should be regarded as absolutely essential for ensuring safety, and desirable for the purpose of obtaining economy and performance from the car.

The maintenance instructions listed are those recommended by Honda, and they are supplemented by tasks which experience has shown need to be carried out.

Weekly, before a long journey, or every 250 miles

1 **Engine:** Check the level of the engine oil, add oil as necessary until the level reaches the full mark on the dipstick.
2 **Battery:** Check the level of electrolyte in the battery and top-up with distilled water as necessary.
3 **Radiator:** Check the coolant level in the reserve tank beside the battery. Top-up the tank to the 'Full' mark with coolant and antifreeze. Use inhibited coolant for the aluminium engine.
4 **Tyres:** Check the tyre pressure with an accurate gauge and adjust as necessary. Inspect the tyre walls and treads for damage; remember that the law (UK) requires the tread should be at least 1 mm deep across three-quarters of the width of the tread around the whole periphery of the tyre.
5 **Hydraulic fluid reservoir:** Check the level of the hydraulic fluid in the reservoirs for the brake systems. It should be between the 'max'-'min' marks on the side of each reservoir. If either needs replenishing weekly, check the brake hydraulic system for leaks.
6 **Wheel bolts:** Check the tightness of the wheel nuts; do not over-tighten.
7 **Windscreen washer:** Refill the windscreen washer sack with soft water. Add an antifreeze satchet in cold weather. (**Do not use ordinary antifreeze**). Check that the jets operate clearly and accurately.
8 **Lights, wipers, horns:** Check for satisfactory functioning of all electrical systems on the car, including the brake lights and 'winkers'.

Every 3,000 miles

Tasks in addition to the 250 mile routine checks:
1 **Engine:** Renew the engine oil and the oil filter. Honda advise that the engine oil be changed every 3,000 miles, or even more frequently if operating conditions are particularly arduous.

Drain the sump when the engine is hot: a container of at least 6 pints will be required to collect the oil.

Once the oil has been drained, replace the plug in the sump and fill to the 'full' mark on the dipstick with new engine oil. Fit a new filter.

Start the engine, and run for a few minutes and re-check the level of engine oil-topping-up as necessary.
2 **Engine:** Adjust and check the following items:

Check the rocker/valve clearance, as detailed in Chapter 1 of this manual.

Check the alternator drivebelt, as directed in Chapter 2.

Check the tightness of the intake and exhaust manifold fasteners.
3 **Carburation:** Check the idle speed setting and idle mixture control with respect to Carbon Monoxide emissions.

Inspect the operation of the choke mechanism throttle opener and control valve. Details in Chapter 3.

Check the fuel lines and connections.
4 **Brake system:** Check the adjustment of the rear brakes - detailed in Chapter 9.

Check the operation and adjustment of the handbrake - detailed in Chapter 9.

Every 6,000 miles

Tasks in addition to the 250 mile routine and 3,000 mile checks:
Brake system: Examine all the brake pipes and hoses - look for leaks, cracks, corrosion and surface deterioration. Details, Chapter 9.

Check the thickness of the friction material on the front brakes and rear brakes. Inspection details in Chapter 9.
Clutch system: Check the clutch pedal travel and adjust if necessary. Refer to Chapter 5.
Exhaust system: Check the condition of the exhaust pipes, silencers and supports.

Every 12,000 miles

Tasks in addition to those listed to be completed at 250, 3,000 and 6,000 miles:
Engine: Examine the vacuum lines and hoses, replace any that are cracked or perished.

Examine all cooling system hoses and connections - Again replace any that are beginning to perish.

Clean the radiator exterior to clear the core of dust and debris.
Air cleaner: Replace the air filter. If the car is used in dusty conditions the filter should be replaced more frequently. It cannot be properly cleaned and re-used.

Carburation: Check the operation of the air intake temperature control system.

Check operation of carbon canister and idle cut off valve.

Check condition of fuel line, one-way valve and fuel filler cap

Refer to Chapter 3, for details of the carburation system checks.
Ignition system: Refer to Chapter 4 of this manual, and complete the following checks and adjustments:
i)   *Replace the contact breaker points and reset gap*
ii)   *Replace spark plugs*
iii) *Check and adjust the engine ignition timing*
iv)   *Examine the distributor cap*
v)   *Check the operation of the vacuum actuated idle retard system.*
Brake system: Clean the air filter on the vacuum servo unit. Refer To Chapter 9.
Front suspension and steering: Refer to Chapter 7, and check the following:
i)   *Front wheel alignment*
ii)   *Ball joints on tie rods and lower control arm*
iii) *Rack play*
iv)   *Steering wheel play, rotation, axial and radial*
Steering system torce at steering wheel

Every 24,000 miles or 2 years (whichever sooner)

All checks, replacements and tasks detailed in intervals of 250, 3,000, 6,000 and 12,000 miles, and then in addition, the following:
Engine: Replace the coolant. Use inhibited coolant for aluminium engines. When new, the strength of antifreeze protects to temperatures of -35°C.
Carburation: Replace the fuel filter. Replace the carbon canister.
Ignition system: Replace the distributor cap and rotor.
Brake system: Replace the hydraulic fluid in the brake system (See Chapter 9).
Transmission: Replace the transmission oil. (Chapter 6).

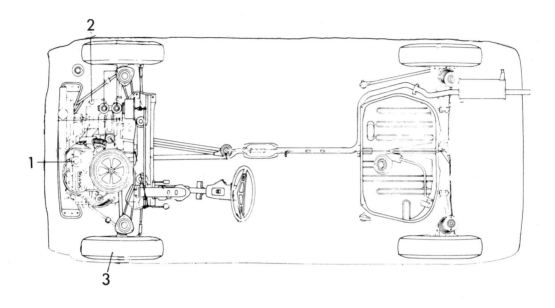

Recommended lubricants

1	Engine	Castrol GTX
2	Gearbox (manual)	Castrol GTX
2	Gearbox (automatic)	Castrol TQ Dexron R
3	Wheel bearings	Castrol LM Grease

Note: the above recommendations are general and are intended for guidance only. Lubrication requirements vary from territory-to-territory. Consult the operators handbook supplied with your car.

Buying spare parts
and vehicle identification numbers

Buying spare parts

Spare parts are available from many sources, for example: Honda garages, other garages and accessory shops, and motor factors. Our advice regarding spare part sources is as follows:

Officially appointed Honda garages - These are the best source of parts which are peculiar to your car and are otherwise not generally available (eg; complete cylinder heads, internal gearbox components, badges, interior trim etc). It is also the only place at which you should buy parts if your car is still under warranty; non-Honda components may invalidate the warranty. To be sure of obtaining the correct parts it will always be necessary to give the storeman your car's engine and chassis number, and if possible, to take the 'old' part along for positive identification. Remember that many parts are available on a factory exchange scheme - any parts returned should always be clean! It obviously makes good sense to go straight to the specialists on your car for this type of part for they are best equipped to supply you.

Other garages and accessory shops - These are often very good places to buy materials and components needed for the maintenance of your car (eg; oil filters, spark plugs, bulbs, fan belts, oils and greases, touch-up paint, filler paste etc). They also sell general accessories, usually have convenient opening hours, charge lower prices and can often be found not far from home.

Motor factors - Good factors will stock all of the more important components which wear out relatively quickly (eg; clutch components, pistons, valves, exhaust systems, brake cylinders/pipes/hoses/seals/shoes and pads etc). Motor factors will often provide new or reconditioned components on a part exchange basis - this can save a considerable amount of money.

Vehicle identification numbers

The chassis number is stamped on a plate attached to the engine compartment bulkhead on the top right-hand side.

The engine number is stamped on the cylinder block casting, adjacent to the starter motor.

Engine and chassis numbers are repeated on the vehicle identification plate attached to the engine compartment front frame.

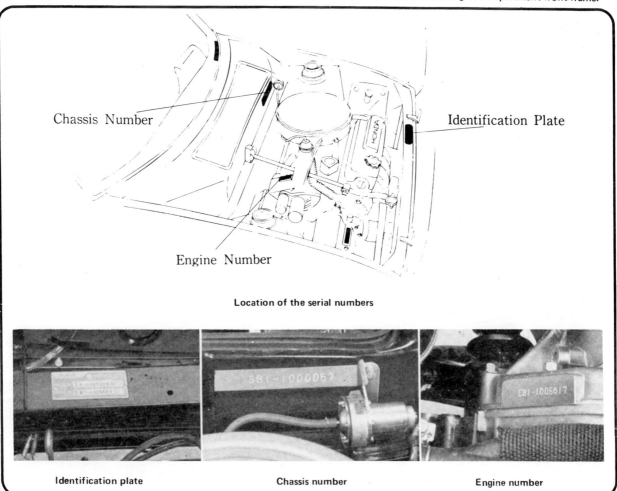

Chassis Number

Identification Plate

Engine Number

Location of the serial numbers

Identification plate   Chassis number   Engine number

Chapter 1 Engine

Contents

Specifications

Dimensions in millimetres, inches in brackets.

Engine (general):

Type	Transverse, 4 cylinder, in-line, ohv, water cooled	
Capacity	1169 cc (71.4 cu in.) or 1237 cc (75.5 cu in.)	
	1169 cc	**1237 cc**
Bore	70 mm	72 mm
Stroke	76 mm	76 mm
Compression ratio	8.3 : 1	8.1 : 1

Crankshaft and main bearings:

Rotation	Anticlockwise (viewed from pulley end)	
	Dimension *	**Service limit ***
Diameter		
Journal	50.0 - 49.97 (1.9685 - 1.9673)	—
Crankpin	40.0 - 39.97 (1.5748 - 1.5736)	—
Out of round		
Journal	0.005 (0.0002), max.	0.010 (0.0004)
Crankpin	0.005 (0.0002), max.	0.010 (0.0004)
Axial play	0.10 - 0.35 (0.0039 - 0.0138)	0.45 (0.0177)
Bend	0.03 (0.0013), max.	0.05 (0.0020)

	Dimension *	Service limit *
Crankpin bearing		
Axial play	0.2 - 0.45 (0.0079 - 0.0177)	—
Oil clearance	0.020 - 0.038 (0.0008 - 0.0015)	0.07 (0.0028)
Main bearing		
Oil clearance	0.024 - 0.042 (0.0009 - 0.0017)	0.07 (0.0028)
Lug axial play	0.2 - 0.45 (0.0079 - 0.0177)	

Gudgeon pins:

Fit	Interference (in connecting rod small end)	
Diameter of gudgeon pin bore in piston	17.01 - 17.016 (0.6697 - 0.6699)	17.03 (0.6705)
Gudgeon pin clearance	0.010 - 0.022 (0.0004 - 0.0008)	0.05 (0.0020)

Connecting rods:

Press-fitting interference with gudgeon pin	0.016 - 0.039 (0.0006 - 0.0015)	0.016 (0.0006)
Big-end axial play	0.15 - 0.30 (0.0059 - 0.0118)	0.4 (0.0157)
Bend between big and small ends	0.08/100 (3/100000), max.	—

Pistons and piston rings:

Note: all pistons and rings can be obtained in four oversizes +0.25 mm, +0.50 mm, +0.75 mm and +1.00 mm.

1169 cc engine

Outside diameter at skirt	69.98 - 70.00 (2.7551 - 2.7559)	69.91 (2.7524)
Minimum clearance in cylinder	0.03 (0.0012)	0.10 (0.0039)
Piston ring groove width:		
Top	1.510 - 1.520 (0.0594 - 0.0598)	1.55 (0.0610)
Second	1.510 - 1.520 (0.0594 - 0.0598)	1.55 (0.0610)
Oil	2.805 - 2.820 (0.1104 - 0.1110)	2.85 (0.1122)
Piston rings:		
Travel in groove:		
Top	0.020 - 0.045 (0.0008 - 0.0018)	0.13 (0.0051)
Second	0.020 - 0.045 (0.0008 - 0.0018)	0.13 (0.0051)
Ring gap:		
Top	0.2 - 0.4 (0.0079 - 0.0157)	0.6 (0.0236)
Second	0.2 - 0.4 (0.0079 - 0.0157)	0.6 (0.0236)
Oil	0.2 - 0.9 (0.0079 - 0.0354)	1.1 (0.0433)

1237 cc engine

Outside diameter at skirt	71.98 - 72.00 (2.8339 - 2.8345)	71.91 (2.8311)
Minimum clearance in cylinder	0.03 (0.0012)	0.10 (0.0039)
Piston ring groove width:		
Top	1.510 - 1.520 (0.0594 - 0.0598)	1.55 (0.0610)
Second	1.510 - 1.520 (0.0594 - 0.0598)	1.55 (0.0610)
Oil	2.805 - 2.820 (0.1104 - 0.1110)	2.85 (0.1122)
Piston rings:		
Travel in groove:		
Top	0.020 - 0.045 (0.0008 - 0.0018)	0.13 (0.0051)
Second	0.020 - 0.045 (0.0008 - 0.0018)	0.13 (0.0051)

Ring gap:	Dimension *	Service limit *
Top	0.25 - 0.40 (0.0098 - 0.0157	0.60 (0.0236)
Second	0.25 - 0.40 (0.0098 - 0.0157)	0.60 (0.0236)
Oil	0.30 - 0.90 (0.0118 - 0.0394)	1.10 (0.0433)

Valves and valve gear:

Valve timing:

1169 cc engine and 1237 cc engine (Valve clearance Zero).

Inlet valve open	10⁰ after top dead centre
Inlet valve closes	20⁰ after bottom dead centre
Exhaust valve open	30⁰ before bottom dead centre
Exhaust valve closes	10⁰ before top dead centre

Valve guide inside diameter:	Dimension *	Service limit *
Inlet	6.61 - 6.63 (0.2602 - 0.2610)	6.65 (0.2618)
Exhaust	6.61 - 6.63 (0.2602 - 0.2610)	6.65 (0.2618)
Valve stem outside diameter:		
Inlet	6.580 - 6.590 (0.2591 - 0.2594)	6.55 (0.2579)
Exhaust	6.55 - 6.56 (0.2579 - 0.2583)	6.52 (0.2567)
Valve guide to stem clearance:		
Inlet	0.01 - 0.04 (0.0004 - 0.0016)	0.08 (0.0031)
Exhaust	0.05 - 0.08 (0.0020 - 0.0031)	0.11 (0.0043)
Valve seat:		
Width:		
Inlet	1.4 (0.0551)	—
Exhaust	1.4 (0.0551)	—
Sinkage	0	0.2 (0.0079)
Valve spring:		
Free length:		
Inner	42.0 (1.6535)	41.0 (1.6142)
Outer	39.95 (1.5728)	38.9 (1.5315)
Squareness (degrees):		
Inner	± 2⁰	1.5⁰
Outer	± 2⁰	1.5⁰
Valve clearances (cold):		
USA type (Inlet and Exhaust)	0.13 - 0.17 (0.005 - 0.007)	—
Other types (Inlet and Exhaust)	0.10 - 0.14 (0.004 - 0.006)	—

Camshaft:

	Dimension	Service limit
Oil clearance	0.05 - 0.09 (0.0020 - 0.0035)	—
Axial play	—	0.5 (0.0197)
Cam height:		
Inlet	36.77 - 36.48 (1.4477 - 1.4363)	0.3 (0.0118)
Exhaust	36.65 - 36.35 (1.4429 - 1.4311)	0.3 (0.0118)
Bend	0.03 (0.0012)	0.05 (0.0020)

Rockers:

Rocker arm shaft to cam holder clearance	0.006 - 0.051 (0.0024 - 0.0020)	0.08 (0.0032)
Inside diameter of rocker arm	15.00 - 15.018 (0.5906 - 0.5913)	15.03 (0.5927)

Cylinder block:

Type	Aluminium alloy, with cast iron liners

Cylinder head:

	Dimension *	Service limit *
Gasketed surface warpage	0.03 (0.0012)	0.10 (0.0039)

Cylinders (1169 cc engines):

	Dimension *	Service limit *
Inside diameter (I.D.)	70.00 - 70.015 (2.7559 - 2.7565)	70.10 (2.7598)
Difference in I.D.s between top and bottom	—	0.05 (0.0020)
Difference in I.D.s between cylinders	0.01 (0.0004), max.	0.05 (0.0020)
Wear	—	1.00 (0.03937), max.

Cylinders (1237 cc engines):

	Dimension *	Service limit *
Inside diameter (I.D.)	72.00 - 72.015 (2.8345 - 2.8352)	72.10 (2.8386)
Difference in I.D.s between top and bottom	—	0.05 (0.0020)
Difference in I.D.s between cylinders	0.01 (0.0004), max.	0.05 (0.0020)
Wear	—	0.50 (0.0197)

Lubrication system:

	Dimension *	Service limit *
Oil regulator pressure setting, kg/cm^2 (lb/in^2)	3.5 - 4.1 (49.77 - 58.30)	1.5 (21.33), min. (at 80° C or 176° F and at idle speed)
Oil pump:		
Displacement, litres (US gal.)/min.	32 (8.4)	—
Inner-to-outer rotor radial clearance	0.15 (0.0059)	0.2 (0.0079)
Outer rotor-to-body radial clearance	0.1 - 0.18 (0.0039 - 0.0071)	0.2 (0.0079)
Rotor-to-body side clearance	0.03 - 0.10 (0.0012 - 0.0039)	0.15 (0.0059)

Table 1 (Main bearing shell selection):

Corresponding crankshaft main journal diameter - bearing shell seat diameter - main bearing shell thickness and colour code.

The figures 1, 2, 3 or 4 are stamped on the crankshaft near to the main journals to indicate dimension class of main bearing.

The letters A, B, C or D are stamped on the sump - cylinder block face to indicate the class of main bearing seat bore for each bearing.

Note: oil clearances are already accommodated. Dimensions are in millimetres (inches in brackets).

Cylinder counterbore 54 (2.13)	A	B	C	D
Journal dia. 50 (1.97)	0 - + 0.006 (+0.0002)	+0.006 - +0.012 (+0.0002 - 0.0005)	+0.012 - +0.018 (0.0005 - 0.0007)	+0.018 - +0.024 (0.0007 - 0.0009)
1	**Red**	**Pink**	**Yellow**	**Green**
0 - −0.006 (−0.0002)	−0.002 - −0.005 (−0.0001 - −0.0002)	+0.001 - −0.002 (0.00004 - −0.0001)	+0.004 - +0.001 (+0.0002 - 0.00004)	+0.007 - +0.004 (+0.0003 - +0.0002)
2	**Pink**	**Yellow**	**Green**	**Brown**
−0.006 - −0.012 (−0.0002 - −0.0005)	+0.001 - −0.002 (0.00004 - −0.0001)	+0.004 - +0.001 (+0.0002 - 0.00004)	+0.007 - +0.004 (+0.0003 - +0.0002)	+0.010 - +0.007 (+0.0004 - +0.0003)
3	**Yellow**	**Green**	**Brown**	**Black**
−0.012 - −0.018 (−0.0005 - −0.0007)	+0.004 - +0.001 (+0.0002 - 0.00004)	+0.007 - +0.004 (+0.0003 - +0.0002)	+0.010 - +0.007 (+0.0004 - +0.0003)	+0.013 - +0.010 (+0.0005 - +0.0004)
4	**Green**	**Brown**	**Black**	**Blue**
−0.018 - −0.024 (−0.0007 - −0.0009)	+0.007 - +0.004 (+0.0003 - +0.0002)	+0.010 - +0.007 (+0.0004 - +0.0003)	+0.013 - +0.010 (+0.0005 - +0.0004)	+0.016 - +0.013 (+0.0006 - +0.0005)

Main bearing centre stock thickness: 2.0 (0.079)

Table 2 (Big-end bearing shell selection):

Corresponding crankpin diameter class - big end bearing seat bore class - big-end bearing shell thickness and colour code.

The figures 1, 2, 3 or 4 are stamped on the connecting rod near to the big-end to indicate the class of the bearing seat diameter. The number should not be confused with any mark indicating the con-rods position on the engine.

The letters A, B, C or D are stamped on the crankshaft to indicate the class of the crankpin diameter. **Note:** oil clearances are already accommodated. Dimensions are in millimetres (inches are in brackets).

Connecting rod dia. 43 (1.69)	1	2	3	4
Crankpin dia. 40 (1.57)	0 - +0.006 (+0.0002)	+0.006 - +0.012 (+0.0002 - +0.0005)	+0.012 - +0.018 (+0.0005 - +0.0007)	+0.018 - +0.024 (+0.0007 - +0.0009)
A	**Red**	**Pink**	**Yellow**	**Green**
0 - −0.006 (−0.0002)	−0.005 - −0.008 (−0.0002 - −0.0003)	−0.002 - −0.005 (−0.0001 - −0.0002)	+0.001 - −0.002 (0.00004 - −0.0001)	+0.004 - +0.001 (+0.0002 - 0.00004)
B	**Pink**	**Yellow**	**Green**	**Brown**
−0.006 - −0.012 (−0.0002 - −0.0005)	−0.002 - −0.005 (−0.0001 - −0.0002)	+0.001 - −0.002 (0.00004 - −0.0001)	+0.004 - +0.001 (+0.0002 - 0.00004)	+0.007 - +0.004 (+0.0003 - +0.0002)
C	**Yellow**	**Green**	**Brown**	**Black**
−0.012 - −0.018 (−0.0005 - −0.0007)	+0.001 - −0.002 (0.00004 - −0.0001)	+0.004 - +0.001 (+0.0002 - 0.00004)	+0.007 - +0.004 (+0.0003 - +0.0002)	+0.010 - +0.007 (+0.0004 - +0.0003)
D	**Green**	**Brown**	**Black**	**Blue**
−0.018 - −0.024 (−0.0007 - −0.0009)	+0.004 - +0.001 (+0.0002 - 0.00004)	+0.007 - +0.004 (+0.0003 - +0.0002)	+0.010 - +0.007 (+0.0004 - +0.0003)	+0.013 - +0.010 (+0.0005 - +0.0004)

Connecting rod bearing centre stock thickness: 1.5 (0.059)

Torque wrench settings:

	kg fm	lb f ft
Crankshaft bearing cap bolt	3.7 - 4.3	27 - 31
Connecting rod bearing cap bolt	2.5 - 2.9	18 - 21
Overhead cam holder	1.8 - 2.2	13 - 16
Flywheel to crankshaft bolts	4.7 - 5.3	34 - 38
Clutch cover to flywheel bolts	1.0 - 1.4	7 - 10
Cylinder head bolts:		
Engine number: up to EB1 - 1019949	4.2 - 4.8	30 - 35
from EB1 - 1019950	5.1 - 5.9	37 - 42
from EB2 - 1000000	5.1 - 5.9	37 - 42
Crankshaft pulley	4.7 - 5.3	34 - 38
Timing belt driven pulley	2.5 - 3.5	18 - 25
Engine mount bracket	31.1 - 31.9	22 - 28
Intake manifold	1.8 - 2.4	13 - 17
Carburettor mount nuts	0.8 - 1.2	6 - 9
Sump	0.3 - 0.7	2 - 5
Clutch housing/sump bracket	0.3 - 0.7	2 - 5
Fuel pump	1.8 - 2.4	13 - 17
Tappet adjusting nut	1.8 - 2.2	13 - 16
Oil filter	1.5 - 2.0	11 - 14
Water pump	1.0 - 1.4	7 - 10
Exhaust manifold	1.8 - 2.4	13 - 17
Oil pump assembly to crank bearing cage	1.0 - 1.4	7 - 10
Oil pass block	1.0 - 1.4	7 - 10
Oil pump gear holder	1.0 - 1.4	7 - 10
Sump drain plug	4.0 - 5.0	29 - 36
Cylinder head cover	0.8 - 1.2	6 - 9
Breather cover	0.7 - 1.1	5 - 8
Tachometer special bolt	1.0 - 1.4	7 - 10
Thermoswitch	2.0 - 2.5	14 - 18
Spark plugs	1.3 - 1.7	9 - 12
Distributor fixing plate	1.0 - 1.4	7 - 10
Oil pressure sensor	1.4 - 1.8	10 - 13
Alternator mounting bolts	4.0 - 4.6	29 - 33
Alternator stay bolt	2.0 - 2.5	14 - 18
Transmission drain plug	3.5 - 4.5	25 - 33
Clutch housing/cylinder block	4.0 - 5.0	29 - 36
Starter motor bolts	4.0 - 5.0	29 - 36
Transmission case to clutch housing	2.3 - 3.1	17 - 22
Transmission end cover	1.0 - 1.4	7 - 10
Reversing light switch	2.3 - 2.7	17 - 20
Timing belt upper cover and lower cover	0.8 - 1.2	6 - 9
Hot air intake bolts	1.0 - 1.4	7 - 10
Speedometer cable gear	0.7 - 1.0	5 - 7
Clutch cable stay	2.0 - 2.8	14 - 20
Exhaust manifold	1.9 - 2.5	14 - 18
Exhaust manifold and pipe	1.9 - 2.5	14 - 18
Engine centre support beam	3.5 - 4.3	25 - 31
Engine mount centre rubber to beam	1.0 - 1.6	7 - 12
Engine mount rubber to engine	1.9 - 2.5	14 - 18
Engine torque reaction rod to body	3.5 - 4.3	25 - 31
Lower control arm balljoint nut	3.0 - 4.0	22 - 29

1 General description

The engine has been designed to provide the Civic with a lively and economical performance; many of the engine's features can be found on the motor cycle engines Honda produce.

Beginning at the top, the cylinder head is of a 'cross-flow' design, the inlet and exhaust valves are arranged on an hemispherical combustion chamber. They are operated by rockers in contact with a single camshaft mounted centrally on the aluminium alloy cylinder head.

The distributor is mounted on the carburettor side of the cylinder head and is driven from a helical gear out at the forward end of the camshaft, next to the camshaft wheel.

A second gear is cut midway on the camshaft and this drives the oil pump coupling shaft which runs vertically through the centre of the engine.

At the rear end of the camshaft there is an additional lobe which activates the mechanical fuel pump mounted beside the inlet manifold. The camshaft is driven from the crankshaft by a toothed fabric belt.

The cylinder block is of aluminium alloy with cast iron inclusions providing for the cylinders themselves.

The crankshaft is supported on five main bearings as is usual, but a new feature is the supporting of the main bearings on a single cradle rather than the conventional individual main bearing caps. This large cradle has oil galleries drilled in to take oil from the pump (also mounted on the cradle) to the main bearings and, via the crankshaft, to the big-ends. The gallery in the cradle also distributes oil to drillings in the cylinder block which take the oil to the camshaft bearings, distributor drive and the oil pump drive.

The engine is equipped with a single compound carburettor which is one of the keys to the engine's economical performance.

Having provided a cross-flow cylinder head and hemispherical combustion chambers, there are naturally four inlet ports and four exhaust. The inlet and exhaust manifolds have been shaped to minimise the resistance to flow of the 'gases' through them.

The inlet manifold is warmed by water from the cylinder head and cylinder block water jacket. The route which the cooling water takes provides another interesting feature of the engine. The cool water from the base of the radiator is impelled around the cylinder, and cylinder head jackets, by a belt driven centrifugal action pump mounted on the front end of the engine. All the water flows from the cylinder head into the inlet manifold jacket. It leaves the inlet manifold block for the top of the radiator via the thermostat housing at the rear end of the inlet manifold.

The impressions gained of this engine are of neat and compact design; these are essential attributes when there is a requirement for an economical, responsive and lightweight unit for a front wheel drive transverse engined small car.

2 Major operations possible with engine in place

The following major operations can be carried out on the engine with it in place in the car:

1 *The removal and refitting of the cylinder head assembly.*
2 *The removal and refitting of the sump/oil pump.*
3 *The removal and refitting of the big-ends.*
4 *The removal and refitting of the pistons and conrods.*
5 *The removal and refitting of the water pump.*

3 Major operations requiring engine removal

The following operations can only be carried out with the engine out of the car:

1 *Removal and refitting of the main bearings*
2 *Removal and refitting of the crankshaft.*
3 *Removal and refitting of the timing belt.*
4 *Removal and refitting of the flywheel.*

4 Methods and equipment for engine removal

1 The engine should be removed together with the transmission, the assembly being separated on the bench. The gearbox and final drive can be removed from the car separately.
2 Essential equipment includes chassis stands to retain the car at a sufficient height to enable access to the exhaust system and transmission supports. The next piece of essential equipment is a hoist - the engine and gearbox together weigh approximately 150 lbs (68 kg); therefore ensure that all the hoist's equipment can handle that load safely.

5 Engine - removal (with the gearbox)

1 Begin by removing the grille and associated brightwork. Undo the two screws retaining the bottom strip of trim, remove the strip. Then undo and remove the four screws which secure the centre section of the grille to the bodyshell. There is one screw midway along the base of the grille, and three screws along the top of the grille. Finally, remove the two screws which retain the headlight trims in position and remove the trims.
2 Next remove the engine compartment hood, by undoing the bolts which secure it to the hinges; store it carefully to avoid damaging paintwork. (See Chapter 11, Section 12).
3 Remove the radiator filler cap and loosen the draining cock at the base of the radiator to drain the engine cooling system. Collect the coolant in a clean container so that it can be re-used. Turn the car interior heater control to 'hot'. Once the system has been drained tighten the draining cock again.
4 The gearbox/differential oil should be drained as well, otherwise oil will spill out of the differential when the driveshafts are extracted and the engine/transmission unit is raised.
5 The positive and negative leads connecting to the battery

should now be removed. This is an essential safety precaution. Detach the braided engine/transmission earthing strip from the transmission tag.
6 Undo the coolant hose clips and remove the lower hose from the water pump connecting tube, and the upper hose off the thermostat cover. Lastly remove the interior heater hose from the pump connecting tube. Remove the transmission oil cooler hoses from the hondamatic transmission if fitted.
7 Disconnect the fuel intake pipe from the fuel pump, and then detach the fuel vapour tube running between the carbon filled canister and the carburettor from the canister. Catch any spillage from the fuel pipe with a dry cloth.
8 Detach the choke and throttle cables from the carburettor and then the clutch activating cable. Detach the speedometer cable from the end of the gearbox and the tachometer cable.
9 Disconnect the electrical lead from the electric motor on the radiator fan, cooling system temperature sensor, reversing light switch (on the end of the manual gearbox) and the LT and HT leads to the distributor.
10 Disconnect the heavy electrical cables from the starter motor and the heavy leads from the alternator.
11 Remove the cooling system bypass hoses from the 'H' pattern joints and then undo and remove the nut and bolt securing the engine torque reaction rod to the engine block.
12 Remove the radiator complete with hoses and electric fan.
13 It is now necessary to detach the driveshafts from the transmission - this is accomplished as follows:
14 Apply the handbrake, and then jack-up the front of the car supporting it on chassis stands situated beneath the front suspension subframe. (Chapter 11, Section 17).
15 Chock the rear wheels and then move the engine hoist over the engine. Attach the lifting sling to the clutch cable stay and cylinder head, then raise the hoist so that it just accepts the weight of the engine and transmission.
16 Undo and remove the nuts and bolts securing the right-hand engine steady rubber mounting to the engine.
17 Next undo and remove the nuts retaining the exhaust pipe in position and lower the pipe from the engine/transmission unit.
18 It is now necessary to remove the balljoints on the ends of the steering rods and on the ends of the lower suspension control arms. Chapter 8, Section 10, gives details of this operation.
19 By grasping the wheel hub/ brake unit the driveshafts may be pulled from the middle of the differential in the transmission. The engine should be inclined slightly to permit the right-hand side driveshaft to be pulled free.
20 The only two connections which remain are the gearshift mechanism and the lower flexible support.
21 The spring pin which secures the gearshift linkage to the shaft in the gearbox should be driven out with a square faced drift. Next remove the panel on the left-hand side wheel arch, to allow more lateral movement of engine and transmission. (photo)
22 With the engine weight taken by the hoist, undo and remove the two nuts which secure the lower mounting to the suspension subframe. (photo)
23 Pack the holes in the differential casing for the driveshafts with clean, non-fluffy rag, to prevent ingress of foreign matter. Then make a final check that all connections, hoses, electrical leads, and control cables have been disconnected from the engine and transmission and that these items have been safely stowed away so that they cannot be damaged as the engine is lifted out of the car.
24 Raise the engine and transmission slowly, tilting slightly so that it clears the brake master cylinder and pipes, as well as the battery tray. (photos)
25 Once the engine and transmission has been removed from the car the engine and gearbox can be separated. Undo and remove the two nuts and bolts securing the starter motor, and then the bolts which secure the clutch bellhousing to the cylinder block. The gearbox and engine can now be moved apart. (photo) Take care to support the gearbox as the two are separated, the clutch friction plate can be damaged if the gearbox and engine become misaligned.
26 If the engine is going to be dismantled and out of the car for

5.21 Wheel arch panel removal.

5.22 Lower centre engine mounting.

5.24A Engine and transmission removal

5.24B Attitude of engine to clear brake system and bodyshell parts

5.25 Engine and transmission on a bench

a day or so, then it is wise to smear oil or grease onto the mating surfaces of the driveshaft, wrapping them with dry rag to prevent corrosion and collection of dirt.

6 Engine dismantling - preparation

1   It is best to mount the engine on a dismantling stand, but if one is not available stand the engine on a strong bench, to be at a comfortable working height. It can be dismantled on the floor, but it is not easy.

2   During the dismantling process greatest care should be taken to keep the exposed parts free from dirt. As an aid to achieving this, thoroughly clean down the outside of the engine, removing all traces of oil and congealed dirt.

3   To clean the exterior of the engine use paraffin or Gunk: the latter compound will make the job much easier, for after the solvent has been applied and allowed to stand for a time, a vigorous jet of water will wash off the solvent with all the grease and dirt. If the dirt is thick and deeply embedded, work the solvent into it with a stiff brush.

4   Finally wipe down the exterior of the engine with a rag and only then, when it is quite clean, should the dismantling process begin. As the engine is stripped, clean each part in a bath of paraffin or Gunk.

5   Never immerse parts with oilways (for example the crankshaft) in paraffin, but to clean wipe down carefully with a petrol dampened cloth. Oilways can be cleaned out with nylon pipe cleaners. If an airline is available, all parts can be blown dry and the oilways blown through as an added precaution.

6   Re-use of the old engine gaskets is false economy and will lead to oil and water leaks, if nothing worse. Always use new gaskets throughout.

7   Do not throw the old gasket away for it sometimes happens that an immediate replacement cannot be found and the old

gasket is then very useful as a template. Hang up old gaskets as they are removed.

8   To strip the engine it is best to work from the top down. The underside of the crankcase when supported on wooden blocks acts as a firm base. When the stage is reached, where the crankshaft and connecting rods have to be removed, the engine can be turned on its side, and all other work carried out in this position.

9   Whenever possible, replace nuts, bolts and washers finger tight from wherever they are removed. This helps to avoid loss and muddle later. If they cannot be replaced, lay them out in such a fashion that it is clear from whence they came.

7 Ancillary engine components - removal

Before basic engine dismantling begins, it is necessary to strip it of ancillary components as follows:

1   Alternator
2   Distributor
3   Inlet manifold and carburettor
4   Oil filter cartridge
5   Fuel pump
6   Exhaust manifold
7   Water pump

It is possible to remove any of these components with the engine in place in the car, if it is merely the individual items that require attention.

Presuming the engine to be out of the car and on a bench, and that the items listed above are still on the engine follow the procedures described below:

1   Slacken off the alternator retaining nuts and bolts, move the alternator towards the engine and remove the water pump/alternator drivebelt. Continue to undo and remove the nuts and

bolts retaining the alternator to the engine block and then remove the alternator.

2 Before removing the distributor mark the distributor body mounting flange and adjacent engine face so that the distributor can be refitted later into the exact position from which it was taken. Then undo and remove the two bolts securing the clamping plate to the cylinder head. Label the distributor HT leads and LT leads to ensure that they can be readily refitted to their correct locations. Carefully extract the distributor from the cylinder head and store in a safe place.

3 The next ancillary component to be removed is the inlet manifold and carburettor. Note that the thermostat housing is part of the inlet manifold. The inlet manifold is mounted on six studs in the cylinder head, therefore all that is required is to undo the six nuts and the inlet manifold can be removed together with the carburettor. Pull the petrol feed pipe from the carburettor to permit complete separation of the inlet manifold assembly and engine block. Recover the gasket and wipe up any spillage of coolant that has remained in the engine.

4 The fuel pump can be removed before, or after, the inlet manifold. It is secured to the cylinder head by two nuts on studs in the cylinder head. Once the two nuts have been removed the pump can be lifted from the engine.

5 The oil filter cartridge on the front side of the engine is of the disposable type and is removed simply by unscrewing from the thread boss in the cylinder block. Wipe up the small spillage of oil.

6 The exhaust manifold should be removed next. Like the inlet manifold, it is retained on the cylinder head by eight nuts on eight studs in the cylinder head. Lift the exhaust manifold from the cylinder head and recover the old gasket.

7 The last of the ancillary components to be removed from the engine is the water pump. This is retained in the cylinder block by four bolts. It is unnecessary to remove the pump pulley. Recover the rubber sealing ring which is seated in a groove in the pump body side of the body/cylinder block joint surfaces.

8 The engine is now stripped of its ancillary components and is ready for the major dismantling tasks to begin.

8 Timing belt - removal, refitting and adjustment

1 The timing belt is a glass fibre reinforced rubber toothed belt, which passes over the camshaft wheel, and the drive wheel on the end of the crankshaft. The belt is maintained at its correct tension by a spring loaded roller.

Adjusting the belt tension
2 This task can be completed while the engine is in the car; the tensioning roller is mounted on a plate. A tension spring acts on the plate to push the roller against the belt. The bolts which retain the plate in position project through the timing belt cover and can therefore, easily be reached.

3 To adjust the belt, loosen both tensioner and adjusting bolts

projecting through the cover. Allow the spring acting on the roller mounting plate to move the roller against the belt and tension it. Once the belt tension has been adjusted, retighten the tension and adjuster bolts.

4 **Do not apply any force other than that of the tension spring on the roller mounting plate to adjust the tension of the belt.** belt.

5 It will be wise to check the ignition timing after the belt has been adjusted, and also watch for any oil or water leaks and abnormal noise.

Timing belt removal
6 The timing belt will need to be removed whenever the engine is going to be fully dismantled or when the tensioning mechanism has reached its limit of travel. The normal life of the timing belt is around 36,000 miles, and therefore it should be replaced in any event at that interval.

7 It will be necessary to remove the engine from the car in order to gain sufficient access to the front of the engine to be able to remove the timing belt.

8 With the engine out of the car and on a bench, proceed as follows:

9 Slacken the alternator retaining bolts and move the unit towards the engine to loosen the water pump/alternator drive-belt. Remove the belt.

10 Turn the engine until No. 1 piston is at tdc, and then hold the engine in that position. Honda do supply a specially shaped block which bolts onto the crankcase cylinder block and which engages a tooth on the flywheel ring gear. If this block is not available from the local agent it is well worth while fabricating a similar block; it will be very useful when either the clutch, flywheel or crankshaft components are being removed and refitted. Loosen the crankshaft pulley bolt. Remove the bolt and pulley; recover the peg which locates the pulley on the end of the crankshaft.

11 Once the crankshaft pulley has been removed, the lower timing belt cover can be unbolted from the cylinder block.

12 If re-use of the timing belt is anticipated, mark the direction in which the belt runs, so that it can be refitted to run in the same direction.

13 In order to free the upper cover it will be necessary to remove the rocker cover first. The rocker cover is secured by two nuts, and is seated on a specially shaped gasket.

14 Once the rocker cover has been removed, unscrew the two long bolts and remove the top timing belt cover.

15 Now loosen the belt tensioner bolts and relax the belt so that the belt can be lifted off the toothed wheel on the crankshaft. Lift the belt up to the camshaft wheel and remove the belt from the wheel. Note the position of the wheel.

Inspection of timing belt
16 Whenever the belt has been removed, or at yearly intervals the condition of the belt should be inspected as follows:

17 Examine the teeth on the inside of the belt, if the rubber jacket is peeling on the tooth faces of the teeth, or if there are

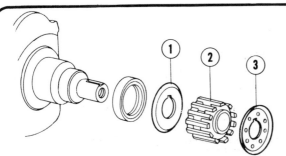

Fig 1.1 Arrangement of timing belt drive components (Sec 8)

1 *Timing guide plate*   3 *Timing guide plate B*
2 *Timing belt drive pulley*

Fig 1.2 Examination of Timing belt (Sec 8) Reject belt if worn as shown

1 *Jacket peeled*   2 *Direction of belt drive*

any cuts and abrasions, the belt should be replaced.
18 Loosen the cylinder head nuts and bolts in the reverse order to that shown in Fig. 1.18.
fibre material which reinforces the belt. Do not allow the belt to become contaminated with oil.

Refitting the timing belt

19 Refitting the belt follows the reversal of the removal procedure, but attention should be paid to the following points:

  i) *Ensure the belt is refitted to the crankshaft and camshaft wheels so that it moves in the same direction as it did before - the direction as indicated by the arrow marked on the belt for its removal.*
  ii) *Tension the belt, as detailed earlier in this Section.*
  iii) *Use new gaskets and locknuts as appropriate.*
  iv) *Tighten the various nuts and bolts to the torques specified at the beginning of this Chapter.*
  v) *Ensure that the belt is fitted when the camshaft and crankshaft are in the correct relative positions.*

20 If the camshaft and crankshaft have been disturbed since the belt was removed; slacken off all the rockers so that crankshaft and camshaft may be turned without risk of interference

between valves and pistons. Turn the crankshaft to tdc for No. 1 piston, then turn the camshaft so that both lobes above the No. 1 cylinder are angled downwards and the reference marks on the camshaft wheel are horizontal and in line with the top of the cylinder head.

9 Cylinder head - removal (engine in car)

1 Drain the cooling system, as directed in Chapter 2.
2 For safety reasons disconnect the battery leads and tuck them safely away.
3 Remove the top radiator hose from the radiator and thermostat housing on the inlet manifold.
4 Remove the bypass hose from the inlet manifold.
5 Disconnect the throttle and choke control cables and stow them carefully aside.
6 Remove the tube connecting the carbon filled canister (if fitted) to the carburettor.
7 Detach the hot air tube and then proceed to remove the air cleaner box.
8 Detach the inlet fuel pipe from the fuel pump on the side of the cylinder head.
9 Remove the exhaust pipe from the exhaust manifold.

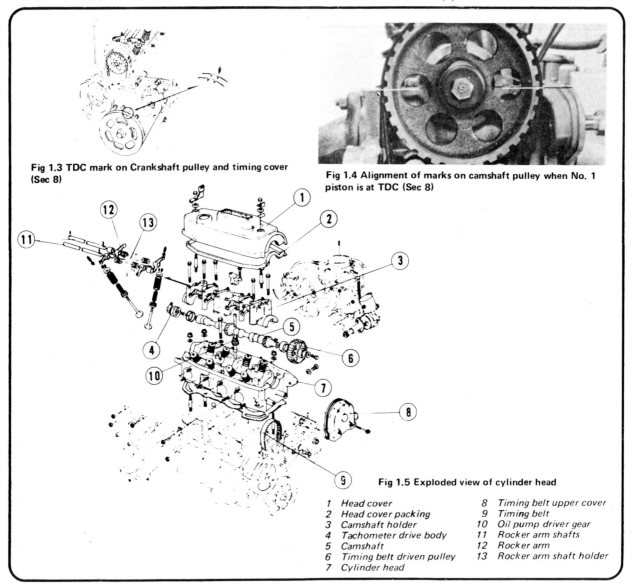

Fig 1.3 TDC mark on Crankshaft pulley and timing cover (Sec 8)

Fig 1.4 Alignment of marks on camshaft pulley when No. 1 piston is at TDC (Sec 8)

Fig 1.5 Exploded view of cylinder head

1 Head cover	8 Timing belt upper cover
2 Head cover packing	9 Timing belt
3 Camshaft holder	10 Oil pump driver gear
4 Tachometer drive body	11 Rocker arm shafts
5 Camshaft	12 Rocker arm
6 Timing belt driven pulley	13 Rocker arm shaft holder
7 Cylinder head	

10 Detach the engine torque stabilising rod.
11 Undo and remove the two nuts which secure the rocker cover to the cylinder head, and then remove the cover. Retrieve the old gasket, then remove the top timing belt cover.
12 Slip the transmission into 1st gear and nudge the car forwards to turn the engine so that the No. 1 piston is at top-dead-centre. This position is indicated by marks on the crankshaft pulley and lower cover of the timing belt.
13 Apply the handbrake and leave the car in gear to ensure that the engine remains in that position. ('P' for hondamatic transmission model).
14 Now loosen the timing belt tensioner bolts and undo and remove the bolts which retain the camshaft toothed wheel to the camshaft.
15 Lift the toothed wheel from the camshaft and allow the timing belt to rest slack in the lower cover. Watch for the Woodruff key which locates the wheel on the shaft - it could fall into the lower cover and its removal from there would be very tedious. It may be necessary to use a small sprocket puller to ease the toothed wheel off the camshaft.
16 Next remove the fuel pump and the distributor. Tag all the HT and LT ignition leads so that they can be refitted to their proper positions. Remember to mark the position of the distributor casing relative to the cylinder head so that refitting and static timing checks can be completed more easily.
17 The shaft driving the oil pump needs to be removed now, it runs vertically through the engine between the 2nd and 3rd cylinders. Undo and remove the two bolts which retain the shaft end block in the centre camshaft holder. Lift the block out of the holder and extract the pump driveshaft complete with gear.
18 Loosen the cylinder head nuts and bolts in the order shown in Fig. 1.18.
19 Lift the cylinder head off the engine complete with inlet manifold, carburettor and exhaust manifold. If the cylinder head appears to be stuck to the engine block, do not try and prise it off the cylinder block with a screwdriver or cold chisel, but tap the cylinder head firmly with a plastic or wooden mallet. The mild shocks should be sufficient to break the bond between the gasket, the cylinder head and the cylinder block.

10 Cylinder head - removal (engine out of car)

The procedure is exactly the same as that detailed in the previous Section, with the exception of the paragraphs numbered 1 to 10 and 16.

11 Cylinder head - dismantling

1 The cylinder head is a casting of aluminium alloy, the camshaft runs centrally in journals machined directly from the cylinder head casting and the camshaft retaining blocks which are also cast aluminium alloy. The retaining blocks support the two rocker shafts as well, so that the blocks, rockers and rocker shafts comprise a sub-assembly of the cylinder head assembly.
2 The exhaust and inlet valves move in steel guides which are an interference fit in the cylinder head. Each valve is returned by live springs, and its head seats on a cast iron insert in the cylinder head casting. It is not possible to replace the seats, only to re-cut and/or regrind them.
3 *Dismantling:* Always work on a clean bench, and support the joint face of the cylinder head on wooden blocks. It is essential that the relatively soft machined surfaces on the cylinder head are not scratched or scored, and that the cylinder head does not rest on open valves.
4 Begin dismantling by unbolting the five camshaft bearing blocks, and then removing the blocks complete with rockers, rocker shafts and springs.
5 Drive out the pins in the two end blocks which retain the rocker shafts in position. Pull off the end blocks and then slide the rockers, intermediate blocks and springs from the rocker shafts.

6 Tag or store all the parts so that they can be refitted into exactly the same positions from which they were removed.
7 The camshaft can now be lifted from the cylinder head.

12 Valves (inlet and exhaust) - removal

1 If it is intended to remove only the valves from the cylinder head, for instance to permit the valve seats to be reground, it will be necessary to have first removed the rocker assembly and camshaft.
2 The valves can be removed from the cylinder head by the following method: Using a valve spring compressor, compress each set of valve springs in turn until the two halves of the split collet near the top of the valve stem can be removed. Release the compressor and then remove the valve springs cap, springs, spring seats and finally the valve itself.
3 If when the valve spring compressor is screwed down the spring cap refuses to free and expose the collets - do not continue to screw the compressor down as there is a likelihood of damaging it.
4 Gently tap the top of the tool directly over the cap with a light hammer. This should free the cap. Hold the compressor firmly with one hand to prevent the compressor jumping off the valve when the cap is released.
5 It is essential that the valves keep to their respective places in the head; therefore, if they are going to be kept and used again, place them on a piece of card with slots cut in it, and numbered 1 to 4 exhaust, and 1 to 4 inlet, corresponding with the positions the valves occupied in the cylinder head. Keep the valve springs, caps and seats in their correct order too.

13 Valve guides - removal and refitting

1 Only remove those guides which on inspection have been found to have worn excessively. The correct bore and tolerance is given in the Specifications at the beginning of this Chapter.
2 The valve guides are an interference fit in the cylinder head block. Remove the guides as follows:
3 Place the cylinder head upside down on a bench on two stout blocks of wood, ensuring that there is sufficient space for the guides to emerge fully from the block.
4 With a suitable diameter drift, carefully drive the guides from the cylinder head.
5 It should be noted that the inlet and exhaust valve guides are not interchangeable.
6 Do not remove all the worn valve guides at one go, always remove one, then refit its replacement. The correct position of the new guide can then be judged against the position of the adjacent guides.
7 Use a steel rule and put it across the existing valve guides so that it bridges or projects over the new guide. Drive the new guide into the top of the cylinder head until it projects from the top of the head to the same extent as its neighbouring guides.
8 Use Honda Reamer '07984 - 6110000' to finish the bore of the valve guide to the correct dimensions given in the Specifications at the beginning of this Chapter.

14 Camshaft, camshaft wheel and rockers - removal

1 The removal procedure for the camshaft, camshaft wheel and rockers is covered in the Sections 9 and 10, of this Chapter.
2 To remove the camshaft wheel follow the instructions detailed in paragraphs 11, 12, 13, 14 and 15, of Section 9.
3 To remove the camshaft and rockers, proceed as directed in paragraphs 11, 12, 13, 14 and 15, of Section 9 and remove the rocker cover and camshaft wheel; then follow the instructions given in paragraphs 4, 5, 6 and 7, of Section 10.

15 Cylinder block - dismantling (engine out of car)

1   It will have been necessary to have removed the engine ancillary components as described in Section 7, of this Chapter.
2   It will also have been necessary to have removed the cylinder head as described in Sections 9 and 10 of this Chapter.
3   Refer to Chapter 5, and remove the clutch assembly or torque converter from the flywheel. The block described in Section 8, of this Chapter will again be of use to lock the flywheel whilst the clutch is removed.
4   The sump is removed after undoing the four nuts and fourteen bolts which secure it to the underside of the cylinder block. If it is difficult to remove the sump once the fastenings have been undone, a few light blows with a wooden mallet should be sufficient to break the bonds between sump, gasket and cylinder block. Do not use a screwdriver or similar tool to prise the sump off the cylinder block.
5   Next unbolt the oil strainer and oil pump assembly from the crankshaft main bearings cap cage. There are two long bolts which secure the pump to the cage casting, and two short bolts secure the inlet shoot and strainer.
6   There will be some loss of oil from the various galleries when the pump assembly is removed.
7   Next unscrew the oil filter element, using a chain wrench or similar tool.
8   Loosen the four bolts securing the water pump to the cylinder block. Remove the bolts and pump body. Recover the water sealing ring.
9   The cylinder block is now sufficiently stripped for the removal of the basic moving parts to be commenced.

16 Big-end bearings - removal (engine out of car)

1   The big-end shell bearings are one of those items which may require attention more frequently than any other moving part on the engine. They are the usual shell bearings, running on a hardened steel crankpin. The shell surface is a soft alloy, and it is not uncommon to be advised to renew the shells every 25,000 miles or so: this interval is probably too short if the engine oil is good and has been changed regularly. A more reasonable life is between 50,000 and 60,000 miles, when it is also advisable to clean up the cylinder head and overhaul the valve mechanisms.
2   The big-ends may be dismantled without removing the engine from the car. It is only necessary to drain the engine oil, followed by the removal of the sump and oil pump. See the following Section (17).
3   Having arrived at the stage when the dismantling of the big-end bearings is the next step - either with the engine in the car and the tasks in paragraph 2 complete - or with the engine out of the car and dismantled as far as described in Section 15 complete; proceed as follows:
4   Check that the connecting rods and big-end bearing caps are correctly marked. Normally the numbers 1 to 4 are stamped on the adjacent sides of the big-end caps and connecting rods, indicating which cap fits on which rod, and which way round the cap fits on the rod. The number 1 should be stamped on the con-rod and cap operating the number 1 piston at the front of the engine, 2 for the second piston/cylinder, and so on. Do not mistake the big-end bearing seat bore code for the con-rod number (Fig. 1.6).
5   If for some reason no numbers or marks can be found, then a centre pop can be used to make dots on the cap and con-rod. One dot on rod and cap in number 1 cylinder, two dots for number 2 and so on.
6   Undo and remove the nuts securing the big-end caps, and then lift off the big-end caps. If they are difficult to remove the 'stiction' bond between cap and rod can be broken by gently tapping the cap with a soft faced hammer.
7   To remove the shell bearings, press the shell opposite the groove in both the connecting rod and bearing cap and the shells will slide out easily.

8   If the bearings are being attended to with the engine in the car, make sure that the pistons do not fall too far down the cylinder bores, so that the pistons could reach a position when the lower piston rings pass out from the bottom of the cylinder bores. It is difficult and tedious using worm drive hose clips to compress the piston rings, so that the piston can be eased back into the cylinder.
9   Now proceed to the next Section, paragraph 6, *et. seq.* for details of crankpin inspection, and selection of big-end shells. Sections 25 and 39, also give details of big-end bearings and their refitting.

17 Big-end bearings - renewal (engine in car)

1   It will be necessary to jack up the front of the car and support it on firmly based chassis stands. The stands to be located underneath the front suspension subframe.
2   Position a hoist over the engine, and position slings around the clutch housing. Raise the hoist so that it *just* accepts the weight of the engine.
3   Next unbolt the centre support beam from underneath the engine, and detach the engine flexible mounting on that beam. Do not disturb the right engine mount or the stabilising rod.
4   The sump can now be unbolted from the crankcase to expose the crankshaft, connecting rod and bearings.
5   The oil pump must be unbolted from the crank bearing cage before the tasks detailed in paragraphs 3 to 7, of the previous Section for the removal of the shell bearings, can be started.
6   Having removed the old bearing shells, the crankpins on the crankshaft should be inspected.
7   The Specifications at the beginning of this Chapter gives details of the sizes and tolerances of the crankpins.
8   Always use a good quality micrometer when measuring the crankpins and remember to check it by measuring a standard length gauge.
9   Having measured the crankpins, compare the dimensions with those given in the bearing shell selection chart in the Specifications at the beginning of this Chapter.
The crankshaft cannot be reground.
10 Fit the appropriate size of new shell to the con-rod and cap. Ensure that the slots in the shells match the slots in the rod and cap, and also ensure that the holes in the upper shell coincide with the oil holes in the connecting rod, which provide for splash lubrication of the cylinder bores.
11 Take great care when handling the new shells; the bearing surface is soft and can easily be damaged.
12 Before offering the connecting rods back onto the crankshaft, coat the crankpins liberally with engine oil.
13 With the con-rods in place on the crankshaft, refit the appropriate caps to the con-rods. Ensure that the identification numbers stamped on the connecting rods and caps correspond, and that all face the same side of the crankcase.
14 Refit the big-end nuts onto the bolts and tighten in pairs to the torque specified.
15 Clean the joint faces of the sump and crankcase of old gasket material. Smear the faces of the new gasket with heavy grease and stick it to the crankcase joint surface. Fit the sump and tighten the fourteen bolts to the torque specified.
16 It is worth while changing the oil filter element when the big-end bearings have been renewed.
17 Refit the engine lower support beam and flexible support and tighten all fasteners to their specified torques.
18 Finally refill the engine with Castrol GTX or equivalent oil.

18 Pistons, piston rings and connecting rods - removal and separation

1   The procedure for piston and connecting rod removal is the same whether the engine is in, or out of, the car.

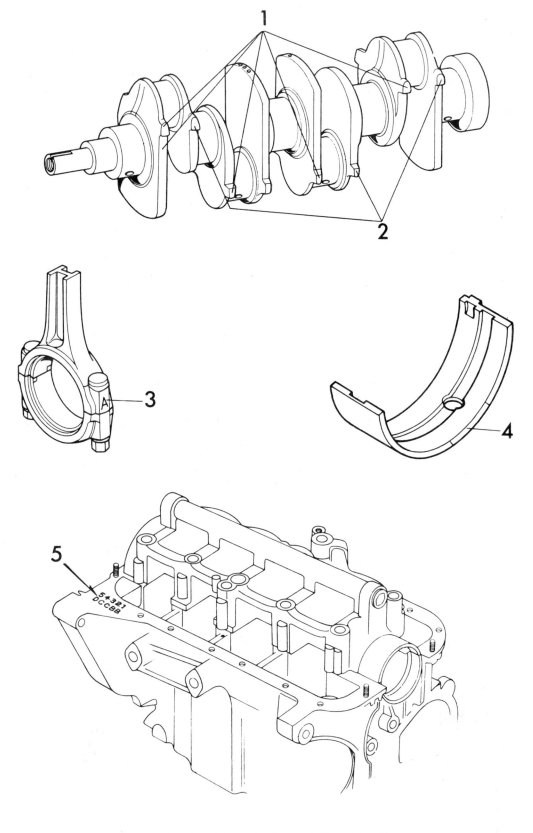

Fig 1.6 Crankshaft main journal and crankpin fit markings (Secs 16 & 35)

1 Crankshaft journal fit markings
2 Crankpin fit markings
3 Connecting rod fit marking
4 Bearing shell identification colour
5 Cylinder block fit markings

2 In either case, the cylinder head needs to have been removed (see Sections 9 and 10) and the big-end bearings dismantled (Sections 16 and 17).

3 The engine having been stripped down as indicated, giving complete access to the basic moving parts of the engine, proceed as follows:

4 The pistons and con-rods are pushed out of the top of the cylinder bores together. Be careful not to allow the rough edges of the connecting rod to score the fine bore of the cylinder.

5 The pistons will not pass the crankshaft downwards out of the crankcase.

6 Once the piston/connecting rod assembly has been removed

from the engine, the piston rings may be slid off the piston.

7 The top piston rings are of cast iron, and the lower ones of steel. It is all too easy to break them as they are expanded during removal, so it is useful to make use of a feeler gauge as described next, to minimise the risk of breakage.

8 Lift one end of the piston ring to be removed, out of its slot in the piston *just* sufficiently to insert the end of a thin feeler gauge underneath it.

9 Move the feeler gauge slowly around the piston and apply upward pressure on the piston ring to move the ring onto the band above the ring slot. Once the ring is completely out of its slot, it can be eased further up and finally off the piston. The

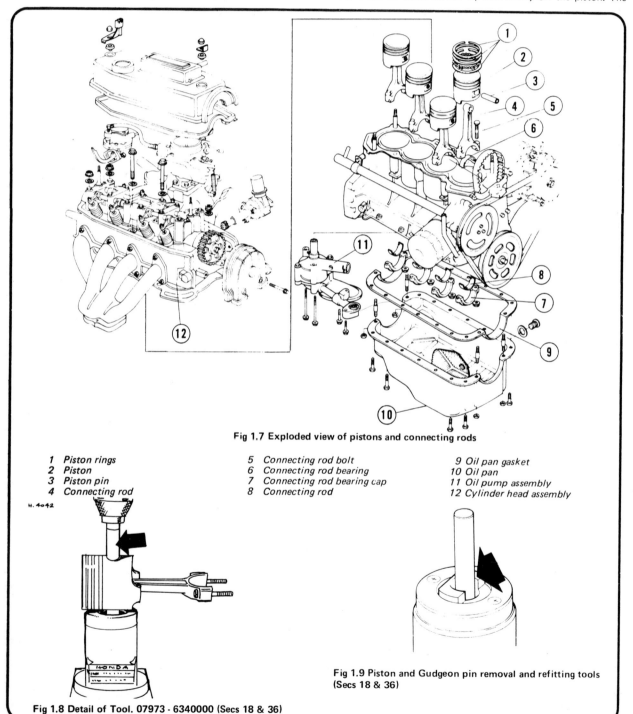

Fig 1.7 Exploded view of pistons and connecting rods

1 Piston rings
2 Piston
3 Piston pin
4 Connecting rod

5 Connecting rod bolt
6 Connecting rod bearing
7 Connecting rod bearing cap
8 Connecting rod

9 Oil pan gasket
10 Oil pan
11 Oil pump assembly
12 Cylinder head assembly

H. 4042

Fig 1.8 Detail of Tool. 07973 - 6340000 (Secs 18 & 36)

Fig 1.9 Piston and Gudgeon pin removal and refitting tools (Secs 18 & 36)

feeler gauge(s) can be used to bridge other slots to prevent the ring slipping into them as they are removed.

10 The piston and connecting rod are held together by a gudgeon pin, which is an interference fit in the small end of the connecting rod and a clearance fit in the piston.

11 Honda supply a special mandrel and piston support, to be used in a hydraulic press to remove - and refit - gudgeon pins. Tool: '07973 - 6340000'. (Fig. 1.8).

12 *Gudgeon pin removal:* Using the Honda tools, if available, or a mandrel and piston support made to the design shown in Fig. 1.9, place the piston on the support and press out the gudgeon pin.

19 Crankshaft and main bearings - removal

1 The crankshaft can be removed once the engine has been stripped of the following items:

   i) *Clutch and flywheel (Section 5, Chapter 5)*
   ii) *Oil pump and sump (Section 15, Chapter 1)*
   iii) *Big-end bearings (Section 16, Chapter 1)*
   iv) *Timing belt, fan belt and the respective crankshaft wheels (Section 8, Chapter 1)*

2 It is not essential to remove the cylinder head in order to complete the task of crankshaft removal, but it makes the cylinder block easier to handle if the head is off as well as avoiding damaging the valves in the cylinder head, should the crankshaft be turned when the timing belt is off. Lastly, the opportunity of inspecting the cylinder head and its components should not be missed.

3 Before beginning on the actual removal of the crankshaft, it is wise to check the endfloat of the crankshaft.

4 Feeler gauges can be used to measure the gap between the centre main bearing journal wall and the thrust washers on the shoulders of the crankcase centre bearing housing.

5 Alternatively, a clock gauge mounted on the crankcase with its probe resting on a suitable part of the crankshaft, can be used to measure the axial movement of the crankshaft.

6 In either case, move the crankshaft as far as it will go, in each direction, with a pair of tyre levers or the like. The endfloat should be between 0.004 and 0.0138 inches (0.10 and 0.33 mm). If it does not fall within those dimensions, oversize washers will need to be fitted when it comes to refitting the crankshaft.

7 This engine has a single member which is bolted to the crankcase to support all five main bearings. Proceed to unbolt the main bearings retainer, and when all bolts have been removed - lift off the retainer. Ensure that all the bearing shells are kept in position to match their respective main bearing journal.

8 The crankshaft can now be lifted out of the crankcase, and the upper shells of the main bearings pressed out of their seatings in the case. Once again, store the shells so that they can be identified individually and if to be re-used, refitted to the same seating from which they were taken. Recover the two semi-circular crankshaft end thrust bearings from the shoulders of the centre main bearing support in the crankcase.

20 Lubrication system (engine) - general description

1 The system is quite conventional. The sump carries some 8 pints of oil; the Trochoidal oil pump is mounted on the crankshaft main bearing retainer cage and is driven by a shaft that runs vertically through the centre of the engine and which is driven by the camshaft.

   The oil pump takes oil from the sump, through a strainer and

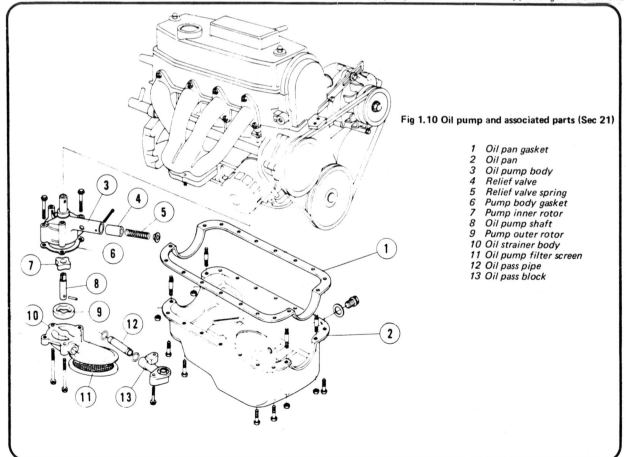

Fig. 1.10 Oil pump and associated parts (Sec 21)

   1 Oil pan gasket
   2 Oil pan
   3 Oil pump body
   4 Relief valve
   5 Relief valve spring
   6 Pump body gasket
   7 Pump inner rotor
   8 Oil pump shaft
   9 Pump outer rotor
   10 Oil strainer body
   11 Oil pump filter screen
   12 Oil pass pipe
   13 Oil pass block

delivers it under pressure into galleries drilled in the main bearing retaining cage. The oil from the pump passes through the cage under pressure into the oil filter cartridge mounted on the crankcase, via drillings in the crankcase. Once through the filter the oil returns to the crankshaft, via galleries in the main bearing retaining cage. Another drilling in the crankcase/cylinder block and cylinder head takes oil under pressure to the camshaft bearings in the cylinder head.

The main crankshaft bearings are fed with oil under pressure, directly from the bearing retaining cage; the big-end bearings however, receive oil under pressure which is bled from the main bearings and flows to the crankpins through drillings in the crankshaft.

The pistons and gudgeon pins receive splash lubrication from the big-end bearings. To improve lubrication of the piston in the cylinder, in the thrust side of the bore, a small hole in the upper big-end shell and in the connecting rod provide for a continuous squirt of oil to spray onto the bore surface just below the piston skirt. The spray of oil provides for hydrodynamic lubrication. There is a pressure relief valve in the oil pump which acts to allow a proportion of the oil from the delivery side of the pump to return to the sump.

21 Oil pump - removal, dismantling and renovation

Oil pump removal:

1 It will be necessary to remove the sump to gain access to the pump. Section 15, of this Chapter, details the operations to be carried out to remove the sump with the engine in place in the car.
2 Having exposed the pump, simply undo and remove the four bolts securing the pump to the main bearing cage, and then undo the two bolts securing the delivery pipe to the cage.
3 Remove the pump together with the inlet strainer and delivery pipe.

Dismantling:

4 Begin by extracting the oil pressure relief valve from the body of the pump as follows: Pull the split pin out of the end of the relief valve housing and then shake the valve spring seat, spring and valve out of the housing.
5 The pump itself can be dismantled once the two bolts holding the pump body to the cover/inlet strainer have been undone and removed. The delivery pipe can be carefully pulled from the pump body and end fitting. Watch for the 'O' rings fitted at each end of the delivery tube. (photo)
6 Recover the gasket between the pump body and cover, and take the strainer off the inlet horn.
7 The pump rotor and trochoidal idler simply slide out of the body. (photo)
8 Now that the pump has been dismantled, clean all the parts in Gunk or equivalent solvent. Make sure that once cleaned all parts are thoroughly dried with a non-fluffy rag and placed on a clean surface ready for inspection.

Inspection of oil pump parts:

9 Refer to the oil pump detail dimensions given in the Specifications, at the beginning of this Chapter. Check the following for compliance with the Specifications:
   i)   Oil pressure relief valve; fit in housing bore.
   ii) Clearance between trochoidal idler and pump body.
   iii) Radial clearance between rotor and idler.
   iv) Axial clearance between rotor and pump cover.
10 In addition inspect the rotor, idler, pump body and relief valve parts for wear and surface marks. If any component has suffered surface wear or been marked, it should be replaced.
11 If the pump's moving parts have worn to the point where one, or more, clearance is beyond the specified limits, it will be as well to replace the pump assembly. In all probability other clearances will be close to limits and would not last another reasonable period of service in the engine.

Reassembly of the pump:

12 The pump is reassembled in a sequence that is the reverse of the dismantling procedure. (photo) Tighten the oil pump body/cover bolts to the specified torque, and once the strainer and delivery parts have been fitted, immerse the inlet strainer side of the pump into a pan of clear engine oil. Reassemble the oil pressure relief valve onto the pump body. (photos)
13 Turn the pump rotor shaft with a screwdriver and check that oil emerges from the delivery pipe. Allow for the pump to be primed. As a last check once it has been established that the pump is moving oil, place a finger over the delivery port of the pipe end fitting. A distinct pressure should be felt on the finger as the pump rotor is turned and oil squeezes out of the delivery port.
14 It will be wise to prime the pump again as described above before it is refitted to the engine.
15 Before refitting the pump ensure that the 'O' ring seals on the delivery pipe, and pipe end fitting are properly seated and not damaged in any way.
16 Remember to tighten the bolts which secure the pump to the main bearing cage to the specified torque.

22 Oil filter cartridge - removal and fitting

1 It will be necessary to use a ratchet and socket spanner to undo and remove the cartridge from the union on the side of the crankcase.
2 Once the filter has been removed, wipe the seal seating on the crankcase clean with a non-fluffy rag, and wipe away any spilled oil from the crankcase and sump.
3 Take the new filter and seal and coat the new seal with clean engine oil. Fit the seal into its seat groove in the base of the filter.
4 Offer the filter to the union on the engine and screw into position.
5 Tighten the filter cartridge to the specified torque with a torque wrench and socket on the hexagon on the top of the filter.
6 Refill the engine with oil if necessary and run the engine to check for leaks around the cartridge seal.

23 Engine components - examination and renovation

1 With the engine stripped and all parts thoroughly cleaned, every component should be examined for wear. The items listed in the Sections following, should receive particular attention and where necessary be renewed or renovated.
2 Many measurements on engine components require accuracies down to tenths of thousands of an inch. It is advisable therefore to either check your micrometer against a standard gauge occasionally to ensure that the instrument zero is set correctly, or use the micrometer as a comparative instrument. This last method however necessitates that a comprehensive set of slip and bore gauges is available.

24 Crankshaft - examination and renovation

1 Examine the crankpin and main journal surfaces for signs of scoring or scratches and check the ovality and taper of the crankpins and main journals. If the bearing surface dimensions do not fall within the tolerance ranges given in the Specifications at the beginning of this Chapter, the crankpins and/or main journals will have to be reground.

Big-end and crankpin wear is accompanied by distinct metallic knocking particularly noticeable when the engine is pulling from low revs.

Main bearing and main journal wear is accompanied by severe engine vibration - rumble - getting progressively worse as engine revs increase.

If when inspected the crankshaft journals are found to have

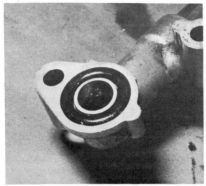
21.5 Oil pump line oil seals

21.7 Oil pump rotors

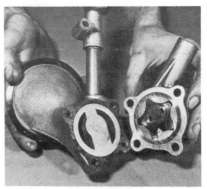
21.12A Assembly of oil pump

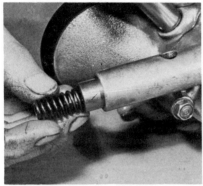
21.12B Inserting relief valve and spring

21.12C Inserting valve spring cap and pin

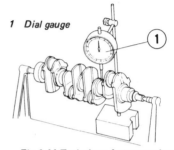
1   Dial gauge

Fig 1.11 Technique for measuring crankshaft runout (Sec 24)

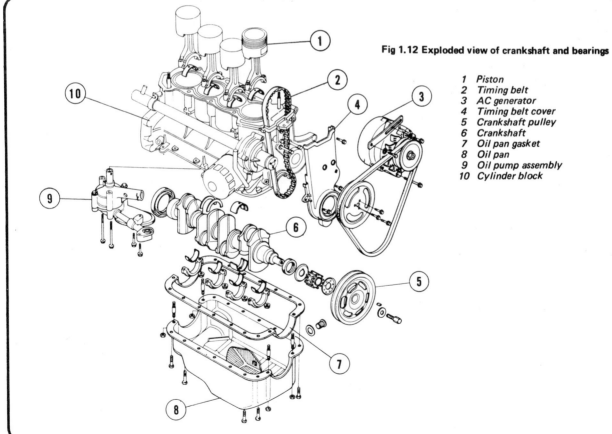

Fig 1.12 Exploded view of crankshaft and bearings

1   Piston
2   Timing belt
3   AC generator
4   Timing belt cover
5   Crankshaft pulley
6   Crankshaft
7   Oil pan gasket
8   Oil pan
9   Oil pump assembly
10 Cylinder block

worn beyond the limits given in the Specifications and no over-size shells are available; the crankshaft must be renewed. **It cannot be reground.**

25 Big-end and main bearing shells - examination

1   Big-end bearing failure is accomplished by a noisy knocking from the crankcase and a slight drop in oil pressure. Main bearing failure is accompanied by vibration which can be quite severe as the engine speed rises and falls, and a drop in oil pressure.

2   Bearings which have not broken up, but are badly worn will give rise to low oil pressure and some vibration. Inspect the big-ends, main bearings and thrust washers for signs of general wear, scoring, pitting and scratches. The bearings should be matt grey in colour. With lead-indium bearings, should a trace of copper colour be noticed the bearings are badly worn as the lead bearing material has worn away to expose the indium underlay. Renew the bearings if they are in this condition, if there is any sign of scoring or pitting, or if the bearings have already been in use for a considerable mileage.

3   The undersizes available are designed to correspond to wear expected on the crankpin. The bearings are, in fact, slightly more than the stated undersize as running clearances have been allowed for during their manufacture.

4   Very long engine life can be achieved by changing big-end bearings at intervals of 30,000 miles (48,000 km) and main bearings at intervals of 50,000 miles (80,000 km) irrespective of bearing wear. Normally, crankshaft wear is infinitesimal and regular changes of bearings will ensure mileages in excess of 100,000 miles (160,000 km) before crankshaft renewal.

26 Cylinder bores - examination and renovation

1   The cylinder bores must be examined for taper, ovality, scoring and scratches. Start by carefully examining the top of the cylinder bores. If they are at all worn a very slight ridge will be found on the thrust side. This marks the top of the piston travel. The owner will have a good indication of the bore wear prior to dismantling the engine, or removing the cylinder head. Excessive oil consumption accompanied by blue smoke from the exhaust is a sure sign of worn cylinder bores and piston rings.

2   Measure the bore diameter just under the ridge with a micro-meter and compare it with the diameter at the bottom of the bore, which is not subject to wear. If the difference between the two measurements is more than 0.15 mm (0.006 inch), then it will be necessary to fit special piston rings or to have the cylinders rebored and fit oversize pistons and rings. If no micro-meter is available, remove the rings from a piston and place the piston in each bore in turn about three-quarters of an inch below the top of the bore. If an 0.25 mm (0.010 inch) feeler gauge can be slid between the piston and the cylinder wall on the thrust side of the bore then remedial action must be taken. Oversize pistons are available in the following sizes:

+0.25 mm (0.010 inch)
+0.50 mm (0.020 inch)
+0.75 mm (0.030 inch)
+1.00 mm (0.040 inch)

3   These are accurately machined to just below these measure-ments so as to provide correct running clearances in bores bored out to the exact oversize dimensions.

4   If the bores are slightly worn but not so badly worn as to justify reboring them special oil control rings can be fitted to the existing pistons which will restore compression and stop the engine burning oil. Several different types are available and the manufacturer's instructions concerning their fitting must be followed closely.

27 Pistons and piston rings - examination and renovation

1   If the old pistons are to be refitted carefully remove the piston rings and thoroughly clean them. Take particular care to clean out the piston ring grooves. At the same time do not scratch the aluminium. If new rings are to be fitted to the old pistons, then the top ring should be stepped to clear the ridge left above the previous top ring. If a normal but oversize new ring is fitted, it will hit the ridge and break, because the new ring will not have worn in the same way as the old, which will have worn in unison with the ridge.

2   Before fitting the rings on the pistons each ring should be inserted approximately 76 mm (3 inches) down the cylinder bore and the gap measured with a feeler gauge. This should be as detailed in the Specifications at the beginning of this Chapter. It is essential that the gap is measured at the bottom of the ring travel. If it is measured at the top of a worn bore and gives a perfect fit, it could easily seize at the bottom. If the ring gap is too small rub down the ends of the ring with a fine file, until the gap, when fitted, is correct. To keep the rings square in the bore for measurement, line each up in turn with an old piston: use the piston to push the ring down about 76 mm (3 inches). Remove the piston and measure the piston ring gap.

3   When fitting new pistons and rings to a rebored engine the ring gap can be measured at the top of the bore as the bore will now not taper. It is not necessary to measure the side clearance in the piston ring groove with rings fitted, as the grooved dimen-sions are accurately machined during manufacture. When fitting new oil control rings to used pistons it may be necessary to have the piston grooves widened by machining to accept the new wider rings. In this instance the ring manufacturer's repres-entative will make this quite clear and will supply the address to which the pistons must be sent for machining.

4   When new 'standard sized' pistons are fitted, take great care to fit the exact size best suited to the particular bore of your engine. Honda go one stage further than merely specifying one size of piston for all standard bores. Because of very slight differ-ences in cylinder machining during production it is necessary to select just the right piston for the bore. A range of different sizes is available either from the piston manufacturer's or from the dealer for the particular model of car being repaired.

5   Examination of the cylinder block face will show, adjacent to each bore, a small diamond shaped box with a number stamped in the metal. Careful examination of the piston crown will show a matching diamond and number. These are the standard piston sizes and will be the same for all four bores. If standard pistons are to be refitted or standard low compression pistons changed to standard high compression pistons, then it is essential that

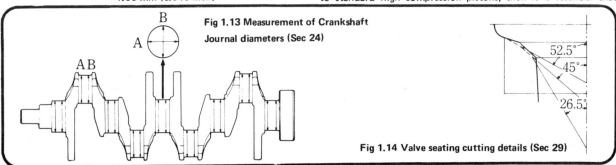

Fig 1.13 Measurement of Crankshaft Journal diameters (Sec 24)

Fig 1.14 Valve seating cutting details (Sec 29)

only pistons with the same number in the diamond are used. With oversize pistons, for rebored cylinders the amount of oversize is stamped in an ellipse in the piston crown.

6 On the engines with tapered second and third compression rings, the top narrow rise of the ring is marked with a 'T'. Always fit this side uppermost and carefully examine all rings for this mark before fitting.

28 Camshaft and camshaft bearings - examination

1 Carefully examine camshaft bearings for wear. If the bearings are obviously worn or pitted or the metal underlay just showing through, then they must be renewed. This is an operation for your local Honda agent or automobile engineering works, as it demands the use of specialised equipment. The bearings are removed using a special drift after which the new bearings are pressed in, care being taken that the oil holes in the bearings line up with those in the block. With another special tool the bearings are then reamed in position.

2 The camshaft itself should show no signs of wear, but, if very slight scoring marks on the cams are noticed, the score marks can be removed by very gentle rubbing down with a very fine emery cloth or an oil stone. The greatest care should be taken to keep the cam profiles smooth.

29 Valves and valve seats - examination and renovation

1 Examine the heads of the valves for pitting and burning; especially the heads of the exhaust valves. The valve seating should be examined at the same time. If the pitting on the valves and seats is very slight the marks can be removed by grinding the seats and the valves together with coarse, and then fine, valve grinding paste. Where bad pitting has occurred to the valve seats it will be necessary to recut them to fit new valves. If the valve seats are so worn that they cannot be recut, then it will be necessary to fit new valve seat inserts. These latter two jobs should be entrusted to the local Honda agent or automobile engineering works. In practice it is very seldom that the seats are so badly worn that they require renewal. Normally, it is the valve that is too badly worn for replacement, and the owner can easily purchase a new set of valves and match them to the seats by valve grinding.

2 Valve grinding is carried out as follows: Place the cylinder head upside down on a bench, with a block of wood at each end to give clearance for the valve stems. Alternatively, place the head at 45° to a wall with the combustion chambers facing away from the wall.

3 Smear a trace of coarse carborundum paste on the seat face and apply a suction grinder tool to the valve heads. With a semi-rotary action, grind the valve head to its seat, lifting the valve occasionally to redistribute the grinding paste. When a dull matt even surface finish is produced on both the valve seat and the valve, then wipe off the paste and repeat the process with fine carborundum paste, lifting and turning the valve to redistribute the paste as before. A light spring placed under the valve head will greatly ease this operation. When a smooth unbroken ring of light grey matt finish is produced, on both valve and the valve seat faces, the grinding operation is complete.
complete.

30 Cylinder head and pistons - decarbonisation

1 This operation can be carried out with the engine either in, or out of, the car. With the cylinder head off, carefully remove with a wire brush and blunt scraper all traces of carbon deposits from the combustion spaces and the ports in the cylinder head. The valve stems and valve guides should also be freed from any carbon deposits. Wash the combustion spaces and posts down with petrol and scrape the cylinder head surface of any foreign matter with the side of a steel rule or a similar article. Take care not to scratch the surface.

2 Clean the pistons and top of the cylinder bores. If the pistons are still in the cylinder bores then it is essential that great care is taken to ensure that no carbon gets into the cylinder bores as this could scratch the cylinder walls or cause damage to the piston and rings. To ensure that this does not happen, first turn the crankshaft so that two of the pistons are at the top of the bores. Place clean non-fluffy rag into the other two bores or seal them off with paper and masking tape. The waterways and push-rod holes should also be covered with a small piece of masking tape to prevent particles of carbon entering the cooling system and damaging the water pump, or entering the lubrication system and damaging the oil pump or bearing surface.

3 We advise that **all** carbon deposits should be removed. There is a school of thought which advocates that a ring of carbon should be left around the edge of the piston and on the cylinder bore wall as an aid to keeping oil consumption low.

4 If all traces of carbon are to be removed, press a little grease into the gap between the cylinder walls and the two pistons which are to be worked on. With a blunt scraper carefully scrape away the carbon from the piston crown, taking care not to scratch the aluminium. Also scrape away the carbon from the surrounding lip of the cylinder wall. When all the carbon has been removed, scrape away the grease which will now be contaminated with carbon particles, taking care not to press any into the bores. To assist prevention of carbon build up the piston crown can be polished with a metal polish. Remove the rags or masking tape from the other two cylinders and turn the crankshaft so that the two pistons which were at the bottom are now at the top. Place non-fluffy rag into the other two bores or seal them off with paper and masking tape. Do not forget the waterways and oilways as well. Proceed as previously described.

5 If a ring of carbon is going to be left round the piston then this can be helped by inserting an old piston ring into the top of the bore to rest on the piston and ensure that the carbon is not accidentally removed. Check that there are no particles of carbon in the cylinder bores. Decarbonising is now complete.

31 Oil pump driveshaft - examination

1 There are no dimensions available for this shaft and its bearings to enable specific statements to be made as to when the shaft assembly has worn to point where renewal is necessary.

2 Therefore, examine the parts visually, and if clear signs exist of bearing surface deterioration, replace the appropriate parts.

3 The same inspection can be made of the shaft drive gear and register spigot.

32 Flywheel and starter ring gear - examination and renovation

1 If the teeth on the flywheel starter ring gear are badly worn, or if some are missing, then it will be necessary to remove the ring. This is achieved by splitting the old ring using a cold chisel. The greatest care must be taken not to damage the flywheel during this process. Check the availability of spare ring gears before proceeding to remove the gear. **Note:** On cars fitted with 'Hondamatic' transmission, the starter ring gear is bolted to the periphery of the torque converter. Refer to Chapter 6 of this manual for details of torque converter and ring gear removal and refitting.

2 To fit a new ring gear, heat it gently and evenly with an oxyacetylene flame until a temperature of approximately 350° C (662° F) is reached. This is indicated by a light metallic blue surface colour. With the ring gear at this temperature, fit it to the flywheel with the front of the teeth facing the flywheel register. The ring gear should be either pressed or lightly tapped gently onto its register and left to cool naturally, when the contraction of the metal on cooling will ensure that it is a secure and permanent fit. Great care must be taken not to overheat the ring gear, as if this happens its temper will be lost.

3 Alternatively your local Honda agent, or local automobile engineering works may have a suitable oven in which the ring

gear can be heated. The normal domestic oven will give a temperature of about 250° C only, at the very most, except for the latest self-cleaning type, which will give a higher temperature. With the former it may just be possible to fit the ring gear with it at this temperature, but it is unlikely and no great force should have to be used.

33 Rockers and rocker shaft - examination and renovation

1 Thoroughly clean out the rocker shaft. As it acts as the oil passages for the valve gear, clean out the oil holes and make sure they are quite clear. Check the shaft for straightness by rolling it on a flat surface. It is most unlikely that it will deviate from normal, but if it does, then a judicious attempt must be made to straighten it. If this is not successful, purchase a new shaft. The surface of the shaft should be free from any wear ridges caused by the rocker arms. If any wear is present renew the rocker shaft. Wear is likely to have occurred only if the rocker shaft oil holes have been blocked.
2 Check the rocker arms for wear of the rocker bushes, for wear at the rocker arm face which bears on the cam, and for wear of the adjusting ball ended screws. Wear in the rocker arm bush can be checked by gripping the rocker arm tip and holding the rocker arm in place on the shaft, noting if there is any lateral rocker arm shake. If any shake is present, and the arm is very loose on the shaft, remedial action must be taken. It is recommended that any worn rocker arm be taken to your local Honda agent or automobile engineering works to have the old bush drawn out and a new bush fitted.

34 Engine reassembly - preparation and sequence

1 To ensure maximum life with minimum trouble from a re-built engine, not only must every part be correctly assembled, but everything must be spotlessly clean, all the oilways must be clear, locking washers and spring washers must always be fitted where indicated and all bearings and other working surfaces must be thoroughly lubricated during assembly. Before assembly begins renew any bolts or studs whose threads are in any way damaged; whenever possible use new springs and washers.
2 Apart from your normal tools, a supply of non-fluffy rag, an oil can filled with engine oil (an empty washing-up fluid plastic bottle thoroughly cleaned and washed out will invariably do just as well), a supply of new spring washers, a set of new gaskets and a torque wrench should be collected together.
3 It will be as well to remember that this engine assembles (and dismantles) in a particular sequence. The reassembly sequence is as follows:

i)   Refit the crankshaft
ii)   Reassemble piston, conrods and piston rings
iii)   Refit the piston/conrod assembly to the engine
iv)   Recouple the conrods to the crankshaft
v)   Refit the oil pump and oil strainer
vi)   Refit the sump
vii)   Refit crankshaft timing belt wheel, and belt tensioner
viii)   Reassemble the cylinder head
ix)   Refit the cylinder head to the engine block
x)   Refit the timing belt to camshaft and refit timing belt
xi)   Refit the flywheel and clutch assembly
xii)   Refit the distributor and establish static timing
xiii)   Refit water pump
xiv)   Refit the fuel pump and inlet manifold with carburettor
xv)   Refit the exhaust manifold
xvi)   Refit the alternator and drivebelt
xvii)   Recouple the engine assembly to the gearbox
xviii) Refit the starter motor
xix)   The engine is now ready for refitment to car

35 Crankshaft - refitting

1 Ensure that the crankcase is thoroughly clean and that all oilways are clear. A thin twist drill is useful for cleaning them out. If possible blow them out with compressed air.
2 Now take note of the alpha-numeric code marked on the crankcase, relating to the main bearings and also note the colour coding on the old main bearing shells - Fig. 1.6, and the table in the Specifications at the beginning of this Chapter.
3 It is necessary to use a 'plastigauge' to determine the oil clearance between the main bearing shells and main journal on the crankshaft. Begin by fitting new shells with the same colour coding as the old ones. Ensure that the shells are properly located in their respective housings. The oil bleed/feed holes in the shells should coincide with the drillings in the bearing seats, and the tabs located in the slots in the seats.
4 Now lower the crankshaft into place, and place a cut length of 'plastigauge' - 0.001 to 0.003 inch (0.025 to 0.076 mm), onto each main bearing journal. Do not cover or restrict the oil holes in the crankshaft or bearing shells with the plastigauge.
5 Lower the main bearing cage into place and screw in all ten retaining bolts. Tighten them to the correct torque working in a diagonal sequence from the centre to each end of the cradle.
6 Then undo all ten bolts and remove the main bearing cage. Examine the plastigauge; this material which is supplied in a precise diameter, squashes to a new width depending on the gap in which it was squeezed. Use the teller on the plastigauge pack to check what the clearance on particular bearings is.
7 Refer to the Specifications at the beginning of this Chapter to find what oil clearances are permitted, and the new size shell required to establish the correct oil clearance.
8 Note that because it is not possible to regrind the crankshaft in order to recondition the journals it is necessary to select from quite a range of shells the correct size to provide for the correct running clearances in the main bearings.
9 It will be necessary to replace the crankshaft if the correct oil clearances cannot be established with the range of shell bearings available from Honda.
10 To determine the thickness of the thrust bearings required by the crankshaft, begin by referring to the note made of endplay and bearing thickness when the crankshaft was originally removed (paragraph 4, Section 19).
11 The required thrust bearing thickness can be deduced from the note made, to establish the endfloat of the crankshaft within the specified limits.
12 However if a new crankshaft is being fitted, it will be necessary to measure the width of the centre main journal, and the distance between the thrust bearing seats across the main bearing seating in the crankcase in order to determine the thickness of the thrust bearings required.
13 In any event, check that the required endfloat has been obtained when the crankshaft has been installed. **Do not check the endfloat when the 'plastigauge' is being used to determine oil clearances in the crankshaft main bearing. Any axial movement of the crankshaft will distort the plastigauge and ruin the measurement.**
14 Having arrived at the correct combination of shell bearings and crankpins, temporarily remove the crankshaft to give it a final clean. Wipe the new bearing shells clean too, and then position them back into their proper seatings. Cover the crank main journals with clean engine oil, and inject some oil into the crankshaft oilways. Lower the crankshaft back into the crankcase. Relocate the main bearing cage and screw in the ten retaining bolts. (photos)
15 Tighten the main bearing bolts in the order indicated to the torque specified. Finally check that the crankshaft rotates freely in its main bearings. (photo)
16 Finish the installation of the crankshaft by fitting the rear crankshaft oil seal and front timing belt wheel and crankshaft oil seal.
17 The rear crankshaft oil seal fits in the seating formed in the crankcase and main bearing cage. Pay attention to the arrow on

35.14A Fitting the crankshaft thrust bearings

35.14B Lowering the crankshaft into the engine block

35.14C Fitting the main bearing cage

35.15 Tightening the main bearing cage bolts

the seal which indicates the proper orientation of the seal with respect to crankshaft rotation. The crank rotates anticlockwise when viewed from the timing belt end.

18 The front crankshaft oil seal also fits in a seating formed in the crankcase and main bearing cage.

19 In both instances, do not use sealing compound between the seals and seatings; fragments could find their way into the oil reservoir and from that into the oilways.

36 Pistons and connecting rods - assembly

1 If the same pistons are being used then they must be mated to the same connecting rod with the same gudgeon pin. If new pistons are being fitted, it does not matter with which connecting rod they are used.

2 Because the gudgeon pin is a tight fit in the small end bearing, it will be necessary to press the gudgeon pin into position. The piston will need to be supported around the gudgeon pin bore, and a special mandrel used to locate the pin whilst it is pressed in position (Figs. 1.8 and 1.9).

3 Ensure that the piston and connecting rod are correctly aligned, as follows, before the pin is pressed into position. The

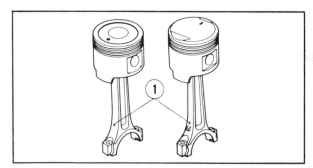

Fig 1.15 Relative positions of oil holes in connecting rod and the piston marks (Sec 36)

1 Oil jets

dimple mark on the top of the piston should be facing the oil jet hole in the big-end of the conrod (Fig. 1.15).

4 Place the piston on the support (Fig. 1.8).

5 Coat the gudgeon pin with hypoid gear oil and slip it into the piston bore.

6 Locate the connecting rod and introduce the pin to the small

end bore in the rod.

7 Position the mandrel in the gudgeon pin and drive the pin home.

8 When the piston and connecting rod have been assembled, check that the piston moves freely on the pin.

37 Piston rings - refitting

1 Check that the piston ring grooves and oilways are thoroughly clean and unblocked. Piston rings must always be fitted over the head of the piston and never from the bottom (Fig. 1.16).

2 The easiest method to use when fitting rings is to wrap a 0.020 inch feeler gauge round the top of the piston and place the rings one at a time starting from the bottom oil control ring, over the feeler gauge.

3 The feeler gauge, complete with ring can then be slid down the piston over the other piston ring grooves until the groove is reached. The piston ring is then slid gently off the feeler gauge into the groove. Set all ring gaps 120° to each other (Fig. 1.17).

4 An alternative method to fit the rings is by holding them slightly open with the thumb and both index fingers. This method requires a steady hand and great care as it is easy to open the ring too much and break it.

5 The two top rings are suitably marked to ensure that they are not fitted the wrong way round.

38 Piston/connecting rod assemblies - refitting

1 Lay-out the piston and connecting rod assemblies in the correct order ready for refitting into their respective bores. These are numbers stamped on the big-end bearing bosses as shown in the photo 38.1.

2 With a wad of clean non-fluffy rag wipe the cylinder bores clean.

3 Position the piston rings so that their gaps are 120° apart and then lubricate the rings. (photo)

4 Fit the piston ring compressor to the top of the piston, making sure it is tight enough to compress the piston ring.

5 Using a piece of fine wire double check that the little jet hole in the connecting rod is clean.

6 The pistons, complete with connecting rods, are fitted to their bores from above.

7 As each piston is inserted into its bore, ensure that it is the correct piston - connecting rod assembly for the particular bore and that the connecting rod is the right way round, also that the front of the piston is towards the front of the bore, i.e. the mark is towards the front of the engine. Lubricate the piston with clean correct grade oil. (photo)

8 The piston will slide into the bore only as far as the bottom of the piston ring compressor. Gently tap the top of the piston with a wooden or plastic hammer whilst the connecting rod is guided into approximate position on the crankshaft. (photo)

9 Repeat the previous sequence for all four pistons and connecting rod assemblies.

39 Connecting rods to crankshaft - reassembly

1 Wipe clean the connecting rod half of the big-end and the underside of the shell bearing. Fit the shell bearing in position with its location tongue engaged with the corresponding groove in the connecting rod. (photo)

2 If the old bearings are nearly new and are being refitted then ensure they are replaced in their correct locations in the correct rods.

3 Generously lubricate the crank pin journals with engine oil, and turn the crankshaft so that the crank pin is in the most advantageous position for the connecting rod to be drawn into it.

4 Wipe clean the connecting rod bearing cap and back of the

shell bearing and fit the shell bearing in position ensuring that the locating tongue at the back of the bearing engages the locating groove in the connecting rod cap.

5 Generously lubricate the shell bearing and offer up the connecting rod bearing cap to the connecting rod. (photo)

6 Fit the connecting rod bolts and tighten in a progressive manner to a final torque wrench setting as specified at the beginning of this Chapter.

40 Sump - refitting

1 Before refitting the sump case, ensure that the following components have been refitted to the engine, and that all fastening nuts and bolts have been tightened to the correct torques.

   i) Crankshaft: Check endfloat (Section 35)
   ii) Main bearing cage (Section 35)
   iii) Big-ends, conrod and piston assemblies (Section 38)
   iv) Crankshaft: freedom to turn (Section 35)
   v) Rear crankshaft oil seal (Section 35) (photo)
   vi) Front crankshaft oil seal (Section 35) (photo)
   vii) Oil pump assembly and intake strainer (Section 21) (photo)

2 Clean mating sump and crankcase surfaces of old gasket material, and place a new gasket - smeared with grease - onto the crankcase face. (photo)

3 Offer the sump onto the crankcase, taking care not to disturb the new gasket resting on the joint face. (photo)

4 Secure the sump with bolts and tighten them progressively.

41 Flywheel and clutch - refitting

1 Stand the engine the right way up on its sump.

2 Offer up the flywheel to the rear end of the crankshaft so that the bolt holes line up and secure the wheel to the shaft with the six bolts.

3 Using the block, described in Section 8 of this Chapter, to hold the flywheel whilst its attachment bolts are tightened to the torque specified at the beginning of this Chapter.

4 Fit the clutch shaft spigot bearing in the centre of the crankshaft and lubricate with some medium grease.

5 Now put the friction disc in position on the flywheel followed by the pressure plate assembly. Align the marks on the pressure plate and flywheel periphery to ensure that they are in the correct relative position.

6 Use a mandrel - a turned down wooden rod, or better still an old clutch/gearbox shaft to hold the friction disc centrally/ concentrically on the flywheel. Screw in the pressure plate retaining bolts and tighten progressively and diametrically to their respective torque - see Chapter 5 for details.

7 When the engine is coupled to 'Hondamatic' transmission a driveplate is bolted to the crankshaft. The torque converter is then secured to the driveplate. Refer to Chapter 6 for further details.

42 Cylinder head fitting - preparation

1 The engine block is nearly ready to receive the cylinder head. The major moving parts, crankshaft, pistons etc., will have been fitted; the sump, flywheel and clutch will also have been fitted. All that remains is the fitting of timing belt, tensioner and sprocket, before the refitting of the cylinder head assembly can commence. Refer to Section 8, of this Chapter.

2 Pay particular attention to the instructions relating to inspection and refitting of the timing belt given in Section 8, of this Chapter.

3 The timing belt must not show any signs of wear or abrasion, and should be refitted so that it moves in the same direction as it

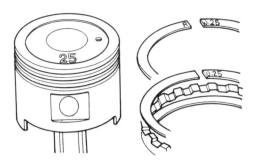

Fig 1.16 Typical piston and piston ring markings when oversize pistons are being fitted (Sec 37)

Fig 1.17 Relative positions of piston ring gaps (Sec 37)

38.1 Crankpin and main journal diameter classification markings

38.3 Oiling Piston Rings

38.7/8 Inserting Piston Assembly into cylinder

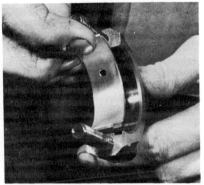

39.1 Fitting big-end bearing shells

39.5 Assembling big-end bearing onto the crank

40.1A Fitting 'rear' transmission end oil seal to the crankshaft

40.1B Fitting 'front' oil seal to the crankshaft

40.1C Fitting the oil pump

40.2 Fitting the sump seal

40.3 Fitting the sump

did before the engine was dismantled. If a new belt is being fitted, it does not matter which way round it is fitted.
4 Ensure that all gasket and sealed joint surfaces are clean and completely free of all old sealing material before refitting commences.

43 Cylinder head - reassembly

The cylinder head reassembly is accomplished in three main phases. Firstly, the valves (exhaust and inlet) are assembled into the cylinder head. Then, secondly, the rockers and camshaft/rocker support pedestals are gathered into a subassembly. Finally, the cylinder head block with valves fitted, the camshaft, and the rockers subassembly are brought together to complete the assembly of the cylinder head. The cylinder head can be fitted to the engine block with only the valves fitted. The camshaft and rockers being fitted afterwards.

44 Valves - refitting

To refit the valves into the cylinder head proceed as follows:
1 Rest the cylinder head block on its side and slide the valves into their appropriate positions. If valves are being reused, they should be fitted into the same position from which they were taken. Apply clean engine oil to the stems before inserting the valves. (photo)
2 Now place the low spring seat in position around the valve guide, and the inlet valve seals into position on top of the valve guide. (photo)
3 Slip the two valve springs in place, followed by the spring's cap. (photos)
4 The valve spring compressor should be used to compress the springs so that the cap presses down the top of the valve stem sufficiently to allow the split collets to be inserted into the cotter groove machined into the stem. (photo)
5 Remove the valve spring compressor and repeat this procedure until all eight valves have been assembled into the cylinder head.
6 It is possible now to refit the cylinder head to the cylinder block (Section 47), and fit the camshaft and rocker assembly afterwards. The photograph sequence shows this method of assembly, although the script assumes the cylinder head is 'completely' assembled before being fitted to the cylinder block.

45 Rockers, rocker shafts and support pedestals - reassembly

1 Place the rockers, rocker shafts, spacing springs, pedestals and pins out on a bench ensuring that components, which are being re-used are in the same position as they occupied before.
2 Check that the rocker shafts have been orientated so that the intake valve rocker shaft (to the right when facing the front of the engine - ie; the water pump end) notch is to the right and that the oil holes are along the bottom of the tube.
3 The exhaust valve rocker shaft (left-hand side) should have the oil holes facing down, and the locating dowel hole to the rear (flywheel) end of the engine.
4 Begin reassembly by fitting the rocker shafts in the rear (flywheel end) pedestal. Drive in the 4 mm dowels which locate the rocker shafts in the pedestals.
5 Slide the rockers, springs and pedestals into position and secure the front pedestals with two 4 mm dowel pins.
6 Once this subassembly is complete, ensure that each rocker is free to move axially and rotationally. (photo)
7 Loosen the rocker adjusting screws and locknuts, and screw them back to the rocker in readiness for its fitting onto the cylinder head.

46 Camshaft - refitting

1 Begin by applying engine oil to the camshaft bearings in the cylinder head, and rocker assembly; and the camshaft journals.
2 Lower the camshaft into position in the cylinder head. (photo)
3 Smear a little gasket sealer compound on the joint surfaces of the front and rear pedestal bases, and then lower the rocker/pedestal assembly onto the cylinder head and camshaft. (photo)
4 The rocker adjusting screws should have been fully screwed back into the rocker lever, so that none of the levers exert any force onto the valves at this stage.
5 Tighten the rocker pedestal bolts to the specified torque.
6 Once the rocker assembly has been refitted, fit the camshaft end plug or tachobody as appropriate. (photo)
7 At the camshaft wheel end, fit the oil seal onto the camshaft into the seating provided by the cylinder head and rocker shaft pedestal. (photo)
8 Next insert the Woodruff key into the camshaft, and slide the camshaft wheel onto the shaft and key. Screw in the fastening bolt and tighten to its specified torque. (photo)
9 The photograph sequence shows the camshaft and rocker assembly installation taking place after the cylinder head has been fitted to the engine block.
   Alternatively, if the assembly of the cylinder head, camshaft and rockers has proceeded with the head on the work bench, it is now the time to refit the cylinder head to the cylinder block.

47 Cylinder head - refitting to the engine

1 It is as well to fit both exhaust and inlet manifolds to the cylinder, before moving the cylinder head to the engine.
2 Clean the manifold/head joint surfaces, ensuring that no fragments of old gasket remain on the surfaces.
3 Always use new gaskets and tighten the fastening nuts to the specified torques. (photo)
4 It is essential to ensure that all valves are kept closed until correct camshaft and crankshaft timing has been established. If the rockers have already been fitted before the cylinder head is refitted to the engine block, then all rocker adjusting screws should be turned right back, so that no cam movement is conveyed to the valve.
5 If the camshaft has not been fitted yet, refer to Sections 45 and 46, of this Chapter, and fit the camshaft now.
6 Turn the camshaft wheel so that the two marks on the periphery of the wheel are parallel with the top of the cylinder head, and the Woodruff key is facing upwards. (photo)
7 Continue and turn the crankshaft so that the 'top-dead-centre' mark on the pulley is with the tdc mark on the timing belt cover. The pistons in the No. 1 and No. 4 cylinders should now be at top-dead-centre. If the engine is being reassembled on the bench, the key slot in the crankshaft should be at tdc. (photo)
8 Ensure that the dowel pins which align the cylinder head and cylinder block are in position in the cylinder head. (photo)
9 Clean the cylinder head and block joint surfaces and position a new gasket on the cylinder head. It is wise to smear a small amount of high temperature melting point grease on the gasket before it is finally put in place. The grease will prevent the gasket sticking to either block or head. (photo)
10 With the cylinder block and head prepared, and crank and camshafts in the correct relative positions, lower the cylinder head into position on the engine. (photo) Screw in the securing bolts and tighten evenly in the order shown in Fig. 1.18 to the torque specified at the beginning of this Chapter.
11 With the cylinder head in position, recheck the positions of the camshaft and crankshaft. The positions should still be as described in paragraphs 7 and 8, of this Section.
12 It is now the time to slip the timing belt cover over the camshaft wheel and to tension it as described in Section 8, of

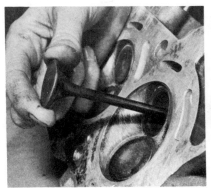
44.1 Fitting valves

44.2 Fitting valve spring seats

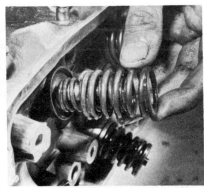
44.3A fitting the valve springs

44.3B Fitting the valve spring cap

44.4 Fitting the split collets onto the valve stem

45.6 The rocker assembly

46.2 Lowering the camshaft onto the cylinder head

46.3 Fitting the rocker assembly

46.6 Fitting the rear camshaft seal

46.7 Fitting the forward camshaft seal

46.8 The camshaft toothed wheel

47.3 Tightening the cylinder head fasteners

this Chapter. Again once the belt has been installed and tensioned ensure that the camshaft and crankshaft are still in the correct relative positions described. (photo)

13 If the engine is being reassembled on a bench, complete the assembly of the crankshaft driving sprocket, fitting the timing belt cover and crankshaft pulley. It is also worthwhile to fit the distributor now. (photos)

48 Distributor - refitting

1 With the crankshaft in position with No. 1 and No. 4 pistons at tdc, and the camshaft wheel marks horizontal, take the distributor and with the cover off, align the metal tag on the rotor arm with the lug on the periphery of the distributor body. Holding the distributor in this position insert the distributor into the bore housing in the cylinder head (Fig. 1.19).

2 The distributor is driven off a helical gear, so expect to allow the unit to rotate as it is fed into its housing bore to permit the gear on the distributor shaft to completely engage the gear cut in the camshaft.

3 Complete the static timing adjustment of the distributor using the technique detailed in Chapter 4, of this manual. The engine will need to be turned to 5° btdc.

49 Fuel pump - refitting

The pump bolts onto the rear end of the cylinder head, as a lever protrudes from the pump to follow an eccentric lobe machined on the camshaft. Ensure that the pump lever is resting on the top of the eccentric lobe and then secure the pump with two bolts. Tighten the fasteners to the specified torque. Refer to Chapter 3, for details of inspection and fitting the fuel pump.

50 Oil pump driveshaft - installation

1 Having fitted the cylinder head and installed the distributor and fuel pump, it is now the time when the oil pump driveshaft needs to be fitted. This shaft runs vertically through the centre of the engine, and the middle rocker/camshaft pedestal houses the shaft end bearing and drive gears.

2 Coat the shaft with clean engine oil and slip it down through the centre pedestal so that it engages first the gear on the camshaft and then the slot in the pump drive. It may be necessary to

turn the engine by hand, a little, to rotate the oil pump driveshaft into a position when it can engage the oil pump. (photo)

3 Once the shaft has bedded down into position the top plate which acts to accept some end thrust, can be bolted into position on top of the centre pedestal. (photo)

4 With all the moving parts of the engine assembled, it only remains to adjust and set the rocker/valve stem gaps as detailed in the next Section.

51 Rocker arm/valve - clearance adjustment

1 If the engine is in place in the car, it will be necessary to remove the rocker cover to gain access to the rockers. Position the car on a level surface and put in gear. It will be necessary to jog the car forwards a little to turn the engine so that respective valves will open and shut as they are needed. On cars fitted with 'Hondamatic' transmission, turn the engine with the crankshaft pulley bolt.

2 The valve adjustments should be made with the engine cold. The importance of correct rocker arm/valve stem clearances cannot be overstressed as they vitally affect the performance of the engine.

3 If the clearances are set too wide, the efficiency of the engine is reduced because the valves open later and close earlier than was intended. If on the other hand the gap is too small, there is a chance that thermal expansion in the valve and operating mechanism may 'overtake' the gap and prevent the valve from seating properly. In such instances the valves overheat and soon become damaged and ineffective.

4 It is important that the gap is set when the rocker acting on the valve being adjusted is away from the peak of the cam. This can be achieved by aligning the crankshaft pulley tdc mark with the index mark on the timing belt cover when number 1 piston is at tdc on its compression stroke (i.e. inlet and exhaust valve are both closed), and adjusting valves 1, 2, 3 and 6; then rotate the crankshaft 360° and adjust valves 4, 5, 7 and 8.

5 The correct valve clearance is given in 'Specifications' at the beginning of this Chapter. The correct clearance is obtained by slackening the hexagonal locknut with a spanner while holding the ball pin against rotation with a screwdriver as shown in the photograph.

6 Insert a feeler gauge of the correct size between the rocker and valve stem, beneath the adjusting screw. Screw down the adjusting screw until the gauge is just gripped between the screw head and valve stem. (photo)

7 When the gauge is being lightly pinched by the adjusting screw, tighten the locknut to secure the adjusting screw.

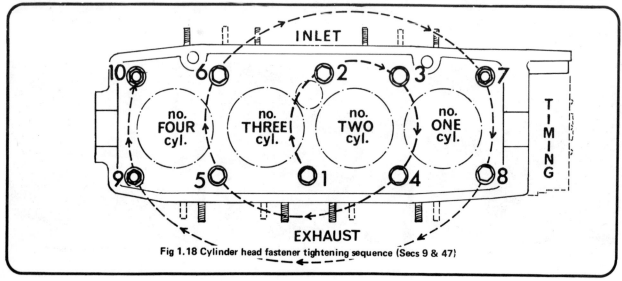

Fig 1.18 Cylinder head fastener tightening sequence (Secs 9 & 47)

47.6 Camshaft wheel marks alignment

47.7 Fitting crankshaft timing sprocket

47.8/9 Cylinder Block prepared for Cylinder Head

47.10 Fitting the cylinder head

47.12 Timing belt fitted

47.13A Woodruff key for crankshaft pulley wheel

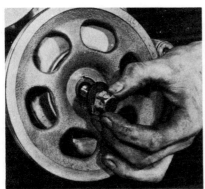
47.13B Fitting crankshaft pulley

47.13C Fitting timing belt cover

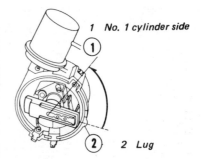
Fig 1.19 Alignment of rotor arm and distributor body when No. 1 piston is at TDC (Sec 48)

1 No. 1 cylinder side
2 Lug

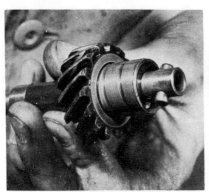
50.2 Oil pump driveshaft and gear

50.3 Oil pump shaft retaining block

51.5/6 Rocker/Valve gap adjustment

52.1A Carburettor

52.1B Inlet manifold refitting

52.1C Thermostat and Elbow

52.1D Water pump

52.1E Oil pressure transducer

52.1F Rocker cover

52.1G Timing belt top cover

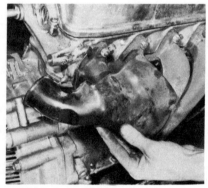
52.1H Exhaust manifold and warm air scoop

53.3 Lowering engine into the car

53.4 Interference of transmission and brake pipes

53.5A Fitting front end engine mounting

53.5B Inserting driveshafts

52 Engine - final assembly

1   The following components need to be refitted to the engine before it is rejoined to the gearbox and transmission.

   i)   Carburettor and inlet manifold - Chapter 3. (photos)
   ii) Thermostat and water outlet elbow - Chapter 2. (photo)
   iii) Alternator - Chapter 10
   iv) Water pump - Chapter 2. (photo)
   v)   Water pump/alternator belt, band tensioning - refer to Chapter 2
   vi) Oil filter cartridge and oil pressure transducer. (photo)
   vii) Cylinder head and timing belt top covers. (photos)
   viii) Exhaust manifold and warm air scoop. (photo)

53 Engine - refitting to the car

Although the engine can be replaced by one man using a suitable hoist, it is easier if two are present. Generally replacement follows the reverse of the removal procedure. It is wise to ensure that all loose leads, cables etc., are tucked out of the way. It is easy to trap one and cause much additional work after the engine has been installed.

1   Begin by joining the engine and gearbox. When offering the gearbox to the engine make sure that the clutch shaft is inserted into the clutch and flywheel carefully, so as not to bend or deform the clutch plate or shaft.

2   Tighten the engine to transmission securing bolts to the torque specified at the beginning of this Chapter.

3   Place a sling around the engine and transmission and hoist it into the engine compartment in the car. (photo)

4   Lower the engine slowly into the engine space, inclining it so that it does not interfere with the battery tray, brake pipes and bodyshell members. (photo)

5   With the engine in its installed position, reconnect the lower engine mount to the suspension subframe. Then introduce the driveshafts into the differential in the transmission. It may be necessary to incline the engine slightly to refit the right-hand shaft. Next refit the end engine support and torque reaction rod. (photos)

6   Reconnect the gearshift mechanism, and then proceed to re-assemble the front suspension - the lower control arm balljoint and the steering arm balljoints - Chapters 7 and 8 detail those tasks.

7   Reconnect the exhaust pipe to the manifold and follow that by refitting the exhaust pipe retainer to the front of the engine.

8   It is now possible to remove the sling and the hoist, and lower the car to the ground.

9   Refit the coolant hoses and bypass hose to the engine inlet and outlet pipes. Refit the radiator, cooling fan and transmission oil cooler hoses if 'Hondamatic' transmission is fitted.

10 Refit the starter if not already on the engine and reconnect the electrical leads to both the starter and alternator.

11 Reconnect the minor electrical leads to the cooling fan, temperature sensor, reversing light switch and LT and HT leads to the distributor.

12 Refit the speedometer cable and tachometer cable as appropriate.

13 Refit the carburettor, the choke cable, accelerator cable and then finally the clutch actuating cable.

14 Reconnect the fuel lines to the fuel pump, and carburettor. Reattach the small hoses - petrol vapour - to the carburettor and carbon filled vapour control canister (Chapter 3).

15 Reconnect the coolant hoses, to the radiator, engine and interior heater.

16 It is now permissible to refit the battery and the positive and negative leads to the battery.

17 Refit the spark plugs and their HT leads.

18 Refill the engine with Castrol GTX, or equivalent oil, and then refill the gearbox and differential with oil as well. (photos) Remember to prime the 'Hondamatic' transmission oil pump if the transmission has been dismantled - Chapter 6.

19 Turn the interior heater to 'hot' and refill the cooling system with water and corrosion inhibitor.

20 Finally refit the engine compartment hood and grille trim.

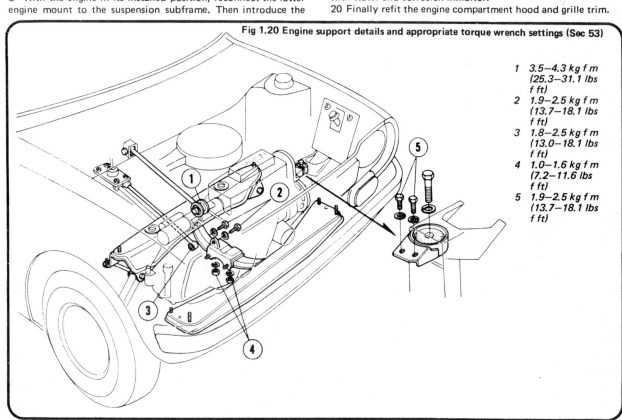

Fig 1.20 Engine support details and appropriate torque wrench settings (Sec 53)

1   3.5–4.3 kg f m (25.3–31.1 lbs f ft)
2   1.9–2.5 kg f m (13.7–18.1 lbs f ft)
3   1.8–2.5 kg f m (13.0–18.1 lbs f ft)
4   1.0–1.6 kg f m (7.2–11.6 lbs f ft)
5   1.9–2.5 kg f m (13.7–18.1 lbs f ft)

53.5C Fitting torque reaction rod

53.18A Refilling the engine with oil

53.18B Refilling the gearbox with oil

54 Engine - initial start-up, after overhaul or major repair

1 Make sure that the battery is fully charged and that all lubricants, coolant and fuel are replenished.

2 If the fuel system has been dismantled it will require several revolutions of the engine on the starter motor to pump the petrol up to the carburettor. An initial prime of about 1/3 of a cupful of petrol poured down the air intake of the carburettor will help the engine to fire quickly, thus relieving the load on the battery. Do not overdo this, however, as flooding may result.

3 As soon as the engine fires, and runs, keep it going at a fast tick over only, (no faster) and bring it up to the normal working temperature.

4 As the engine warms up there will be odd smells and some smoke from parts getting hot and burning off oil deposits. The signs to look for are leaks of water or oil which will be obvious if serious. Check also the exhaust pipe and manifold connections, as these do not always 'find' their exact gas tight position until the warmth and vibration have acted on them, and it is almost certain that they will need tightening further. This should be done, of course, with the engine stopped.

5 When normal running temperature has been reached adjust the engine idling speed as described in Chapter 3.

6 Stop the engine and wait a few minutes to see if any lubricant or coolant is dripping out when the engine is stationary.

7 Road test the car to check that the timing is correct and that the engine is giving the necessary smoothness and power. Do not race the engine - if new bearings and/or pistons have been fitted it should be treated as a new engine and run in at a reduced speed for the first 300 miles (500 km).

55 Fault diagnosis - engine

Symptom	Reason/s	Remedy
Engine fails to turn when starter operated	Flat or defective battery	Charge or replace battery, push start car.
	Loose battery leads	Tighten both terminals and earth ends of earth leads.
	Defective starter solenoid or switch or broken wiring	Run a wire direct from the battery to the starter motor or bypass the solenoid.
	Engine earth strap disconnected	Check and retighten strap.
	Jammed starter motor drive pinion	Place car in gear and rock to and fro. Alternatively, free exposed square end of shaft with spanner.
	Defective starter motor	Remove and recondition.
Engine turns on starter but will not start	Ignition damp or wet	Wipe dry the distributor cap and ignition leads.
	Ignition leads to spark plugs loose	Check and tighten at both spark plug and distributor cap ends.
	Shorted or disconnected low tension leads	Check the wiring on the CB and SW terminals of the coil and to the distributor.
	Dirty, incorrectly set, or pitted contact breaker points	Clean, file smooth, and adjust.
	Faulty condenser	Check contact breaker points for arcing, remove and fit new.
	Defective ignition switch	Bypass switch with wire.
	Ignition leads connected wrong way round	Remove and replace leads to spark plugs in correct order.
	Faulty coil	Remove and fit new coil.
	Contact breaker point spring earthed or broken	Check spring is not touching metal part of distributor. Check insulator washers are correctly placed. Renew points if the spring is broken.
	No petrol in petrol tank	Refill tank!
	Vapour lock in fuel line (in hot conditions or at high altitude)	Blow into petrol tank, allow engine to cool, or apply a cold wet rag to the fuel line.
	Blocked float chamber needle valve	Remove, clean and replace.
	Fuel pump filter blocked	Remove, clean and replace.
	Choked or blocked carburettor jets	Dismantle and clean.
	Faulty fuel pump	Remove, overhaul and replace.
Engine stalls and will not re-start	Too much choke allowing too rich a mixture to wet plugs	Remove and dry spark plugs or with wide open throttle, push start the car.
	Float damaged or leaking or needle not seating	Remove, examine, clean and replace float and needle valve as necessary.
	Float lever incorrectly adjusted	Remove and adjust correctly.
	Ignition failure - sudden	Check over low and high tension circuits for breaks in wiring.
	Ignition failure - misfiring precludes total stoppage	Check contact breaker points, clean and adjust. Renew condenser if faulty.
	Ignition failure - in severe rain or after traversing water splash	Dry out ignition leads and distributor cap.
	No petrol in petrol tank	Refill tank!
	Petrol tank breather choked	Remove petrol cap and clean out breather hole or pipe.
	Sudden obstruction in carburettor(s)	Check jets, filter, and needle valve in float chamber for blockage.
	Water in fuel system	Drain tank and blow out fuel lines.
Engine misfires or idles unevenly	Ignition leads loose	Check and tighten as necessary at spark plug and distributor cap ends.
	Battery leads loose on terminals	Check and tighten terminal leads.
	Battery earth strap loose on body attachment point	Check and tighten earth lead to body attachment point.
	Engine earth lead loose	Tighten lead.
	Low tension leads to coil terminals loose	Check and tighten leads if found loose.
	Low tension lead from coil to distributor loose	Check and tighten if found loose.
	Dirty, or incorrectly gapped plugs	Remove, clean and regap.
	Dirty, incorrectly set, or pitted contact breaker points	Clean, file smooth, and adjust.
	Tracking across inside of distributor cover	Remove and fit new cover.

Symptom	Reason/s	Remedy
	Ignition too retarded	Check and adjust ignition timing.
	Faulty coil	Remove and fit new coil.
	Mixture too weak	Check jets, float chamber needle valve, and filters for obstruction. Clean as necessary. Adjust carburettor(s)
	Air leak in carburettor	Remove and overhaul carburettor.
	Air leak at inlet manifold to cylinder head, or inlet manifold to carburettor	Test by pouring oil along joints. Bubbles indicate leak. Renew manifold gasket as appropriate.
Lack of power and poor compression	Incorrect valve clearances	Adjust to take up wear.
	Burnt out exhaust valves	Remove cylinder head and renew defective valves.
	Sticking or leaking valves	Remove cylinder head, clean, check and renew valves as necessary.
	Weak or broken valve springs	Check and renew as necessary.
	Worn valve guides or stems	Renew valve guides and valves.
	Worn pistons and piston rings	Dismantle engine, renew pistons and rings.
	Burnt out exhaust valves	Remove cylinder head, renew defective valves.
	Blown cylinder head gasket (accompanied by increase in noise)	Remove cylinder head and fit new gasket.
	Worn or scored cylinder bores	Dismantle engine, rebore, renew pistons and rings.
	Ignition timing wrongly set. Too advanced or retarded	Check and reset ignition timing.
	Contact breaker points incorrectly gapped	Check and reset contact breaker points.
	Incorrect valve clearances	Check and reset rocker arm to valve stem gap.
	Incorrectly set spark plugs	Remove, clean and regap.
	Carburation too rich or too weak	Tune carburettor for optimum performance.
	Dirty contact breaker points	Remove, clean and replace.
	Fuel filters blocked causing poor top end performance through fuel starvation	Dismantle, inspect, clean, and replace all fuel filters.
	Distributor automatic balance weights or vacuum advance and retard mechanisms not functioning correctly	Overhaul distributor.
	Faulty fuel pump giving top end fuel starvation	Remove, overhaul, or fit exchange reconditioned fuel pump.
Excessive oil consumption	Excessively worn valve stems and valve guides	Remove cylinder head and fit new valves and valve guides.
	Worn piston rings	Fit oil control rings to existing pistons or purchase new pistons.
	Worn pistons and cylinder bores	Fit new pistons and rings, rebore cylinders.
	Excessive piston ring gap allowing blow-up	Fit new piston rings and set gap correctly.
	Piston oil return holes choked	Decarbonise engine and pistons.
	Leaking oil filter gasket	Inspect and fit new gasket as necessary.
	Leaking rocker cover gasket	Inspect and fit new gasket as necessary.
	Leaking timing gear cover gasket	Inspect and fit new gasket as necessary.
	Leaking sump gasket	Inspect and fit new gasket as necessary.
	Loose sump plug	Tighten, fit new gasket if necessary.
Unusual noises from engine	Worn valve gear (noisy tapping from rocker box	Inspect and renew rocker shaft, rocker arms, and ball pins as necessary.
	Worn big-end bearing (regular heavy knocking)	Drop sump and check bearings - remedy as necessary.
	Worn main bearings (rumbling and vibration)	Drop sump and check bearings - remedy as necessary.

Chapter 2 Cooling system

Contents

Specifications

System type ... ... Pressurized, pump assisted

Cooling system capacity (including heater) ... ... 4.2 litres (4.4 quarts US)

Thermostat (wax filled)
  Opening temperature ... ... 80° to 84° C (176° to 183° F)
  Fully open ... ... 95° C (203° F)
  Valve lift ... ... 8 mm (0.315 inch)

Radiator cap blow-off pressure ... ... 0.75 - 1.05 kg f cm^2 (10.67 - 14.93 lb f in^2)

Water pump/alternator belt tension ... ... 12 mm   9 kgf 12 mm (0.5 inch)   9 kgf (20 lb f)

Fan operating temperature ... ... 88.5° to 91.5° C (191° to 197° F)

Fan to core clearance ... ... 8 mm (0.3 inch)

Torque wrench settings:

	kg fm	lb f ft
Water pump	1.0 - 1.4	7 - 10
Thermoswitch	2.0 - 2.5	14 - 18
Radiator to bodyshell	0.7 - 1.2	5 - 9

1 General description and maintenance

1 Engine cooling is achieved by a conventional pump assisted thermosyphon system, inlet manifold and heating is included, and car interior heating is also part of the engine cooling system as usual.

The coolant is pressurized to prevent premature boiling in adverse conditions and to allow the engine to run at temperature appropriate to maximum efficiency.

The system functions as follows: cold water from the radiator circulates up the lower radiator hose to the water pump where it is impelled into the water passages in the cylinder block helping to keep the cylinder bores and pistons cool.

The water then travels up to the cylinder head, around the combustion chambers and valve seats absorbing more heat before finally passing out into the inlet manifold water jacket. The thermostat is mounted beneath the outlet elbow in the inlet manifold water jacket.

When the engine is running at its correct operating temperature, the thermostat is open to allow the coolant to flow to the radiator. The coolant is cooled as it passes down the radiator by the air being drawn through by the electrically driven fan. However, if the engine has not attained its proper running temperature, the thermostat valve will be closed and will inhibit the flow of coolant through the engine. When the thermostat valve is closed, coolant can only flow through the car interior heater and engine. The restriction to coolant flow ensures a rapid warming of the engine, and this warming is accelerated by the use of a thermal switch operated fan. This means that the fan will not begin to operate and cool the coolant flowing in the radiator until the coolant temperature at the bottom of the radiator has reached between 88 and 92° C (191° to 197° F).

The temperature of the water is monitored by a transmitter in the inlet manifold water jacket, which gives a continuous indication of coolant temperature.

Hot water for the heating and ventilation system is supplied from a union on the inlet manifold water jacket and returned to the lower radiator hose between the radiator and pump inlet.

Normal maintenance consists of checking the level of water in the radiator at regular intervals, and to inspecting hoses and joints for signs of leaks or deterioration.

2 Cooling system - draining

1 With the car on level ground, drain the system as follows:
2 Turn the car interior heater control to hot, and undo the radiator filler cap. Unscrew the plug at the bottom of the radiator and collect the coolant in a suitable receptacle. **Do not**

remove the drain plug when the engine is hot.

3 The coolant antifreeze solution can be reused.

4 When the coolant has finished running out of the cylinder block drain orifice, use a short length of wire to dislodge any sediment which may be blocking the orifice inhibiting complete draining.

3 Cooling system - flushing

1 Generally even with proper use, the cooling system will gradually lose its efficiency as the radiator becomes choked with deposits/sediment from the coolant passages. To clean the system out, remove the radiator filler cap and bottom hose, and leave a hose running in the radiator filler hose for fifteen minutes.

2 Reconnect the bottom hose, refit the drain plug if it has been removed and refill the cooling system as described in Section 4, adding a proprietary cleaning compound. **Remember the engine is aluminium,** some cleaning compounds will corrode aluminium. Run the engine for fifteen minutes: the sediment and sludge should have now been loosened, and may be removed by draining and flushing.

3 Refill the cooling system with a water/antifreeze solution, as directed in Section 4.

4 **Note:** If the sediment in the radiator is particularly difficult to remove, the radiator may be 'reverse flushed'. This involves leaving a hose pipe in either the drain plug orifice or bottom hose union, and forcing water up through the radiator and out of the filler orifice at the top of the radiator. Reverse flushing can be carried out with the radiator in position.

4 Cooling system - filling and bleeding

1 Fit the radiator drain plug, and if the bottom hose has been removed, it should be reconnected.

2 Fill the system slowly to ensure that a minimum number of airlocks form. Check that the car interior heat valve is set at 'hot'. The water used in the cooling system ought to be soft - rain water is ideal.

3 Mix antifreeze with the water, according to the antifreeze manufacturer's instructions. The antifreeze should contain an inhibitor to protect the aluminium from which the engine is constructed.

4 Attach a clear plastic tube to the cooling system bleed screw (near the thermostat on the inlet manifold water jacket) and undo the bleed screw. Continue to add coolant until no air bubbles can be seen in the coolant coming out of the bleed screw through the plastic tubing. When no air bubbles appear from the bleed screw tighten the screw and remove the clear plastic tube.

5 Top up the radiator until the coolant level is about ¾ inches above the tube core in the radiator. Refit the radiator cap.

6 Start the engine and run for about 10 minutes until thoroughly warmed up. Keep the car interior heater control at 'Hot'.

7 Stop the engine and attach the clear plastic tube to the cooling system bleed valve screw. Undo the screw and do not retighten until the coolant running from the bleed screw is free of bubbles (Fig. 2.2).

8 Remove the radiator cap and top-up as necessary, then top-up the expansion bottle to the 'hot' level.

5 Radiator - removal and refitting

1 Drain the cooling system as detailed in Section 2, of this Chapter.

2 Next remove the front grille and the associated bright work. Undo the two screws retaining the bottom strip of trim; remove that strip. Then undo and remove the four screws which secure the centre section of the grille to the bodyshell. There are three screws along the top of the grille and one in the middle of the

bottom edge.

3 Finally the two screws which retain the headlight trims should be removed. Remove all the trims and grille.

4 Disconnect the electrical leads from the battery, this is an essential safety measure. It is all too easy to accidentally short wires and leads to the car bodyshell when dismantling a system.

5 Separate the fan power lead connector and pull the leads from the fan thermoswitch on the bottom of the radiator. (photo)

6 Next remove the top and lower radiator hoses from the unions and then remove the four bolts which secure the radiator to the bodyshell.

7 Lift the radiator clear, complete with fan. The fan and cage may then be unbolted from the radiator itself. (photo)

8 Refitting follows the exact reversal of the removal procedure.

6 Radiator - inspection and cleaning

1 With the radiator out of the car any leaks can be soldered up or repaired with a compound such as Cataloy. Clean out the radiator by flushing as described in Section 3. It should be mentioned that solder repairs are best completed professionally; it is too easy to damage other parts of the radiator by excessive heating.

2 When the radiator is out of the car, it is advantageous to turn it upside-down for reverse flushing. Clean the exterior of the radiator by hosing down the radiator matrix with a strong jet of water to clean away road dirt, dead flies, etc.

3 Inspect the radiator hoses for cracks (internal and external), perishing and damage caused by over-tightening of the hose clips. Renew the hoses as necessary.

4 Examine the hose clips and renew them if they are rusted or distorted. The drain plugs and washers should be renewed if leaking.

7 Fan and motor - inspection and renovation

1 Remove the radiator and separate the fan, motor and cage.

2 The fan motor is mounted on the cage with three bolts and bushes. The fan itself is retained on the motor shaft by a single nut.

3 It will be necessary to remove the fan before the motor can be detached. Hold the fan, whilst the motor shaft nut is undone, then jolt the fan off the shaft.

4 If the fan motor shaft bearings are sloppy or the motor does not run, or runs unevenly, the only remedy is to replace the motor.

5 The motor unit has no facility for repair.

6 The fan itself is of moulded nylon and is not repairable.

7 Reassembly of the fan unit follows the reversal of the dismantling procedure.

8 Thermostat - removal, testing and refitting

Removal

1 Drain the cooling system, as directed in Section 2, of this Chapter.

2 Remove the top radiator hose from the thermostat cover on the inlet manifold water jacket.

3 Undo and remove the two bolts which secure the cover to the manifold jacket. Lift the cover away to reveal the thermostat. (photo)

4 Lift out the thermostat ready for testing.

Testing

5 The thermostat may be tested for correct functioning by suspending it together with a thermometer in a saucepan of cold water. Heat the water and note the temperature at which the thermostat begins to open. This temperature should be between 80 and 84° C (178 - 183° F). Discard the thermostat if it is open

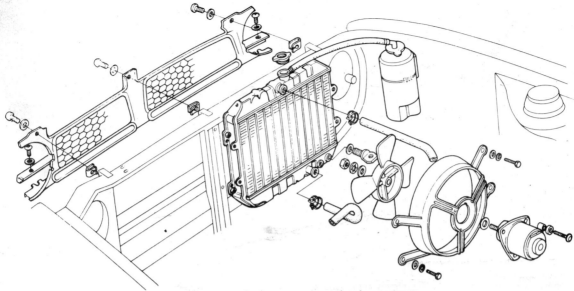
Fig. 2.1 Radiator, fan, motor and associated components

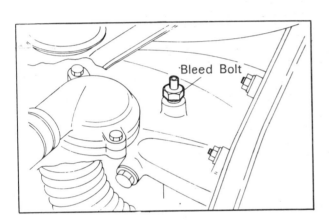
Fig 2.2 Cooling system bleed screw on inlet manifold water jacket (Sec 4)

5.5 Thermoswitch connections

5.7 Radiator removal

8.3 Thermostat removal

too early. Continue heating the water until the thermostat is fully open and note that temperature - 95° C (203° F). Turn off the heat to allow the thermostat to cool down. If the thermostat **does** not open fully in near boiling water, or close completely when cooled, the unit must be discarded and a new thermostat fitted.

Refitting

6   Lower the thermostat into its housing and fit the cover, using a new gasket to seal the joint between the cover and the thermostat housing. Fit the upper hose.
7   Refill the cooling system, as directed in Section 4, of this Chapter.

9   Fan thermoswitch - removal, testing and refitting

1   Drain the cooling system, as directed in Section 2, of this Chapter.
2   Disconnect the electrical leads from the battery; this is an essential safety measure when any electrical circuit in the vehicle is being separated.
3   Pull the electrical leads from the thermoswitch. (photo 5.5).
4   Unscrew the switch from the base of the radiator.
5   A continuity testing circuit is required. This consists of a battery, bulb and three lengths of wire. Connect the thermoswitch and bulb in series with the battery. When the switch is cold the bulb should **not** glow. Lower the switch into a saucepan of water, together with a thermometer. Heat the water and note its temperature when the thermoswitch turns 'on' and the bulb

glows. This 'on' temperature should be 90° C - 1.5° C (191 to 197° F). Once the switch is 'on', turn off the heat, and as the switch cools. note the temperature at which the thermoswitch turns off. 85° C - 1.5° C (182 - 188° F) (Fig. 2.4). The switch should be discarded and a new one fitted if it does not perform as required.
6   Screw the thermoswitch into the radiator, refit the electrical leads to the switch and battery. Refill the cooling system, as directed in Section 4, of this Chapter.

10 Water pump - removal and refitting

1   Drain the cooling system, as directed in Section 2, of this Chapter.
2   Loosen the alternator bolts and move the unit toward the engine so that the drivebelt can be removed from the crankshaft, water pump and alternator pulleys.
3   Undo and remove the four water pump bolts.
4   Extract the water pump from the cylinder block. Part of the pump body passes between the timing belt cover and engine block. The pump should be removed with the rubber dust seal which sits between pump and timing belt cover. (photo)
5   Once the pump has been removed and it has been found to be faulty, the only action is to discard it and fit a new pump.
6   Before refitting the pump, check that the seal ring is in good condition and not cracked or broken. Clean the joint faces of the pump and cylinder block.
7   Position the timing belt cover seal on the pump body and offer the pump into position. Once the impeller has entered the

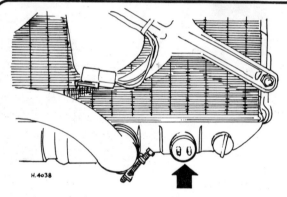

Fig 2.3 Thermoswitch location on radiator (Sec 9)

10.4 Water pump removal

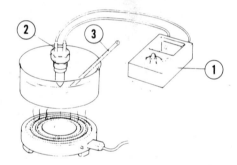

Fig 2.4 Testing the thermoswitch (Sec 9)

1   Multimeter to read electrical resistance of switch   2   Thermoswitch
3   Thermometer

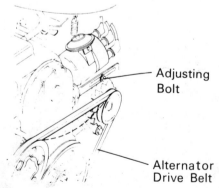

Fig 2.5 Alternator and water pump drivebelt tensioning (Secs 11 & 12)

pump housing in the cylinder block the pump can be slid into position. Ensure that the timing cover seal is properly seated.
8 Insert the four pump bolts and tighten to the specified torque.

11 Pump/alternator drivebelt - removal and refitting

1 Loosen the alternator bolts and move the unit towards the engine so that the drivebelt can be removed from the crankshaft/alternator/pump pulley wheels.
2 If the belt is worn or has overstretched, it should be renewed. Often the reason for replacement is that the belt has broken in service. It is therefore recommended that a spare belt is always carried in the car. Replacement follows the reversal of the removal procedure but if replacement is due to breakage, proceed as follows:
3 Loosen alternator pivot bolts and slotted link bolts and move the unit towards the engine, then carefully fit the belt over the crankshaft, alternator and water pump pulleys.
4 Adjust the belt, as described in Section 12, of this Chapter and tighten the alternator mounting bolts. **Note:** After fitting a brand new belt, it will probably be necessary to re-tension the belt after some 250 miles (Fig. 2.5).

12 Pump/alternator drivebelt - tensioning

1 It is important to keep the drivebelt correctly adjusted: it should be checked every 6,000 miles or 6 months. If the belt is slack, it will slip, wear rapidly and cause water pump and/or alternator malfunction. If the belt is too tight, the alternator and water pump bearings will wear rapidly.
2 The belt tension is correct when there is just ½ inch (13 mm) of vertical movement at the mid-point position between water pump and alternator pulleys. (Fig. 2.5).
3 To adjust the belt tension, slacken the alternator pivot and slot arm bolts, just sufficiently for the unit to be levered away from the engine, with a long screwdriver. Once the new position of the alternator has been obtained for the correct belt tension, the unit's bolts can be tightened.

13 Thermal transmitter - general

1 The thermal transmitter is a device which varies in electrical resistance with temperature. Chapter 10 details the testing procedure for the temperature monitoring system. The transmitter is screwed into the inlet manifold water jacket below the carburettor.
2 Should it be necessary to remove the transmitter, drain the cooling system first, as directed in Section 2, of this Chapter.

14 Fault diagnosis - cooling system

Engine overheating

This is characterised by **all** of the following:
Engine 'pinking' and slightly rough when running.
Excessive evaporation of coolant.

Engine running on when switched off (and high temperature indication).
Reasons for overheating and remedy:
1 Insufficient coolant in system: check for leaks in system. Examine all hoses and gaskets and top-up radiator.
2 Water pump drivebelt slipping: characterised by a shriek as engine speed varies, and possibly a weakening battery and dimmer lights. Tighten the drivebelt.
3 Radiator fan malfunction: if the fan does work sometimes, remove and check the fan thermal switch. If the fan is not seen to work, remove the leads from the thermal switch and join together. The fan motor should run smoothly when the vehicle ignition is switched on. If the fan motor does not run when the switch is bypassed, check that power is reaching the fan by connecting a voltmeter across the fan motor terminals. Remove and replace the fan motor when it has been established as faulty. If the fan motor does run when the thermal switch is bypassed - remove and check the thermal switch.
4 Ignition timing incorrectly set: this will be accompanied by a significantly worsened petrol consumption. Retime engine, as detailed in Chapter 4, of this manual.
5 Carburettors incorrectly adjusted to give a weak mixture: this fault too gives rise to a deterioration in petrol consumption.
6 Thermostat not opened fully: remove and check the thermostat operation.
7 Blown cylinder head gasket: check the compression in each cylinder.
8 Brakes are binding: identified by the vehicle not tending to roll on gentle slopes. Adjust the brakes.
9 Partial blockage in exhaust system: check the exhaust pipe for restrictions and replace any dented sections.
10 Engine not yet 'run-in': it is characteristic of newly machined engines to run hot if driven too hard - do not drive so hard!
11 Insufficient oil in sump: it is unlikely that the oil level could be neglected sufficiently to allow it to fall to a level when the engine will overheat.

Engine running cool

Characterised by reduced effectiveness of car interior heater, higher petrol consumption than usual, low temperature indication.
1 Thermostat malfunction. Remove the thermostat and check its operation. Check also that it is the correct thermostat.

Loss of coolant

1 Check the hoses and gaskets in the cooling system first, but if no leakage can be found, check the radiator pressure cap, it may not be holding the correct pressure in the cooling system.
2 Cracks in the radiator core or cylinder head could lose coolant.

Engine temperature indicator not giving sensible reading

This fault is characterised by the temperature gauge showing a temperature which does not agree with other indications of engine running condition. It may be accompanied by an incorrect fuel level indication. When in doubt on the temperature indication, remove the transmitter and check its electrical resistance at various temperatures. See Chapter 10, for details.

Chapter 3 Carburation;
fuel, exhaust and emission control systems

Contents

Specifications

Fuel pump

Type	Diaphragm unit operated from overhead camshaft
Delivery pressure	2.5 lb f in^2 $\qquad$ 0.18 kg cm^{-2}
Displacement	
$\quad$ Engine R.P.M. 3000	700cc (43 m^3) per minute

Fuel tank capacity ... ... 10 US gallons, 37.8 litres, 8.4 Imp. gallons

Carburettor

Type	Hitachi
1169cc engine - DCG306 - 45	Manual transmission
$\qquad$ - DCG306 - 46	Hondamatic transmission
1237cc engine - DCG306 - 45A	Manual transmission
$\qquad$ - DCG306 - 46A	Hondamatic transmission
Float level	11 mm (0.4331 inch)
Needle valve stroke	1.3 - 1.7 mm (0.05 to 0.067 inch)
Accelerator pump displacement	0.6 cc per stroke (0.037 in^3)
Fast idle at first detent on choke cable:	
$\quad$ throttle valve to barrel clearance - DCG306 - 45, 46 ...	1.48 mm (0.058 inch)
$\qquad$ - DCG306 - 45A, 46A ...	0.8 mm (0.031 inch)
$\qquad$ - DCG306 - 41, 42 ...	1.22 mm (0.048 inch)
Secondary throttle valve opening point	5.83 mm (0.2295 inch)
Number of idle screw turns for nominal adjustment	2¾ ± ¼

Torque wrench settings

	kg f m	lb f ft
Intake manifold	1.8 - 2.4	13 - 17
Carburettor nuts	0.8 - 1.2	6 - 9
Fuel pump	1.8 - 2.4	13 - 17
Exhaust manifold	1.8 - 2.4	13 - 17
Hot air intake	1.0 - 1.4	7 - 10
Exhaust manifold/pipe	1.9 - 2.5	14 - 18
Exhaust pipe/silencer	1.9 - 2.5	14 - 18
Silencer mount	1.9 - 2.5	14 - 18
Fuel tank to body shell	1.9 - 2.5	14 - 18

1 General description

The fuel tank is mounted between the rear wheels, beneath the car. The fuel pump is mechanically actuated and is mounted on the cylinder head alongside the inlet manifold. The carburettor receives petrol under pressure from the pump, and meters it into the air being sucked into the engine, in correct proportions for economical and efficient running.

An emission control system has been added to the fuel/ carburation system to ensure that petrol vapour or noxious combustion products are kept to a minimum. The emission control system provides a sealed fuel system where vapours from the fuel tank are fed to a carbon filled canister. The carbon is bleached of vapour by clean air drawn through it into the engine when it is running. The engine is completely airtight; crankcase vapours are fed into the inlet manifold so that they can be burnt by the engine.

The emission control system also includes several additional devices fixed to the carburettor and air cleaner; the whole system is described fully in Section 9, of this Chapter.

2 Air cleaner element - removal and fitting

1 The air, before it enters the carburettor, is filtered in a dry paper cartridge cleaner. The filter element should be removed and dust tapped off every 2 to 3,000 miles and the element renewed every 6 to 8,000 miles depending on operating conditions. A clogged and dirty filter can be solely responsible for bad starting and lower than usual fuel economy.

2 To remove the filter element, unscrew the wing nut on the top of the cleaner box; then pull off the top of the box carefully. (photo)

3 Once the top of the box is off, the element may be lifted out. If the same element is to be refitted, tap it on a flat surface to remove any loose accumulation of dust. **Do not** try and wash it, brush it, or blow it with compressed air.

4 When reassembling the unit, make sure that the sealing rims on the periphery of the box and in the box cover, are both in position.

5 Take care not to damage the thermal trip device which is in the air cleaner box; the device is part of the emission control system. The cleaner box inlet has an inlet vacuum actuated flap mechanism fitted, again as part of the emission control system. This mechanism works with the thermal trip to ensure that moderately warm air is always supplied to the carburettor. The flap mechanism acts to allow warm air to be drawn into the carburettor from the vicinity of the exhaust manifold. The warm air in the carburettor helps to ensure proper dispersion of the petrol/air emulsion in the air stream passing through the carburettor.

3 Carburettor - description and modes of operation.

The carburettor fitted to the Honda Civic is termed a fixed choke compound carburettor. It has five modes of operation, each one being particular to a range of airflow and operating demands on the carburettor. These separate modes of operation are necessary to allow the carburettor to cope with the wide range of airflows and demands an automatobile engine creates.

The modes are:

(i) Cold start	*Low air flow and enriched fuel air mixture*
(ii) Slow Running - (600 to 1,200 rpm)	*Low air flow - economical fuel air mixture*
(iii) Medium speed running (1,200 to 3,500 rpm)	*Medium air flow and economical fuel air mixture*
(iv) High speed running 3500 + rpm)	*High air flow and economical fuel air mixture*
(v) Acceleration -	*An enriched fuel air mixture imposed at any airflow rate*

The carburettor has been designed with two barrels. One barrel has been fitted with petrol jets for cold start, slow running, medium running and acceleration. The second barrel is used to augment the first for fast running, and the butterfly valve which controls the airflow through the second barrel, only opens when the engine demands more air than the first barrel is capable of handling.

The jets and orifices which control the flow of petrol and air in the carburettor are all fixed with the exception of the slow running jet. It follows therefore, that this is only a minimal capability of adjustment to these carburettors.

If it happens that the carburettor is suspected of not functioning properly when heavy fuel consumption is experienced, the only course of action is to visually examine each jet, orifice and valve in the carburettor for wear, and replace them as necessary.

2.2 Air cleaner

First though, it is necessary to know what the function of each jet and orifice is:

Cold start (Low air flow and enriched fuel/air mixture)

Carburettors fitted to the Honda Civic 1200 manual or automatic transmission have a manually controlled choke butterfly valve. This valve is positioned at the top of the primary barrel, and is closed or nearly closed for cold start, and should be fully open for normal running.

The function of this valve is to increase the vacuum (depression) in the middle of the barrel, at low airflows, so that more fuel is drawn from the float chamber through the main jet and idle jets into the air stream.

Once the engine has reached its proper running temperature the choke valve can be fully opened, to reduce the amount of vacuum in the primary barrel and thereby return the petrol/air mixture to economical proportions.

An enriched mixture is required for cold starting because some petrol condenses out onto the walls of the inlet manifold. This condensation effectively weakens the mixture, and therefore enrichment is necessary in the carburettor in order to maintain a proper mixture to the combustion chambers.

The inlet manifold is fitted with a drain system which collects the condensate and returns it to the carburettor.

Slow running (Low airflow - economical fuel/air mixture) mode of operation when engine rpm is between 600 and 1200.

In this condition the airflow through the primary barrel is not sufficient to draw petrol from the float chamber into the main jet and emulsion tube located adjacent to the primary venturi. The velocity of air through the central venturi is too low and does not create a sufficient vacuum to operate the main jet system. However, the speed of the air around the periphery of the throttle butterfly valve in the base of the barrel is high enough to create sufficient vacuum locally to draw petrol from the slow running jets into the air stream.

The slow running jets situated around the barrel near to the throttle valve feed an air/petrol emulsion to the air stream. The concentration of this emulsion is set by the 'idle mixture screw', and the air mixes with the petrol in drillings within the carburettor body. As may be expected there is an orifice insert to govern the flow of air from the top of the primary barrel into the slow running jet system, and a jet insert to govern the flow of petrol to the system from the float chamber.

Medium speed running (Medium airflow - economical fuel air mixture) mode of operation when engine rpm is 1200 to 3500.

The airflow rates through the primary barrel are the highest it is designed for; when more air is demanded, the throttle valve in the secondary barrel opens and it handles the increased demand.

During medium speed running the primary barrel functions, and the air speeds through the venturis in the middle of the barrel are now sufficient to operate the main jet and emulsion tube system.

High air speeds in the venturi create a vacuum locally in the venturi throat which is sufficient to draw petrol from the float chamber, through the main jet and into the emulsion tube. In the emulsion tube the petrol mixes with a small amount of air which is entering the tube via the 'air correction orifice'. Both air and fuel, mixing into an emulsion, are drawn to the dispersal orifice in the middle of the primary barrel venturi by the vacuum created by the airflow.

The petrol/air emulsion completes its dispersion in the air stream in the lower region of the primary barrel.

High speed running (High airflow + economical mixture) mode of operation typically when engine rpm is 3500 plus.

If the air speed in the primary barrel were allowed to rise, the main jet/emulsion tube system would no longer operate properly because too much air would enter the emulsion tube, via the air correction orifice, and weaken the emulsion of air and petrol passing to the dispersal orifice.

On single barrel carburettors this high speed mixture weakening is offset by a crude enrichment device. The device comprises a single tube which passes directly from the float chamber to the top of the barrel. At high air speeds there is sufficient vacuum created in this upper region of the barrel to draw fuel from the float chamber directly into the air stream via this tube. The turbulence of the air at this speed provides adequate mixing.

The secondary barrel is a far more effective and economical method of handling high airflow demands. On the compound carburettors fitted to the Honda Civic, the secondary barrel is coupled mechanically to the airflow control system. The linkage on the carburettor transmits movement of the accelerator pedal onto the secondary barrel throttle valve, when the primary barrel valve is fully opened.

The operation of the secondary barrel is exactly that of the primary barrel in slow, and medium running. When the secondary barrel throttle valve is just open, slow running jets (which are fixed) ensure that the extra air being admitted to the engine via this barrel is mixed with the appropriate quantity of petrol.

As the secondary barrel valve opens more, the main jet and emulsion tube system in that barrel comes into operation.

Acceleration (Enriched fuel/air mixture at any airflow rate)

The petrol internal combustion engine demands an enriched fuel/air mixture in order to increase its power output for accelerating the car.

This demand is met at any airflow rate by a device called the acceleration pump. The pump comprises a one way valve and a piston, and is mechanically actuated by a linkage connected to the throttle mechanism on the carburettor. Whenever the accelerator/throttle pedal is depressed, the movement is transmitted to the pump. The pump then forces a reserve of petrol to a special jet positioned near the main venturi in the primary barrel. This added fuel enriches the fuel/air mixture in the carburettor (Fig. 3.2).

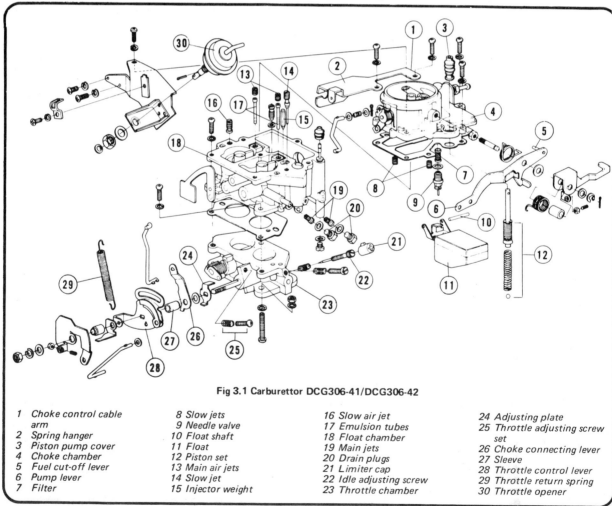

Fig 3.1 Carburettor DCG306-41/DCG306-42

1 Choke control cable arm	8 Slow jets	16 Slow air jet	24 Adjusting plate
2 Spring hanger	9 Needle valve	17 Emulsion tubes	25 Throttle adjusting screw set
3 Piston pump cover	10 Float shaft	18 Float chamber	26 Choke connecting lever
4 Choke chamber	11 Float	19 Main jets	27 Sleeve
5 Fuel cut-off lever	12 Piston set	20 Drain plugs	28 Throttle control lever
6 Pump lever	13 Main air jets	21 Limiter cap	29 Throttle return spring
7 Filter	14 Slow jet	22 Idle adjusting screw	30 Throttle opener
	15 Injector weight	23 Throttle chamber	

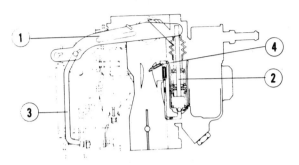

Fig 3.2 Details of the accelerator pump (Sec 3)

1 Pump lever
2 Accelerator pump piston
3 Pump rod
4 Pump ejector

4 Carburettor - removal and refitting

1 As an essential safety precaution remove both main electrical leads from the battery terminals, and stow them so that there is no chance of them inadvertently touching the battery terminals.

2 As another safety precaution, work in a well ventilated area, preferably in the open air. Petrol vapours can easily disperse into explosive concentrations in air which could be ignited by tools or bystanders smoking.

3 Begin the removal of the carburettor by disconnecting the following items:

i)   The hot air tube from the air cleaner box inlet
ii)   The hose from the air cleaner box to the cylinder head cover
iii) The vacuum hose between the thermal-trip actuated one way valve beneath the air cleaner box and the inlet manifold at the manifold
iv)   The hose between the carburettor and carbon canister at the carburettor
v)   The throttle opener hose at the throttle opener device

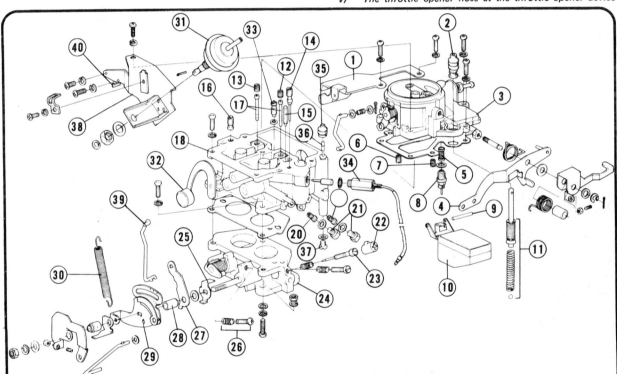

Fig 3.3 Carburettor DCG-306-45A/DCG-306-46A

1 Spring hanger
2 Pump cover
3 Air horn
4 Pump lever
5 Filter
6 Secondary slow air jet
   - size 130
7 Primary slow air jet
   - size 210
8 Needle valve
   - size 200
9 Float pin
10 Float
11 Pump assembly

12 Primary main air jet
    - size 60 (70) *
13 Secondary main air jet
    - size 50
14 Slow air jet
    - size 45
15 Pump needle
16 Slow air jet
    - size 70
17 Emission tubes
18 Main body
19 Primary main jet
    - size 96 (97) *

20 Secondary main jet
    - size 135 (150) *
21 Drain plugs
22 Limiter cap
23 Idle mixture screw
24 Throttle body
25 Adjusting plate
26 Throttle adjusting screw
27 Choke connecting lever
28 Sleeve
29 Throttle control lever
30 Throttle return spring
31 Throttle opener

32 Secondary air valve
33 Economizer valve
    - size 45 (50) *
34 Fuel shutoff solenoid
35 Secondary main jet valve
    cover
36 Secondary main jet valve
    needle
37 Secondary main jet valve
    screw
38 Throttle opener bracket
39 Choke rod
40 Reference tab

* Differences for 4 speed models.

vi) *The hose to the breather chamber beneath the air cleaner box from the inlet manifold, at the breather chamber*

4 Having disconnected the multitude of tubes, go on to detach the choke and throttle cables. Undo their respective clamps and clamping screws.
5 Disconnect the fuel line from the carburettor.
6 Disconnect the fuel shut off solenoid wires.
7 Undo the air cleaner box to carburettor clamps, and remove the air cleaner box.
8 The carburettor should now be sufficiently exposed to allow the four nuts which retain it to the inlet manifold to be undone and removed. Lift the carburettor clear to a clean bench. (photos)
9 Cover the inlet manifold ports exposed, to prevent dust and foreign matter falling into the manifold.

Refitting
10 Refitting as usual follows the reversal of the removal procedure, but as refitting proceeds pay attention to the following points:

i)   *Ensure that the throttle valves open and close fully when the accelerator pedal is functioned. (photo)*
ii) *Ensure that the choke valve closes and opens fully as the choke knob is functioned. (photo)*
iii) *Set the idle speed at 750 to 800 rpm with the engine warm, and check with the instructions in Section 9, Emission Control System, for final idle speed and Carbon Monoxide emission adjustment.*
iv) *Ensure that all hose connections are proper and gastight. Do not reconnect hoses which are frayed or split.*

5 Carburettor - dismantling, inspection and reassembly

1 Do not dismantle the carburettor unless it is absolutely necessary, after systematic diagnosis indicates that there is a fault with it. The assembly is delicate and finely made and unnecessary tinkering will almost certainly do more harm than good.
2 It follows as well that when it is necessary to work on the carburettor, it should be carried out in very clean conditions. The smallest amount of foreign matter in some parts of the carburettor will cause malfunction.
3 With the unit on a clean bench, commence dismantling by removing the throttle return spring, then proceed to remove the snap-ring and split pin which retain the accelerator pump lever in position. Once removed lift off the accelerator pump lever, and detach the pump plunger, and throttle lever link at the same time.
4 Finally remove the throttle cable bracket and the throttle opener bracket on models fitted with the vacuum actuated throttle opened device as part of the emission control system.
5 Now the screws which retain the top of the carburettor can be undone and removed. As the top of the carburettor is lifted off, the choke/throttle link can be detached from the throttle quadrant assembly.
6 Take care as the top of the carburettor is lifted clear, it has several delicate items assembled in, and on, it. Pay particular attention to the float mechanism and fuel feed needle valve. Place the top carburettor assembly aside on a clean area, for inspection. Cover it with a non-fluffy clean cloth until required.
7 Next the centre carburettor assembly, comprising the two barrels and venturis, is separated from the lower throttle valve assembly. The throttle valve assembly is in a cast iron body for

4.8A Carburettor rearward side

4.8B Carburettor R.H. side choke and throttle controls

4.8C Carburettor L.H. side Float chamber

4.10(i) Throttle cable termination

4.10(ii) Choke cable termination

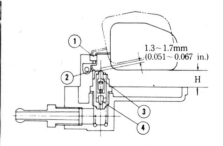
Fig 3.4 Details of the Float needle valve
(Sec 6)
1 Float stopper   3 Valve stem
2 Float seat   4 Needle valve

thermal control of the main carburettor assembly. Cast iron is a poor conductor of heat. It is also a good material for valve spindle bearings.

8 Three screws secure the throttle body assembly to the centre carburettor, once they have been undone and removed the two units may be separated.

9 *Dismantling the top carburettor assembly:* Ensure that there is adequate clean space to lay out the individual items as they are removed, so that there are no mistakes on reassembly.

10 Begin by extracting the accelerator pump and cover, then proceed to detach the float and float pivot pin.

11 Next remove the needle valve assembly by extracting the spring clip.

12 Remove the filter sleeve from the inlet union.

13 Finally unscrew the two slow air jets. Make a note of their size and location.

14 *Dismantling the centre carburettor assembly:* Unscrew the fuel shut off solenoid. Next unscrew primary and secondary petrol jets from the float chamber casing. They are situated in the petrol galleries which convey petrol from the float chamber to the emulsion tubes. Again make a note of the position and size of each jet.

15 Next unscrew the main air jets which admit air to the emulsion tubes beside each barrel. Then invert the centre body to extract the emulsion tubes, which are beneath the air jets. Yet again make a note of the position and size of the jets and emulsion tubes.

16 Unscrew the economiser valve and retain the washer.

17 After the economiser valve, remove the two slow running petrol jets and once again note their size and position on removal.

18 Finally remove the secondary main jet petrol valve plunger cover, and then its retaining screw, followed by plunger spring and ball.

19 *Dismantling the throttle valve assembly:* There is not a great deal which can be achieved by dismantling the valve block assembly; the idle jet screw can be removed so that the petrol/air passages can be cleaned. It is not advised to dismantle the throttle valve, spindle and lever fittings.

Carburettor parts inspection

20 All the parts which have been separated should be thoroughly cleaned in methylated spirits or clean petrol by hand, and without the help of anything more than a soft non-fluffy cloth. Do not use any scrapers, emery paper, wire wool or hard projections such as a pin, on any carburettor parts; all have been machined to extremely fine tolerances. Blow parts dry.

Inspect the carburettor bodies for blockages in petrol/air ways.

Check the float for puncture (any liquid heard inside) and the needle valve for easy operation.

Examine the petrol filter, replace it if it is broken or corroded.

Examine each jet, and reject any which are damaged. Check the accelerator pump parts, in particular the piston cup: fit a new one if the cup edges are frayed and worn.

Examine the idle mixture adjusting screw and its seat in the throttle block. If either part shows signs of wear, it should be replaced.

Check the throttle and choke valve and spindles. In some instances it is possible to replace the valve spindle and bush in the valve body in order to restore smooth operation.

Worn valve spindles and seats can lead to uneven running and poor acceleration, because air can be drawn into the inlet manifold, weakening the air/petrol mixture.

Reassembly of carburettor

21 Refit all parts in the exact reverse order of their removal. Use new copper washers, gaskets and seals. Do not overtighten anything, and do not use gasket cement. If the top of the carburettor does not fit flat, it should be replaced. As reassembly proceeds, pay attention to the settings and adjustments to be made, as detailed in the next Section.

6 Carburettor - settings and adjustments

The following items should be checked and adjusted when the carburettor has been dismantled:

   i)   *Float and needle valve*
   ii) *Primary throttle opening*
   iii) *Preliminary idle mixture screw adjustment*

The next items should be checked with the carburettor installed on the engine:

   i)   *Accelerator pump displacement (tested with air cleaner box removed)*
   ii) *Choke idle running (engine running)*
   iii) *Emission control system checks*

The following paragraphs detail the setting and adjustment techniques for the aforementioned items. Any engine running adjustments must only be made after it has been established that engine ignition timing and valve tappet gaps, are correct and that there are no air leaks in any of the vacuum lines and the inlet manifold.

Float and needle valve contact adjustment

(Carburettor dismantled) (Fig. 3.4).

Turn over the top piece of the carburettor and then carefully lower the float until the tag on the float just touches the needle valve stem. Do not permit the float to compress the spring load needle valve. The distance between the facing float surface and carburettor top should be 11 mm (0.44 inches). This is best checked by making a gauge block of metal and offering it between float and carburettor top. Bend the float tag until the required gap between float and carburettor is obtained.

The final check to be made is to measure the clearance with feeler gauges, between the float tag and needle valve stem, when the float is raised until the float stop contacts the butt on the carburettor top. Adjust this gap by bending the stop tag to obtain needle valve/float tag gap of 1.3 to 1.7 mm (0.040 to 0.042 inches) (Fig. 3.4).

When the carburettor is installed, the adjustments that have been made can be checked by viewing the fuel level in the sight glass on the float chamber. The fuel level should be within the range of the marker dot on the glass.

Primary throttle valve opening

(Carburettor assembled, but on bench)

There are two opened positions to be checked on the primary barrel throttle valve. The first position is that created by the linkage on the carburettor when the choke valve is at the top.

1 Throttle valve opening, choke valve closed; move the linkage to close the choke valve, and check the gap between the primary throttle valve and barrel side with a 16 swg wire (0.050 to 0.066 inch diameter). Bend the link rod between choke and throttle levers to obtain the desired gap (Fig. 3.5).

2 Throttle valve opening, secondary barrel valve just beginning to open: Turn the primary throttle valve lever and check that the primary valve fully opens and closes (choke valve fully open). Then turn the primary throttle valve open until the linkage begins to open the secondary barrel valve. Check the opening on primary valve with a piece of metal made to gauge 5.63 to 6.03 mm (0.221 to 0.237 inch) (Fig. 3.6).

Bend the link rod between the primary and secondary barrel valve levers to obtain the opening gap required. Once all adjustments have been completed, check the primary, secondary and choke valve linkages for binding as they are operated.

Preliminary idle mixture screw adjustment

Screw the idle mixture screw lightly into the primary barrel until it touches the seat, and then undo by some 2½ to 3 turns.

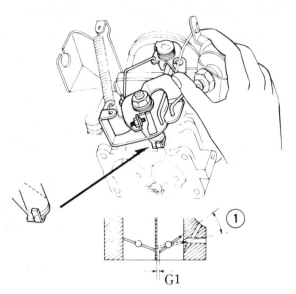

Fig 3.5 Setting of Primary throttle valve - fast idle (Sec 6 & 14)

1   19.5^o for model DCG306-45. DCG306-46
    17° for model DCG306-41. DCG306-42

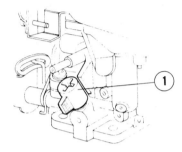

Fig 3.6 Position of primary throttle valve at commencement of secondary valve movement (Sec 6 & 14)

In regions not covered by exhaust emission legislation, the idle mixture - engine running - adjustment may be made as follows:

Adjust the throttle stop screw to bring the idling speed to between 750 and 800 rpm (engine warm), then turn the idle mixture adjustment screw in or out to obtain the highest smooth engine speed. Readjust throttle stop to restore proper engine idle speed. Repeat adjustment of idle mixture.

Accelerator pump displacement

This task requires the air cleaner box to have been removed, then operate either the throttle lever or accelerator pump lever, and watch the accelerator jet in the primary barrel. As the accelerator pump is slowly depressed, a consistent squirt of petrol should come into the primary barrel for the whole of the pump plunger travel.

Choke idle running

This is an adjustment of the idle speed of the engine when it has warmed up, and the choke is pulled out to the first detent. The engine speed should be between 1500 and 2000 rpm. Adjust by bending the choke and primary throttle link rod.

Emission control system checks

There are numerous checks and adjustments to be made on the carburettor and associated items as part of the emission control system. These checks and adjustments are detailed in Section 9, of this Chapter. Idle mixture adjustment - engine running - should be entrusted to a specialist garage who will have the carbon monoxide monitoring instrument which is required.

7 Fuel pump - removal and refitting

1   As usual it is an important safety precaution to disconnect both leads from the battery terminals and stow the leads away.
2   Then detach inlet and outlet petrol lines from the petrol pump.
3   Once the lines have been detached and any spilt petrol mopped up, the two nuts which retain the pump to the cylinder head can be undone and removed.
4   Remove the pump.
5   All Civics are fitted with fuel pumps which are not to be dismantled. This later type is inspected visually and if deemed faulty, replaced as a whole.
6   Refitting the pump follows the reversal of the removal procedure. Tighten the fixing nuts to the specified torque, and ensure that the petrol line connections are liquid tight.

8 Fuel pump - inspection

Only visual checks can be made on the pump, and if it is deemed faulty, the pump is replaced as a whole: it is not repairable.
1   Carry out the following checks:
   i)   *Ensure that the fixing screws of the upper body, lower body and cover are tight.*
   ii) *Ensure that the petrol unions are tight.*
   iii) *Inspect the air hole in the lower body. If there are signs of oil or petrol in the air hole, the diaphragm is most certainly faulty. Replace the whole pump.*
2   Delivery pressure data is included in the Specifications at the beginning of the Chapter, for those fortunate enough to have an appropriate pressure gauge with fittings to join it into the delivery line from the pump to the carburettor.

9 Fuel filters - general

1   There is no filter in the fuel pump, and there is a minor one in the float chamber inlet. The proper fuel filter is in the fuel feed line to the pump.
2   Remove the fuel lines from each end of the filter package. Unclip the package, and remove the filter element. If the filter appears dirty, replace it.

10 Emission control system

The emission control system governs two sources of gas emission:
   i) *Exhaust emissions from the engine*
   ii) *Crankcase oil and petrol vapour emissions*

Taking exhaust emissions first, the following components are directly associated with the exhaust emission control system: distributor, throttle control valve, throttle opener, solenoid valve, air cleaner box, air bleed valve, coolant temperature sender unit, vacuum actuated inlet air flap, transmission gear selector sensor, air valve, and the inlet manifold vacuum actuated ignition advance and retard mechanism (Fig. 3.7).

The crankcase oil and petrol vapour emissions are controlled by a system comprising the following main components: breather tubes and condensation chamber, carbon filled canister, petrol tank vapour line (incorporating a one way valve), a liquid/vapour separator, and finally the fuel filler cap.

The function of the exhaust emission control system is to minimise the emission of carbon monoxide (CO) Hydrocarbon (HC) and Oxides of Nitrogen (NOx), by means of special control devices and engine modifications, the control devices and engine modifications are formed into several sub-systems which together form the whole exhaust emission control system. The sub-systems are described below, together with details for inspection and renovation.

Intake air temperature control (Fig. 3.8)

The intake air temperature control system serves to maintain a feed of warm air to the carburettor in all conditions. The warm air will ensure consistent and more effective dispersal of the petrol/air emulsion in the carburettor barrels.

The system functions as follows: a warm operated device in the air cleaner box controls a valve in a vacuum line from the inlet manifold to a vacuum diaphragm mechanism in the air cleaner inlet.

When the air in the cleaner box is cold - below 100° F (37.8° C) - the thermal trip closes the air bleed line to the control valve. The valve then opens the vacuum line between the inlet manifold and the flap mechanism on the inlet to the air cleaner. The

mechanism then opens the flap to admit warm air from the scoop around the exhaust manifold.

When the air in the cleaner box is warm the thermal device opens the bleed line from the control valve. The valve closes the vacuum line to the flap mechanism, which then closes the flap to stop the flow of air from the exhaust manifold and restore flow through the air cleaner inlet snorkel.

Inlet air control system checks

Begin by checking for loose or disconnected hoses and vacuum lines. Then remove the top of the air cleaner box, detach the LT wire to the distributor and turn the engine over with the starter motor. If the system is working properly the inlet manifold vacuum should open the flap in the inlet snorkel. When the engine stops the flap should remain open if the system is properly airtight. Should the flap close, indicating a leak in the system, check the vacuum diaphragm device as follows:

Vacuum diaphragm check: Lift the flap up in the snorkel, and then close the device vacuum inlet with one finger. If the device is working properly, the flap should remain up. Replace the device if the flap falls indicating a leak in the diaphragm.

Control valve and thermal trip tests

These tests require vacuum pumps and special gauges which only larger garages might have. It is necessary to disconnect the vacuum line to the inlet manifold and connect a pump and gauge to the system. The pump is used to create a vacuum in the system and the gauge is connected in the lines between the diaphragm and control valve, and valve to thermal trip line.

If a leak is detected in the diaphragm line and the diaphragm has already been found to be alright, replace the control valve. If a leak is detected in the thermal trip line, suspect the trip. Function the trip by blowing warm air on it (from a hair drier for instance). The trip should open and cut off the vacuum from the

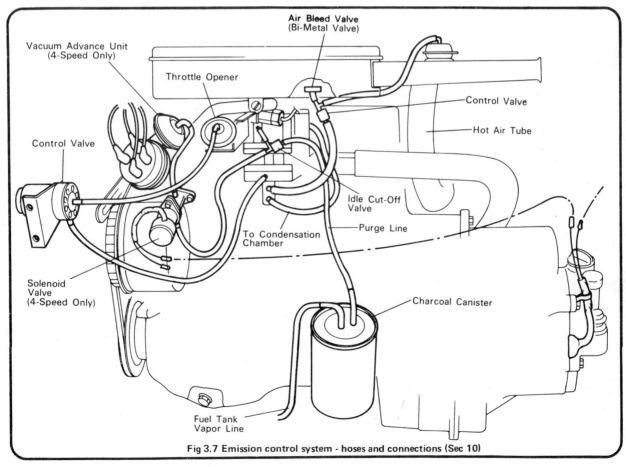

Fig 3.7 Emission control system - hoses and connections (Sec 10)

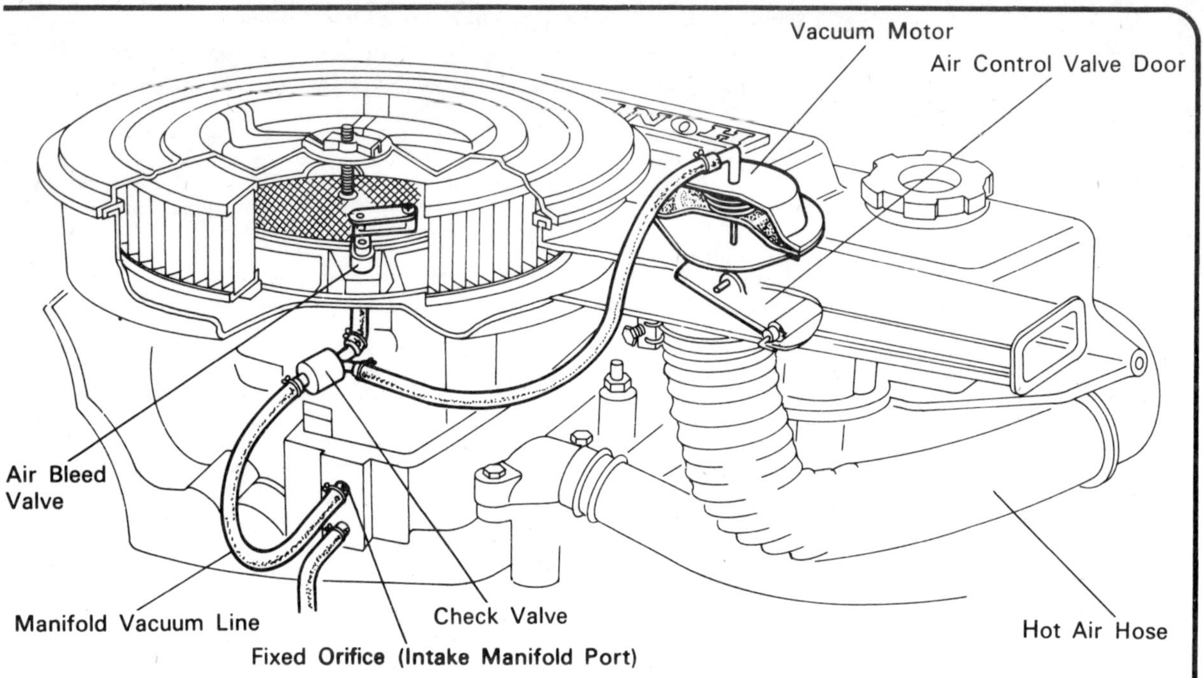

Vacuum Motor

Air Control Valve Door

Air Bleed
Valve

Manifold Vacuum Line

Check Valve

Fixed Orifice (Intake Manifold Port)

Hot Air Hose

Fig 3.8 Intake Air Temperature control system (Sec 10)

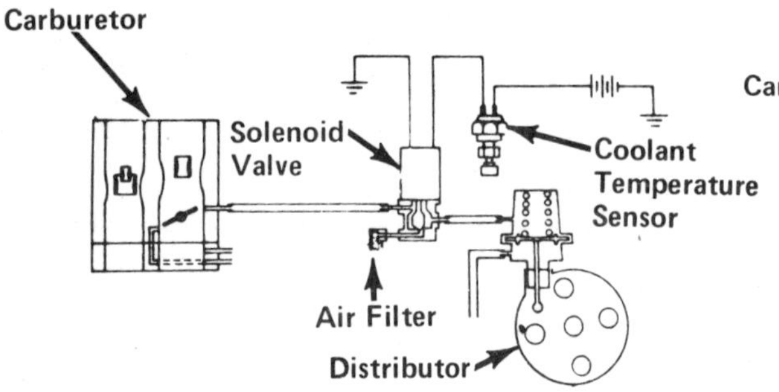

Carburetor

Solenoid
Valve

Coolant
Temperature
Sensor

Air Filter

Distributor

Transmission Sensor

Carburetor

Solenoid
Valve

Coolant
Temperature
Sensor

Air Filter

Distributor

Fig 3.9 Temperature controlled ignition advance system (Sec 10) (Hondamatic transmission only)

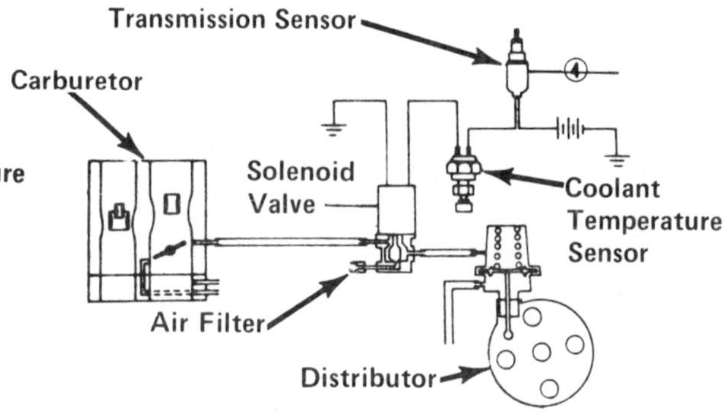

Fig 3.10 Transmission and Engine temperature controlled ignition advance system - 4 speed transmission (Sec 10)

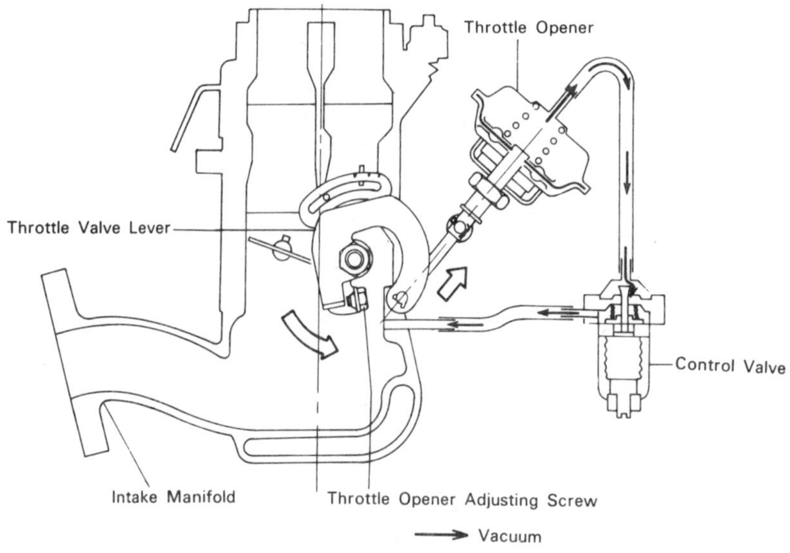

Throttle Opener

Throttle Valve Lever

Control Valve

Intake Manifold

Throttle Opener Adjusting Screw

→ Vacuum

Fig 3.11 Throttle opener system (Sec 10)

diaphragm. The diaphragm will close the flap. If the trip does not function properly, replace it.

Temperature controlled ignition advance system

(Hondamatic transmission cars only) (Fig. 3.9).

This system functions to reduce the emission of nitrogen oxides by disconnecting the vacuum from the vacuum advance mechanism on the distributor, when the engine is warm and no longer needs a vacuum advance facility.

Temperature sensor switch: disconnect the leads and attach a bulb and battery circuit. When the engine is cold the switch should be open, and the bulb should not glow. The switch should close, and the bulb glow when the engine temperature is greater than 120° F (48.9° C). Replace the switch if it does not function as described.

Solenoid vacuum valve: to test this device a vacuum gauge is required to measure vacuums of 3 inches of mercury or more. Connect the gauge into the vacuum line between the solenoid valve and distributor. When the engine is started and is cold the vacuum gauge should record vacuums of 3 inches mercury (Hg) or more at engine speeds of 2,000 rpm. When the engine temperature reaches 120° F (48.9° C) and the radiator fan starts, the vacuum recorded should fall to zero.

If the sensor switch has been found to be satisfactory, yet the vacuum gauge does not show the readings described, replace the solenoid valve.

Temperature and transmission controlled ignition advance system

(Manual transmission cars only) (Fig. 3.10).

This system serves the same function as the temperature operated vacuum advance system on cars with Hondamatic transmission. It reduces Nitrogen Oxides emissions during normal car operation. When the engine is warm, and the transmission is in first, second or third gears, the sensors actuate the solenoid valve to disconnect the vacuum from the ignition advancing unit on the distributor.

Vacuum advance is restored when top gear is engaged. Check the engine temperature sensor as described under 'Temperature controlled ignition advance system' above.

Check the transmission sensor with a continuity tester circuit; a bulb and battery. When first, second or third gears are selected the switch should be closed and the bulb should glow. When fourth is selected, the switch should open and the bulb go out. If the switch does not operate as described - replace it.

Proceed to check the solenoid valve operation with the

technique described under 'Temperature controlled ignition advance system' above.

Throttle opener system

(Fig. 3.11).

This system functions to prevent the emission of hydrocarbons when the throttle is closed swiftly. The throttle opener holds the throttle open during acceleration to allow better mixture control in the carburettor and prevent misfiring. The system comprises a vacuum actuated throttle opener, and a control valve.

The control valve is designed to transmit vacuum to the throttle opener when the inlet manifold vacuum is equal to or greater than 57 ± 2 cm Hg.

The system is checked as follows: Check the vacuum ports in the inlet manifold; clean if necessary with a 0.016 inch drill or pin. Examine all vacuum lines and replace any that have signs of deterioration.

Throttle opener

(Fig. 3.12).

Disconnect vacuum line from the opener to the control valve from the control valve, and reconnect it to the inlet manifold port used by the control valve line. Run the engine up to 1,500 to 2,000 rpm and observe the opener device. The device should move its full stroke. Replace the opener, if it does not work connected directly to the inlet manifold.

Control valve

Run the engine up to 3,500 rpm or more and then release the accelerator. The control valve should operate the throttle opener so that after 1 to 3 seconds the opener has moved one half of its 2/10th inch full travel. The delay time can be adjusted with the screw beneath the control valve. Clockwise will increase the delay, anti-clockwise decrease delay.

Replace the control valve, if it does not actuate the throttle opener when the opener has already proved satisfactory.

Ignition timing retard system

(Fig. 3.13).

This system improves engine timing when the engine is idling. The vacuum in the primary barrel of the carburettor is connected to the advance/retard vacuum actuated device on the distributor, to retard the ignition timing by 5° when the engine is idling. As usual inspect the vacuum lines and replace any that show signs of deterioration. Remove the distributor cap, and

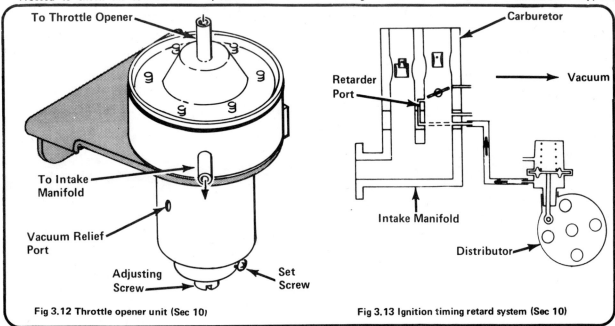

Fig 3.12 Throttle opener unit (Sec 10)   **Fig 3.13 Ignition timing retard system (Sec 10)**

check that the contact breaker plate is free to move around the cam.

Having satisfied yourself of the general condition of the system, connect a strobe light and run the engine at idling speed (800 to 750 rpm).

Observe the position of the white timing mark on the crankshaft pulley relative to the datum mark on the timing cover with the strobe light. The white notch (TDC) should be exactly aligned to the datum. Disconnect the vacuum line from the carburettor to the distributor, as the engine is running, and check that the red notch on the crankshaft pulley is now aligned with the datum mark when viewed with a strobe light.

If the system does not operate as described, and it is certain that there are no blockages in the vacuum lines, the vacuum advance/retard unit should be replaced. The vacuum in the line from the carburettor when the engine is idling should be around 12 inches Hg.

Crankcase emission control system

(Fig. 3.14).

This system feeds oil vapours from inside the engine into the inlet manifold so that the vapours are burnt. The checks on this system are as follows:

    i)   *Squeeze the end cap of the condensation chamber drain tube, to allow any water or oil collected to drain.*

    ii)   *Clear the intake manifold tee-joint with a 0.035 inch drill.*

    iii)   *Check all hoses and pipes and replace any that show signs of deterioration.*

Evaporative emission control system

(Fig. 3.15).

This system serves to prevent fuel vapour escaping to the atmosphere from the carburettor and fuel tank. Fuel vapours in the tank are contained in the expansion chamber in the tank. A pipe line runs from the expansion chamber to a carbon filled canister in the engine compartment. A valve is situated in the pipe line which acts to permit vapour to flow to the canister only when the pressure in the expansion chamber has reached a preset level.

When vapours reach the canister they are absorbed by the carbon. The carbon is purged of the vapour by clean air drawn through the canister when the engine is running. A pipe line connects the canister to the inlet manifold for this purpose.

An excessive vapour pressure in the fuel tank is relieved by a two way valve in the fuel filler cap.

The checks which can be made on this system are as follows:

    1   *Check for loose pipe connections, and pipe deterioration. Refit or replace as necessary.*

    2   *All other checks require specialist equipment, including vacuum gauges and should be entrusted to your local Honda dealer.*

11 Exhaust system

1 The exhaust system comprises a manifold, twin downpipes, or single downpipe, and a tail pipe with silencer. Flange joints are used throughout, and the down and tail pipes are suspended from rubber rings (Fig. 3.16 and photos).

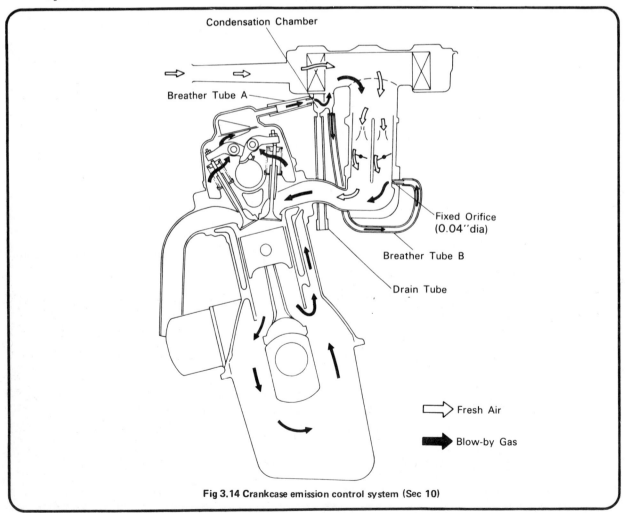

Condensation Chamber

Breather Tube A

Fixed Orifice (0.04"dia)

Breather Tube B

Drain Tube

⇨ Fresh Air

➡ Blow-by Gas

Fig 3.14 Crankcase emission control system (Sec 10)

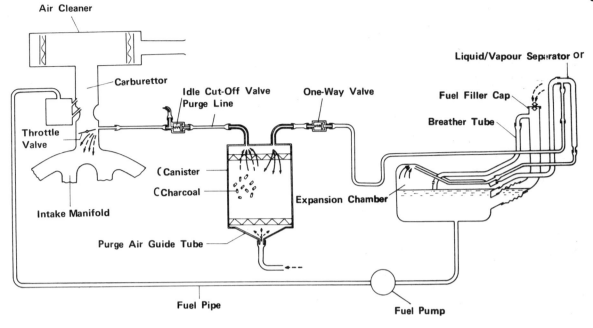

Fig 3.15 Evaporative emission control system (Sec 10)

← Fuel Vapour

←-- Fresh Air

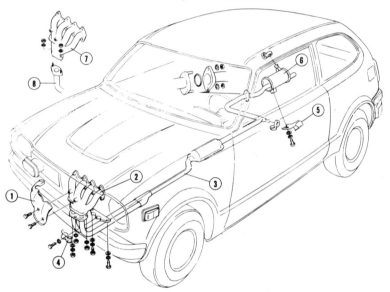

Fig 3.16 Exhaust system (Sec 11)

1   Hot air cover
2   Exhaust manifold
3   Exhaust pipe
4   Pipe clamp
5   Silencer mount
6   Exhaust silencer
7   Exhaust manifold
8   Exhaust pipe

11.1A Exhaust pipe/manifold joint

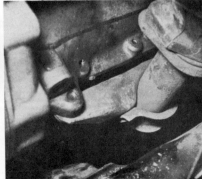

11.1B Exhaust pipe/cylinder block retention

11.1C Exhaust pipe/rear flanged joint

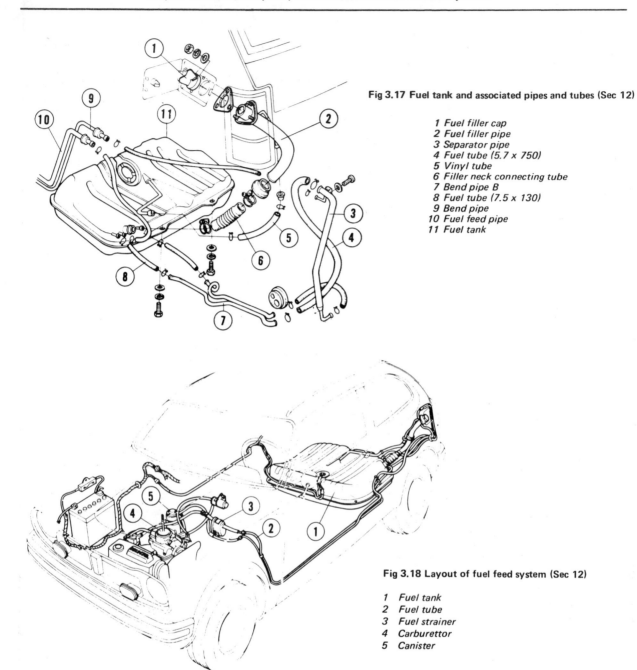

Fig 3.17 Fuel tank and associated pipes and tubes (Sec 12)

1 Fuel filler cap
2 Fuel filler pipe
3 Separator pipe
4 Fuel tube (5.7 x 750)
5 Vinyl tube
6 Filler neck connecting tube
7 Bend pipe B
8 Fuel tube (7.5 x 130)
9 Bend pipe
10 Fuel feed pipe
11 Fuel tank

Fig 3.18 Layout of fuel feed system (Sec 12)

1 Fuel tank
2 Fuel tube
3 Fuel strainer
4 Carburettor
5 Canister

When repairing the system it is wise to use only the original type of exhaust fittings and properly made parts.

2   When any one section of the exhaust system needs renewal it often follows that the whole lot is best replaced.

3   It is most important when fitting exhausts that the twists and contours are carefully followed and that each connecting joint overlaps the correct distance. Any stresses or strain imparted, in order to force the system to fit the hanger rubbers, will result in early fractures and failures.

4   When fitting a new part or complete system it is well worth removing **all** of the system from the car and cleaning up all the joints so that they fit together easily. The time spent struggling with obstinate joints whilst flat on your back under the car is eliminated and the likelihood of distorting or even breaking a section is greatly reduced. Do not waste a lot of time trying to undo rusted and corroded clamps and bolts. Cut them off. New ones will be required anyway if they are that bad.

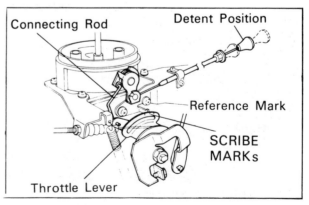

Fig 3.19 Choke linkage and settings (Sec 14)

12 Fuel tank and fuel feed line

Fuel tank removal and refitting

(Fig. 3.17).

1 Work in a well ventilated space, preferably in the open air. Disconnect both electrical cables from the battery terminals. Do not use any electrical tools.

2 Having complied with the safety precautions described, commence to drain the fuel tank. Undo and remove the drain plug. Collect the fuel in a proper metal container. Do not use plastic containers. Small amounts of plastic material may dissolve into the petrol and be precipitated in the carburettor when the petrol vapourises.

3 Disconnect the filler neck tube and vapour tubes. Remove their retaining clips carefully.

4 Remove the fuel tank contents sender unit electrical connections.

5 Undo and remove the fuel tank retaining bolts, and lower the tank from the car.

6 Remove the fuel tank sender unit. Take care as the unit is lifted clear; the float arm is easily bent.

7 Refitting the fuel tank follows the exact reversal of the removal procedure.

Fuel feed lines

8 The feed lines are routed inside the car for the most part. From the engine compartment they pass through the compartment bulkhead at the top right-hand corner, and then pass down into the door sill. They emerge from the sill to pass underneath the rear seat cushion before passing through the bodyshell to the fuel tank (Fig. 3.18). Remove the interior front and rear side garnishes and rear seat cushion to gain access to the tubes. Inspect the pipes for signs of leaks and/or material deterioration.

13 Fuel gauge sender unit

1 Full details of this unit's operation and fault diagnosis are given in Chapter 10 of this manual. However if the unit is to be replaced, proceed to remove the petrol tank as detailed in the previous Section. The unit is retained to the tank by screws and sealed with a gasket.

When the unit is being refitted, take the following precautions: do not use excessive amounts of sealant on the gasket, and take care not to harm the delicate float and arm as the unit is inserted into the tank.

14 Carburettor controls - accelerator and choke

The DCG-306-45A and 46A are fitted with a flexible tag adjacent to the throttle control quadrant. The tag is used to indicate the 'fast idle' position of the throttle valve.

There are scribe marks on the quadrant which should be aligned with the tag when the throttle is at fast idle. If the carburettor controls have been dismantled, the tag can be adjusted to align with the quadrant marks when a 0.032 inch diameter drill is inserted between the throttle valve and barrel side.

Choke cable adjustment: Check that when the choke knob is pushed fully in that the choke valve is fully open. Move the knob in and out to check for slack in the cable, and then move the knob to the first detent. When the knob is at the first detent, the throttle control quadrant markings for fast idle should be aligned with the tag. Bend the choke to throttle link rod to correct any misalignment between quadrant and tag (Figs. 3.5, 3.6 and 3.19).

15 Fault diagnosis - fuel system and carburation

Unsatisfactory engine performance and excessive fuel consumption are not necessarily the fault of the fuel system or carburettor. In fact they more commonly occur as a result of ignition and timing faults. Before acting on the following it is necessary to check the ignition system first. Even though a fault may lie in the fuel system it will be difficult to trace unless the ignition is correct. The faults below, therefore, assume that this has been attended to first (where appropriate).

Symptom	Reason/s	Remedy
Smell of petrol when engine is stopped	Leaking fuel lines or unions	Repair or renew as necessary.
	Leaking fuel tank	Fill fuel tank to capacity and examine carefully at seams, unions and filler pipe connections. Repair as necessary.
Smell of petrol when engine is idling	Leaking fuel line unions between pump and carburettor	Check line and unions and tighten or repair.
	Overflow of fuel from float chamber due to wrong level setting, ineffective needle valve or punctured float	Check fuel level setting and condition of float and needle valve, and renew if necessary.
Excessive fuel consumption for reasons not covered by leaks or float chamber faults	Worn jets	Renew jets or carburettor body if not removable.
	Over-rich jet setting	Adjust jet.
	Sticking mechanism	Check correct movement of mechanism.
Difficult starting, uneven running, lack of power, cutting out.	One or more jets blocked or restricted	Dismantle and clean out float chamber and jets.
	Float chamber fuel level too low or needle valve sticking	Dismantle and check fuel level and needle valve.
	Fuel pump not delivering sufficient fuel	Check pump delivery and clean or repair as required.

Chapter 4 Ignition system

Contents

Specifications

Spark plugs

1169 cc engine	NGK BP - 5ES, BP - 6ES
	Denso W - 20EP, W - 22EP
Gap	0.7 - 0.8 mm (0.028 - 0.031 inch)
1237 cc engine	NGK BP - 6ES
	ND W - 20EP
Gap	0.7 - 0.8 mm (0.028 - 0.031 inch)

Coil

Primary coil resistance	3.8 ± 0.38 ohms (20° C)
Secondary coil resistance	8.0 ± 1.6 ohms (20° C)
Specified voltage	12 volts
Test gap at 8 volts	8 mm (0.315 inch)
Insulation resistance	10 meg. ohms minimum

Ignition sequence ... ...   1, 3, 4, 2.

Distributor

Advance method	Centrifugal and vacuum
Contact breaker gap	0.4 - 0.6 mm (0.017 to 0.022 inch)
Condenser	0.22 to 0.24 mf
Rotation	Counter-clockwise when viewed from cap side

Centrifugal advance characteristics

USA models

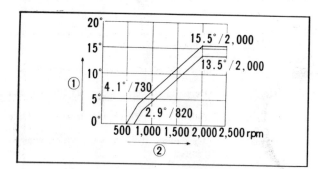

① Distributor advance angle   ② Distributor rpm

UK models

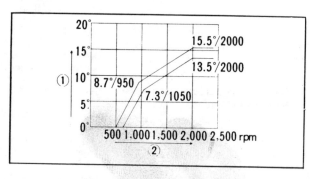

① Distributor advance angle
② Distributor rpm.

Vacuum advance characteristics

USA models

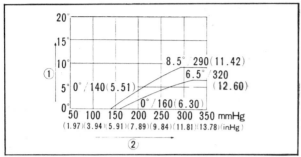

① Distributor advance angle
② Vacuum mmHg (in.Hg)

UK models

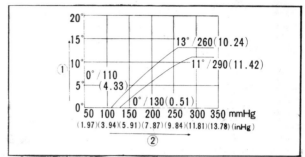

① Distributor advance angle
② Vacuum mmHg (in.Hg)

Torque wrench settings

	kg f m	lb f ft
Timing belt driven pulley	2.5 - 3.5	18 - 25
Spark plug	1.3 - 1.7	9 - 12
Distributor fixing plate	1.0 - 1.4	7 - 10
Timing belt upper cover	0.8 - 1.2	6 - 9
Timing belt lower cover	0.8 - 1.2	6 - 9

1 General description

In order that the internal combustion engine with spark ignition can operate properly, the spark which ignites the air/fuel charge in the combustion chamber must be delivered at precisely the correct moment. This correct moment is that which will allow time for the charge to burn sufficiently to create the highest pressure and temperature possible in the combustion chamber as the piston passes top-dead-centre and commences its power stroke. The distributor and ignition coil are the main devices which ensure that the spark plug ignites the charge as required.

Very high voltages need to be generated in the ignition system in order to produce the spark across the plug gap which ignites the fuel/air charge. The device in which these high voltages - several thousand volts - are generated is the coil (or electronic ignition pack, if fitted). The coil contains two sets of windings - the primary and the secondary windings. A current at 12 volts is fed through the primary windings via the contact breaker mechanism in the distributor. It is precisely when the flow is interrupted by the contact breaker that the huge voltage is momentarily induced in the secondary windings and that voltage is conveyed via HT leads and the rotor arm in the distributor cap to the appropriate spark plug.

It follows therefore that the contact breakers must part the

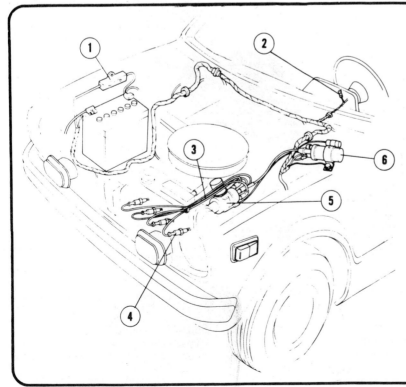

Fig 4.1 Layout of the ignition system

1 Main fuse
2 Ignition switch
3 High tension
4 Spark plug
5 Distributor
6 Ignition coil

instant a spark is required and the rotor arm must be aligned to the appropriate stud in the distributor cap which is 'connected' to the spark plug which 'needs' the spark. The distributor shaft revolves at half crankshaft speed, and there are four lobes on the distributor cam and four studs in the distributor cap, to cater for the four sparks the engine requires each two revolutions of the crankshaft.

On this Honda the timing of the ignition is set by three means:
   i)   *Static timing*
   ii) *Fully automatic centrifugal advance*
   iii) *Inlet manifold vacuum advance/retard (automatic)*

The static timing is that nominal setting which accounts for the time for combustion at the idling speed of the engine. It is necessary therefore when carrying out ignition or carburation adjustments, to ensure that the engine is turning at the speed appropriate to that test or adjustment.

The centrifugal advance mechanism ensures that the spark arrives in the cylinder in that interval of time for combustion which corresponds to a greater angle of crankshaft movement when the engine is turning quickly than when it turns slowly. The mechanism comprises two weights on an arm on the distributor shaft. As the shaft speed increases the weights move outwards against their restraining spring. The contact breaker cam is attached to the weights so that as they move out, it is rotated some 29° relative to the distributor shaft, and therefore the contact breaker will open earlier relative to the distributor shaft and crankshaft as required.

The vacuum advance/retard system functions to alter ignition timing to cater for mixture strength. The time for combustion of the fuel/air mixture will vary slightly with mixture strength. The richer the mixture, the longer time it takes to burn. The system comprises a diaphragm device actuated by inlet manifold and carburettor throat pressure, attached to the distributor. The diaphragm is connected to the contact breaker plate to rotate it relative to the cam, to obtain the required variation of ignition timing.

The vacuum advance is a fine adjustment system and is deactivated by the emission control system in various engine operating conditions because it can have detrimental effects on the engine exhaust gas.

2   Routine maintenance

a) *Spark plugs*
Remove the plugs and thoroughly clean away all traces of carbon. Examine the porcelain insulator round the central electrode inside the plug; if damaged discard the plug. Reset the gap between the electrodes. Do not use a set of plugs for more than 9,000 miles. It is false economy.

b) *Distributor*
Every 9,000 miles remove the distributor cap and rotor arm and put one, or two, drops of engine oil into the centre of the cam recess. Smear the surfaces of the cam itself with petroleum jelly. Do not over lubricate as any excess could get onto the contact point surfaces and cause ignition difficulties.

Every 9,000 miles examine the contact point surfaces. If there is a build-up of deposits on one face and a pit in the other it will be impossible to set the gap correctly and they should be refaced or renewed. Set the gap when the contact surfaces are in order.

c) *General*
Examine all leads and terminals for signs of broken or slackness or signs of fracturing of some strands of wire. Partly broken wire should be renewed.

The HT leads are particularly important as any insulation faults will cause the high voltage to 'jump' to the nearest earth and this will prevent a spark at the plug. Check that no HT leads are loose or in a position where the insulation could wear due to rubbing against part of the engine.

3   Contact breaker points - gap adjustment

1   Remove the distributor cap by prising back the two spring clips holding the cap to the distributor body.
2   Clean the inside and outside of the cap with a dry cloth. It is unlikely that the four studs will be badly burned or corroded, but if they are, the complete cap should be renewed. If only small deposits are on the studs, these may be scraped away with a small screwdriver.
3   Push in the carbon brush, located in the centre of the cap, several times to ensure that it moves freely; the brush should protrude at least one-quarter of an inch.
4   Gently prise open the contact breaker points to examine the condition of the contact faces. If they are rough, pitted or dirty, it will be necessary to remove them for resurfacing, or for replacement points to be fitted.
5   Lift the rotor arm off the cam, and clean with a dry cloth. Scrape away any small deposits with a screwdriver. It will be noticed that the rotor arm cannot be replaced in the wrong position, because of an assymetric joint between rotor and cam.
6   Presuming the points are satisfactory, or that they have been cleaned or replaced, measure the gap between the points once the engine has been turned over until the contact breaker arm is on the peak of one of the four cam lobes. Insert a 0.020 inch feeler gauge between the contact points. (photo)
7   If the gap is not as specified, slacken the contact plate securing screw and adjust the contact gap by turning the adjustment screw in the breaker support plate (Fig. 4.2).
8   Once the desired gap has been established, tighten the contact plate securing screw and check the gap again. Refit the rotor and finally fit the distributor cap. Reconnect HT leads as appropriate.

4   Contact breaker points - removal and replacement

1   If the contact breaker points are burned, pitted or badly worn, they must be removed and either replaced or their faces must be filed smooth.
2   To remove the points, undo and remove the two securing screws, and lift away the plate earthing wire. Detach the LT wire from the contact breaker spring.
3   Lift away the contact breaker set.
4   To reface the points, rub the faces on a fine carborundum stone or on fine emery paper. It is important that the faces are rubbed flat and parallel to each other so that there will be complete face to face contact when the points are closed. One of the points will be pitted and the other will have deposits on it.
5   It is necessary to completely remove the built up deposits but not necessary to rub the pitted point to the stage where all the pitting has disappeared, though obviously if this is done it will prolong the time before the refacing task needs to be repeated.
6   Refitting the contact breaker points follows the reversal of the removal sequence. It will be necessary to adjust the gap, as detailed in the previous Section.

5   Condenser - testing, removal and replacement

1   The purpose of the condenser (sometimes known as a capacitor), is to ensure that when the contact breaker points open there is no sparking across them which would waste voltage and cause wear.
2   The condenser is fitted in parallel with the contact breaker points. If it develops a short circuit, it will cause ignition failure as the points will be prevented from interrupting the low tension circuit.
3   If the engine becomes very difficult to start or begins to miss

after several miles running, and the breaker points show signs of excessive burning, then the condition of the condenser must be suspect. A further test can be made by separating the points by hand with the ignition switched on. If this is accompanied by a flash it is indicative that the condenser has failed.

4 Without special test equipment the only sure way to diagnose condenser trouble is to replace a suspected unit with a new one and note if there is any improvement.

5 To remove the condenser from the distributor, first remove the distributor cap.

6 Detach the condenser cable from the terminal block and remove the condenser fixing to the body. Lift away the condenser.

7 Replacement of the condenser is the reversal of removal.

6 Distributor - removal and replacement

1 Begin by removing the main cables to the battery, this is a safety precaution to prevent sparks when leads are disconnected in the ignition circuits.

2 Next remove the HT leads from the spark plugs and identify the leads with labels to ensure correct refitting.

3 Remove the distributor cap.

4 Rotate the engine until the rotor arm in the distributor is pointing to the position occupied by the stud in the distributor cap connected to the spark plug in the No. 1 cylinder (Figs. 4.3 and 4.4).

5 On the manual transmission cars the easiest way of turning the engine is to select bottom gear and nudge the car so that the engine turns to the desired position. Then apply the handbrake and leave in gear, to ensure that the engine does not subsequently move.

6 On automatic transmission cars the only method available for moving the engine is by actuating the starter motor. There is no firm mechanical link between the transmission and the engine through the torque converter. Consequently there is no means of mechanically fixing the engine, while the distributor is being removed and replaced, if the engine and automatic transmission is in place in the car. If the distributor is being removed with the engine out of the car, use a block bolted to the cylinder block to lock the flywheel and engine in position whilst the distributor is off.

7 Make a pair of marks with a centre pop on the distributor body, and cylinder head to indicate their alignment before removal.

8 Undo and remove the two bolts which secure the distributor to the cylinder head.

9 Disconnect vacuum lines if you have not already done so, and identify them with labels to ensure correct refitting.

10 Now the distributor can simply be pulled out of the cylinder head. (photo)

Refitting the distributor

11 The procedure is basically the reversal of the removal sequence, but the following extra precautions and tasks are involved.

12 As the distributor is inserted back into the cylinder head, hold the rotor arm and distributor body so that the arm is pointing to the position of the No. 1 cylinder stud. Allow the

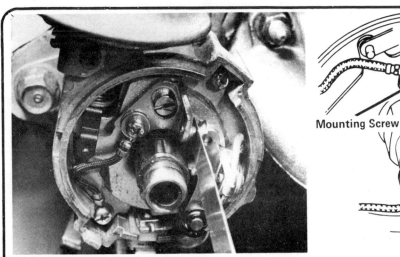

3.6 Measuring contact breaker gap

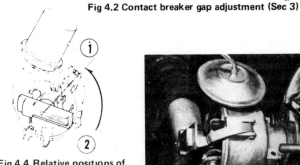

Mounting Screw

Adjusting Screw

Fig 4.2 Contact breaker gap adjustment (Sec 3)

Wrench

0° Mark (TDC)

5° BTDC Mark

Crankshaft Pulley

Reference Mark

Fig 4.3 Moving the crankshaft to 0° and 5° BTDC (Secs 3 & 8)

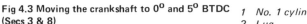

Fig 4.4 Relative positions of rotor arm and distributor when No. 1 piston is in firing position (Sec 6)

1 No. 1 cylinder side
2 Lug

6.10 Removing the distributor

distributor and shaft to rotate as the shaft gear feeds around the drivegear on the camshaft in the cylinder head. It will be necessary to determine this rotation as the distributor is fed into position, so that it can be anticipated when the distributor is inserted for the final time. It is desirable to align the distributor case/cylinder head marks made before removal, as well as the essential alignment of rotor with No. 1 cylinder stud.

13 If the crankshaft has been rotated, before the distributor was to be refitted, it will be necessary to retime the ignition as described in Section 8, of this Chapter.

7 Distributor - dismantling, inspection and reassembly

1 If the distributor is to be dismantled further than the contact breaker support plate; for instance, if the centrifugal advance mechanism has to be taken apart, the distributor will need to be removed from the engine. Always work on a clean bench, with clean tools. The distributor is a fine mechanism, and will malfunction if foreign matter is introduced into the device.

2 Having removed the distributor cap, lift away the rotor arm, then proceed to remove the contact breaker set as detailed in Section 4, of this Chapter.

3 Next detach the vacuum actuated ignition advance/retard unit. It will be necessary to undo and remove the clip retaining the advance/retard link rod to the contact breaker support plate. Then undo and remove the two screws securing the diaphragm unit to the distributor body. Lift the device link rod, rotate the contact breaker support plate and remove the advance/retard unit.

4 Now undo and remove the two screws which retain the contact breaker support plate assembly in the distributor body. Lift away the support plate (Fig. 4.6)

5 The centrifugal advance mechanism is now revealed.

6 Remove the rubber cap from the top of the distributor cam, and undo and remove the screw which has been revealed. Once the screw is removed the cam can be lifted off the distributor shaft and centrifugal advance mechanism.

7 Turning the distributor on its side drive out the pin which retains the driven gear to the distributor shaft. Remove the gear.

8 Once the driven gear has been removed, pull the distributor shaft upwards out of the distributor case, so that the weights and

springs of the centrifugal advance mechanism can be removed. Be careful to recover the washers and seals on the distributor shaft. Note their position ready for reassembly.

Distributor parts inspection

9 If the centrifugal advance mechanism and/or the distributor shaft in the case was found to be sloppy, you should check what spares are available and consider an exchange distributor. Very often in fine mechanisms as distributors it will not be a case of needing to renew just one component.

10 Carry out visual inspection of all parts, examine for wear,

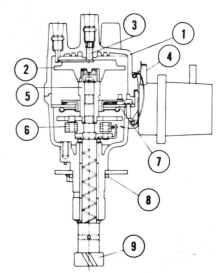

Fig 4.5 Section through distributor (Sec 7)

1 Distributor cap	6 Governor weight
2 Head rotor	7 Breaker plate
3 Carbon point	8 'O' ring
4 Vacuum controller	9 Pinion
5 Cam	

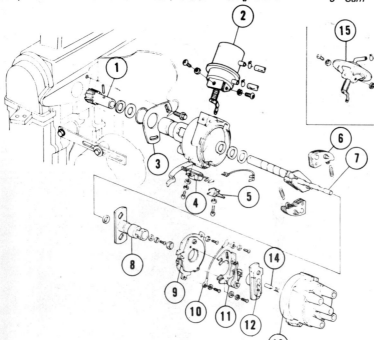

Fig 4.6 Exploded view of distributor (Sec 7)

1 Pinion
2 Vacuum controller
3 Set plate
4 Capacitor
5 Terminal
6 Governor weight
7 Shaft
8 Cam
9 Breaker plate
10 Ground cord
11 Contact breaker
12 Head rotor
13 Cap
14 Carbon point
15 Vacuum controller -
    'Hondamatic'

scoring or corrosion. Replace parts as necessary, but remember it might well be worth while in the case of a distributor obtaining a new or reconditioned exchange unit.

Reassembly of distributor

11 Reassembly is a straightforward reversal of the dismantling sequence, but there are a few points to be watched:

12 Lubricate the balance weights and other parts of the centrifugal advance mechanism, and the main distributor shaft with clean engine grade oil during assembly. Do not oil excessively, but ensure adequate lubrication.

13 Check the movement of the centrifugal advance mechanism throughout the whole advance/retard range; ensure that there is no binding and that movement is smooth.

14 Check that the contact breaker support plate turns smoothly on its mounting plate and ensure that there is no radial movement on the centre bearing.

15 Make certain that the vacuum advance/retard mechanism functions smoothly, without any jerks or binding.

16 Finally, when the distributor is fully assembled on the engine, check the contact breaker gap and static ignition timing in that order. If you have the chance check the dynamic timing as well.

8 Ignition timing

Static timing

(Fig. 4.7).

1 Static timing is that nominal setting which accounts for the time for combustion at the idling speed of the engine.

2 If the distributor clamp plate bolt has been loosened and the static timing lost or if for any other reason it is necessary to set the static ignition timing, proceed as follows:

3 Refer to Section 3, of this Chapter and set the contact breaker gap; do not refit the distributor cap just yet.

4 Remove the cylinder head-rocker-cover and the plastic top timing belt cover, in that order.

5 Turn the engine slowly until the red notch on the crankshaft pulley is aligned with the timing datum mark on the lower timing belt cover. Remember the engine turns anticlockwise when viewed from the crankshaft pulley end. The white notch is Top-Dead-Centre. The red notch is 5o BTDC (Fig. 4.3).

6 Check the cam lobes operating the No. 1 cylinder valves. Both lobes should be angled downwards, both rockers slack and valves closed. If the camshaft is not in this position turn the engine again through 360°, align the red notch on the pulley with the datum on the timing cover and inspect the No. 1

cylinder cam lobes again.

7 Having satisfied yourself that the engine is in the right position, that is 5o BTDC, No. 1 cylinder firing stroke; lock the engine in position by leaving it in gear and applying the handbrake if the car has manual transmission, or if manual or automatic by holding the crankshaft pulley centre bolt with a suitable spanner.

8 Now take hold of the distributor case and turn it about the distributor shaft and rotor, until the rotor arm is pointing to the position of the No. 1 cylinder spark plug stud in the distributor cap. If the distributor had been removed or disturbed for renovation and refitted properly, and if the engine had not moved whilst the distributor was off, the distributor body will require little or no position adjustment to bring the rotor arm and distributor body into the desired relative position.

9 The next task is to adjust the distributor case position more finely now, because it is necessary to bring the contact breakers into the position where they just begin to open.

10 This instant can be determined satisfactorily by connecting a 12 volt bulb across (in parallel) the contact breaker points (one lead to earth, and the other to the contact breaker LT terminal). Switch on the ignition and nudge the distributor body around as necessary (very little movement is required) until the bulb lights up: indicating that the points have just opened.

11 Clamp the distributor in position by tightening the two pinch clamp bolts. Remove wires and bulb. Refit the distributor cap, and undo the means used to lock the engine in the 5o BTDC No. 1 cylinder firing position. (photo)

12 If it was not found possible to align the rotor arm correctly, one of two things is wrong: either the distributor driveshaft has been incorrectly fitted to the engine camshaft - in which case the distributor must be removed and refitted again as described in Section 6, of this Chapter or, alternatively, the distributor cam assembly has been incorrectly fitted to the distributor shaft. To rectify this it will be necessary to partially dismantle the distributor and check the position of the cam member on the centrifugal advance mechanism: it may be 180° out of position.

13 It should be noted that this adjustment is nominal and final adjustment should be made under running conditions.

14 First start the engine and allow to warm up to its proper running temperature, then in a road test accelerate the car in top gear from 30 to 59 mph, whilst listening for pinking from the engine. If pinking is heard, retard the timing slightly by nudging the distributor case clockwise after slackening the clamp bolts (Fig. 4.8).

15 Lastly it is essential if at all possible, to check the operation of the engine temperature actuated ignition advance inhibit system which has been incorporated on the engine as part of the emission control system. Refer to Chapter 3, for this test.

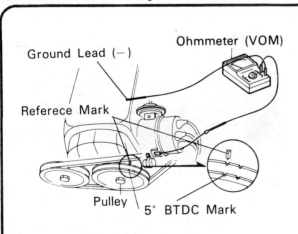

Fig 4.7 Typical equipment for checking static timing of ignition (Sec 8)

8.11 Timing marks on crankshaft pulley. TDC shown pulley turns anticlockwise

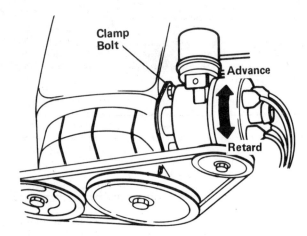

Fig 4.8 Advance and retard adjustment of distributor (Sec 8)

Centrifugal advance

16 The centrifugal advance mechanism ensures that the spark arrives in the cylinder in that interval of time for combustion which corresponds to a greater angle of crankshaft movement when the engine is turning quickly than when it turns slowly.

17 It will be necessary to procure a strobe light and scale so that the variation of engine timing with engine speed may be monitored. Generally this is a specialist task and should be entrusted to your local Honda agent. The test should also include a vacuum advance system test. The advance characteristic is shown in the Specifications at the beginning of this Chapter.

Vacuum advance

18 The vacuum advance/retard system functions to alter ignition timing to cater for variation of mixture strength. The time for combustion of the fuel/air mixture will vary with the mixture strength.

19 It is impractical to test the vacuum advance system without checking the exhaust emission control systems and the centrifugal advance system at the same time. These tests require special equipment and should be entrusted to your local Honda dealer. Again the advance characteristic is shown in the Specifications at the beginning of this Chapter.

9 Spark plugs and HT leads

1 The correct functioning of the spark plugs is vital for the correct running and efficiency of the engine.

2 At intervals of 6,000 miles (10,000 km) the plugs should be removed, examined, cleaned, and if worn excessively, replaced. The condition of the spark plug will also tell much about the overall condition of the engine (Fig. 4.10).

3 If the insulator nose of the spark plug is clean and white, with no deposits, this is indicative of a weak mixture, or too hot a plug. (A hot plug transfers heat away from the electrode slowly - a cold plug transfers heat away quickly).

4 The plugs fitted as standard are one of those as specified at the beginning of this Chapter. If the top and insulator nose is covered with hard black-looking deposits, then this is indicative that the mixture is too rich. Should the plug be black and oily, then it is likely that the engine is fairly worn, as well as the mixture being too rich.

5 If the insulator nose is covered with light tan, to greyish brown, deposits, then the mixture is correct and it is likely that the engine is in good condition.

6 If there are any traces of long brown tapering stains on the outside of the white portion of the plug, then the plug will have to be renewed, as this shows that there is a faulty joint between the plug body and the insulator, and compression is being allowed to leak away.

7 Plugs should be cleaned by a sand blasting machine, which will free them from carbon more than cleaning by hand. The machine will also test the condition of the plugs under compression. Any plug that fails to spark at the recommended pressure should be renewed.

8 The spark plug gap is of considerable importance as, if it is too large, or too small, the size of the spark and its efficiency will be seriously impaired. For the best results the spark plug gap should be set in accordance with the Specifications at the beginning of this Chapter.

9 To set it, measure the gap with a feeler gauge, and then bend open, or close, the outer plug electrode until the correct gap is achieved. The centre electrode should never be bent as this may crack the insulation and cause plug failure if nothing worse.

10 When replacing the plugs, remember to use new washers, and replace the leads from the distributor in the correct firing order, which is 1, 3, 4, 2 (No. 1 cylinder being the one nearest the distributor).

11 The plug leads require no routine attention other than being kept clean and wiped over regularly. At intervals of 6,000 miles (10,000 km) however, pull each lead off the plug in turn and remove them from the distributor. Water can seep down into these joints giving rise to a white corrosive deposit which must be carefully removed from the end of each cable.

10 Ignition coil

1 Maintenance of the coil involves keeping its surfaces clean and dry. Many water repellent sprays are available for this purpose. The high voltages generated by the coil can easily short to earth over the surface of the device and prevent the spark plugs from receiving the pulses of electricity.

2 Damp, or dirty surfaces on the coil, HT leads and distributor cap can cause ignition system malfunction.

3 Tests for the coil are outlined in the following Section 11.

4 The coil is easily removed and refitted: it is retained by two screws.

11 Fault diagnosis - ignition system

Engine troubles normally associated with, and usually caused by faults in the ignition system are:

a) *Failure to start when the engine is turned.*
b) *Uneven running due to misfiring or mistiming.*
c) *Smooth running at low engine revolutions but misfiring when under load or accelerating or at high constant revolutions.*
d) *Smooth running at higher revolutions and misfiring or cutting-out at low speeds.*

a) First check that all wires are properly connected and dry. If the engine fails to catch when the starter is operated do not continue for more than 5 or 6 short burst attempts or the battery will start to get tired and the problem made worse. Remove the spark plug lead from a plug and turn the engine again holding the lead (by the insulation) about ¼ inch from the side of the engine block. A spark should jump the gap audibly and visibly. If it does then the plugs are at fault or the static timing is very seriously adrift. If both are good however, then there must be a fuel supply fault, so go on to that.

If no spark is obtained at the end of a plug lead detach the coil HT lead from the centre of the distributor cap and hold that near the block to try and find a spark. If you now get one, then there is something wrong between the centre terminal of the distributor cap and the ends of the plug leads. Check the cap itself for damage or damp, the 4 terminal lugs for signs of corrosion, the centre carbon brush in the top (is it jammed?) and the rotor arm.

If no spark comes from the coil HT lead check next that the contact breaker points are clean and that the gap is correct. A

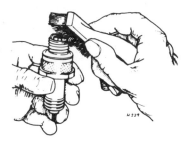

Cleaning deposits from electrodes and surrounding area using a fine wire brush.

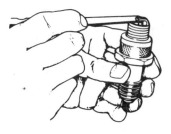

Checking plug gap with feeler gauges

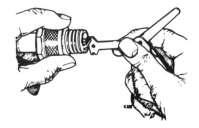

Altering the plug gap. Note use of correct tool.

Fig 4.9 The method of adjusting the spark plug electrodes (Sec 9)

White deposits and damaged porcelain insulation indicating overheating

Broken porcelain insulation due to bent central electrode

Electrodes burnt away due to wrong heat value or chronic pre-ignition (pinking)

Excessive black deposits caused by over-rich mixture or wrong heat value

Mild white deposits and electrode burnt indicating too weak a fuel mixture

Plug in sound condition with light greyish brown deposits

Fig 4.10 Spark plug conditions (Sec 9)

quick check can be made by turning the engine so that the points are closed. Then switch on the ignition and open the points with an insulated screwdriver. There should be a small visible spark and, once again, if the coil HT lead is held near the block at the same time a proper HT spark should occur. If there is a big fat spark at the points but none at the HT lead then the condenser is faulty and should be renewed.

If neither of these things happen, then the next step in this tale of woe, is to see if there is any current (12 volts) reaching the coil (+ terminal). (One could check this at the distributor, but by going back to the input side of the coil a longer length of possible fault line is bracketed and could save time).

With a 12 volt bulb and piece of wire (or of course a voltmeter if you have one handy), connected between the + or SW terminal of the coil and earth and switch on the ignition. No light means no volts so the fault is between the battery and the coil via the ignition switch. This is moving out of the realms of just ignition problems - the electrical system is becoming involved in general. So to get home to bed get a piece of wire and connect the terminal + of the coil to the + terminal on the battery and see if sparks occur at the HT leads once more.

If there is current reaching the coil then the coil itself or the wire from its terminal to the distributor is at fault. Check the CB terminal with a bulb with the ignition switched on. If it fails to light then the coil is faulty in its LT windings and needs renewal.

b) Uneven running and misfiring should first be checked by seeing that all leads, particularly HT, are dry and connected properly. See that they are not shorting to earth through broken or cracked insulation. If they are, you should be able to see and hear it. If not, then check the plugs, contact points and condenser just as you would in the case of total failure to start.

c) If misfiring occurs at high speed check the points gap, which may be too small, and the plugs in that order. Check also that the spring tension on the points is not too light thus causing them to bound. This requires a special pull balance so if in doubt it will be cheaper to buy a new set of contacts, rather than go to a garage and get them to check it. If the trouble is still not cured, then the fault lies in the carburation or engine itself.

d) If misfiring or stalling occurs only at low speeds the points gap is possibly too big. If not, then the slow running adjustment on the carburettor needs attention.

Chapter 5 Clutch

Contents

Specifications

Type ... ...   Single dry disc with diaphragm spring

Clutch disc

Friction area	146 sq cm (22.6 sq in)
Thickness	8.3 to 9.0 mm (0.33 to 0.35 inch)
Thickness, minimum	5.9 to 6.6 mm (0.23 to 0.26 inch)
Face runout (maximum)	0.5 to 0.6 mm (0.020 to 0.023 inch)
Radial play on splines	0.04 to 0.10 mm (0.0016 to 0.004 inch)
Limit for service	0.4 mm (0.016 mm)

Clutch actuation ... ...   Mechanical

Clutch pedal

Free play	15 to 20 mm (0.6 to 0.79 inch)
Full stroke	145 mm (5.7 inch)
Clearance to floor	30 mm (1.2 inch)

Clutch release bearing holder

Internal diameter	$29.0 ^{-0.00}_{+0.03}$ mm (1.14 to 1.15 inch)
Service limit	29.06 mm (1.14 inch)
Clearance case/holder	0.02 to 0.8 mm (0.001 to 0.003 inch)

Torque wrench settings

	kg f m	lb f ft
Flywheel to crankshaft	4.7 - 5.3	34 - 38
Clutch cover to flywheel	1.0 - 1.4	7 - 10
Clutch case cover/oil pan	0.3 - 0.7	2 - 5
Clutch spring stopper	0.7 - 1.1	5 - 8
Clutch release arm bolt	2.0 - 2.8	14 - 20
Clutch case to cylinder block	4.0 - 5.0	29 - 36
Clutch control cable stay	2.0 - 2.8	14 - 20

1 General description

The Honda Civic has been fitted with a single dry plate, diaphragm spring clutch. The unit is conventional and operates as follows: When the clutch pedal is depressed, the clutch thrust bearing moves towards the centre of the clutch. The bearing acts on the inner fingers of the single piece diaphragm spring, thereby reducing the force exerted by the periphery of the spring on the pressure plate in the clutch. The pressure plate holds the clutch friction disc against the flywheel, and when the force exerted on the pressure plate and disc reduces to zero, the disc is free to move relative to the flywheel, and will not transmit engine power to the transmission.

Once the gearbox is not receiving power from the engine, gear selection can be made, followed by release of the clutch pedal. As the pedal is released, the thrust bearing moves away from the centre of the clutch. The diaphragm spring force on the pressure plate is restored and the disc is now held firmly against the flywheel so that engine power is transmitted via the flywheel and clutch disc to the transmission.

Detail features of the clutch include the fitting of four coil springs in the friction disc, which smooth out any shock when the disc is brought into contact with the flywheel. The disc periphery with the friction material is not connected directly to the splined hub, the torque is transmitted via the springs which are arranged circumferentially on the disc hub.

2 Clutch actuating system - general

Honda have fitted a mechanical clutch actuating system: it comprises a cable and sleeve assembly which connects the clutch pedal to the actuating lever on the thrust bearing pivot axle.

The sleeve containing the clutch cable is retained by a grommet in the forward bulkhead, and by an eyelet bolted to the gearbox housing (Fig. 5.1).

3 Clutch cable assembly - removal and refitting

1 The clutch cable needs to be slackened first before removal can commence. The cable is slackened by undoing the clutch travel adjusting nut on the engine end of the cable sleeve (Fig. 5.2).
2 Once the cable and sleeve is completely slack, the cable may be unhooked from the top of the clutch pedal lever, and the top end cable and sleeve drawn out of the engine bulkhead into the engine compartment.
3 Finally the lower end of the cable and sleeve are unhooked from the clutch actuating lever and sleeve retainer bolted to the transmission casing.
4 Refitting the clutch cable follows the reversal of the removal procedure, and before the car is taken onto the road, the clutch pedal free-travel should be adjusted. The following Section details the technique for free travel adjustment.

4 Clutch pedal free-travel adjustment

1 Begin by comparing the heights of the clutch and brake pedals when they are on their respective stops. Ensure that the brake pedal free-travel is correctly adjusted and then align the clutch pedal to the brake pedal (Fig. 5.3).
2 Then proceed to turn the cable sleeve position adjusting screw at the lower end of the cable sleeve, so that the clutch actuating lever play is brought to between 3 and 4 mm. Once the correct play has been obtained tighten the adjusting nut and its locknut (Fig. 5.2).
3 Lastly the clutch pedal release height should be checked as follows:
4 Raise the car onto chassis stands placed beneath the strengthened parts of the bodyshell just rearward of the front wheel. Support the car so that the front wheels are off the ground.
5 Now place the car in top gear, depress the clutch and start the engine; then raise the clutch pedal until the front wheels just begin to turn. Measure the distance between the pedal and carpet and check it against the Specifications at the beginning of this Chapter (Fig. 5.3).

5 Clutch unit and flywheel - removal

1 It is possible to remove the clutch by two methods. If no hoist is available, then the method which involves separating the engine and transmission with the engine in place in the car, should be followed. On the other hand, if a hoist is available, it will be more straightforward to remove the engine and transmission unit as a whole and separate the two units remote from the car.
2 If it is intended to remove the engine and gearbox as a unit, and separate them when they are on a bench, refer to Chapter 1, which details the engine and gearbox removal.
3 Alternatively, if it is intended to separate the engine and transmission in-situ in the car, refer to Chapter 1, Section 5 and follow the instructions down to paragraph 20. Use jacks to support the engine and transmission units.
4 Once the lower engine mounts have been removed, re-install the centre beam, without mounts and lower the engine until it rests on the beam.
5 Remove the panel in the lower part of the front wheel arch next to the gearbox. It is necessary to remove this panel in order to provide space for the gearbox when it is separated and moved away from the engine.
6 Support the gearbox on a jack whilst the four main bolts which secure the transmission to the engine, are removed. Note that one of the starter motor bolts passes right through the clutch housing and is retained by a nut on the engine side of the clutch housing.

7 Once the retaining bolts have been removed, the transmission can be carefully moved away from the engine, and once clear lowered to the ground. Move the transmission unit to a bench, to provide space to work on the clutch.

Clutch separation from flywheel
8 It will be necessary to hold the flywheel securely to allow the clutch retaining bolts to be removed. Honda provide a special block (Part No. 07924 - 6340100) which bolts to the cylinder block and engages the starter ring gear to lock the flywheel in

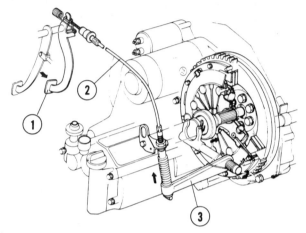

Fig 5.1 Clutch actuation system (Sec 2)

1 *Clutch pedal*   3 *Clutch release lever*
2 *Clutch control cable*

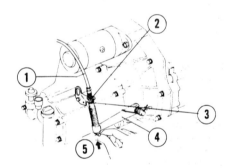

Fig 5.2 Clutch cable adjustment (Secs 3 & 4)

1 *Clutch control cable*   4 *Clutch release lever*
2 *Adjusting nut*   5 *Clutch release lever play*
3 *Locknut*

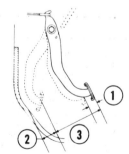

Fig 5.3 Clutch pedal movement (Sec 4)

1 *Clutch pedal play*   *mat when depressed*
2 *Pedal height above floor*   3 *Effective stroke*

position. This tool can easily be improvised if necessary.

9 Using a centre pop make a mark on the clutch assembly cover and flywheel to indicate the correct reassembled position (Fig. 5.5).

10 Undo and remove the eight clutch assembly retaining bolts. Now carefully lift the clutch assembly from the flywheel and recover the clutch friction disc.

6 Clutch components - inspection and renovation

1 Unfortunately it is not possible to inspect the clutch without going to the considerable trouble of removing the assembly. Consequently, one waits for trouble to develop or makes a decision to check and overhaul it anyway, at a specific mileage. Wear of the clutch friction disc depends a great deal on how the car has been driven. Habitual clutch slipping will obviously cause rapid wear. If it is assumed that the friction disc will need replacement at 35,000 miles and will be worth replacing at 25,000 miles there will be no significant waste of time and money if the work is

done. Of course, a history of the car is very valuable for this decision. If, on the other hand, trouble is awaited, action must be taken immediately it occurs; otherwise further more costly wear could occur. Trouble usually comes in the form of slipping, when the engine speeds up and the car does not; or squealing, denoting that the friction material is worn to the rivets; or juddering denoting all sorts of things (see Fault diagnosis). Wear on the ball release bearing which presses onto the centre of the diaphragm every time the clutch is operated could also cause squealing if the wear was extreme. If the clutch is not examined when wear is apparent, the faces of the flywheel and pressure plate may be severely scored and call for costly replacement.

2 Having decided to dismantle the clutch, first examine the faces of the flywheel and the pressure plate. They should be smooth and shiny. If they are slightly ridged or scored, a new friction disc will be enough to regain satisfactory performance. If there is severe scoring, be prepared to buy a new pressure plate assembly and/or flywheel. It is possible to skim the face of the flywheel but engineering advice should be sought. If a new flywheel is obtained it will have to be matched to balance the

Fig 5.4 Crankshaft centre bearing

Fig 5.5 Clutch cover/flywheel alignment marks (Sec 5)

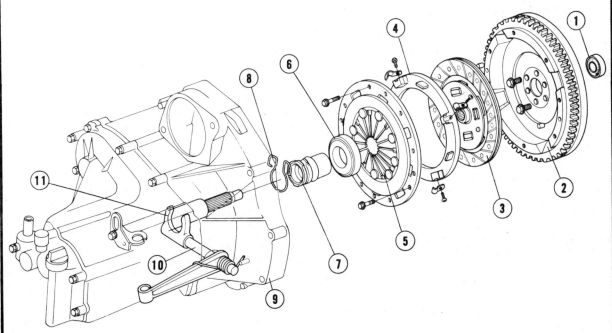

Fig 5.6 Exploded view of clutch mechanism

1 Clutch pilot bearing	*5 Diaphragm spring*	*8 Release arm clip*	*11 Clutch release arm A*
2 Flywheel	*6 Release bearing*	*9 Clutch case*	
3 Friction disc	*7 Release bearing holder*	*10 Release shaft complete*	
4 Pressure plate			

same as the original. (Make sure it is the correct flywheel). If you hurriedly put the badly scored surfaces back together with a new friction plate you will achieve short-lived results only. After a few thousand miles the same trouble will recur and judder will always be present.

3 The friction plate lining surfaces should be at least 0.8 mm above the heads of the rivets, otherwise the disc is not really worth putting back. If the friction lining material shows signs of chipping or breaking up or has black areas caused by oil contamination it should also be renewed. Oil contamination will be confirmed by signs of oil which may be visible on the flywheel or in the release bearing (on the gearbox). Consideration must be given to curing any such leaks before refitting the existing clutch discs but it is hardly worth it. With a new assembly you know that the splines and the disc itself are in good condition.

Fig 5.7 Removal of clutch thrust bearing (Sec 8)

7 Clutch - refitting

1 If the original cover is being reused, line up the marks made before removal and support the friction disc on one finger between cover and flywheel, so that the shortest boss faces the flywheel. It is important to align the clutch cover and flywheel properly, otherwise the assembly will be unbalanced. The cover and flywheels have marks made by the manufacturer for aligning purposes.

2 Locate the cover on the flywheel and then place all the cover bolts in position and screw them up lightly by hand.

3 It is necessary to line up the centre of the friction disc with the exact centre of the flywheel. This is easily done if a piece of shouldered bar can be placed in the bearing in the middle of the flywheel, and with the large diameter supporting the friction disc. If you do not have such a thing the disc may be lined up by eye if the engine is out of the car. For the man flat on his back on a cold concrete floor with his eyes full of grime, it is certainly worthwhile making up some sort of centralising tool from a broom handle to get reasonably accurate positioning.

4 If the clutch disc is not positioned correctly, it will be difficult (and may result in damage to the gearbox input shaft and friction disc) to refit the gearbox to the engine.

5 Having satisfied yourself that the friction plate is correctly positioned, the clutch cover bolts should be tightened up diagonally evenly and progressively to the torque specified at the beginning of this Chapter.

6 Refitting the gearbox to the engine follows the reversal of removal procedure, and is detailed in Chapter 1.

7 Do not forget to inspect and satisfy yourself of the condition of the clutch release thrust bearing.

8 Clutch operating lever and thrust bearing - removal, dismantling and refitting

1 When the clutch pedal is depressed, the cable link moves the operating lever in the clutch housing. The lever forces the ball race thrust bearing against the centre of the diaphragm spring which holds the friction plate against the flywheel.

2 Although the clutch thrust (release) bearing has been packed with grease during manufacture, the grease is eventually lost and the bearing runs dry. A worn, dry bearing is characterised by a whine whenever the clutch pedal is depressed.

3 In order to remove the clutch operating lever and thrust bearing, it will be necessary to remove the transmission by one of the methods described in Section 5, of this Chapter.

4 Once the transmission has been separated from the engine and moved to a clean bench, a visual inspection may be made of the thrust bearing operating lever and shaft.

Dismantling

5 Do not attempt to remove the thrust bearing with the actuating lever, shaft and bearing holder still in place in the clutch housing. Straighten the tabs on the forked bearing lever bolt locking washer, and undo and remove the bolt. Remember

that the actuating lever is spring loaded. Hold the lever as the arm bolt is removed and note the spring pretension.

6 Pull the actuating lever and shaft from the clutch housing so that the thrust bearing, its holder and forked arm can be removed along the input shaft and its sleeve.

7 Now that the thrust bearing, holder and forked arm are free, they may be separated by removing the wire clip which retains the bearing and holder in the forked arm.

8 The thrust bearing is an interference fit on the holder. If the bearing is to be replaced, it must be tapped off the holder with a light mallet.

9 When fitting a new bearing to the sleeve holder, ensure that the rounded side is opposite to the holder and forked arm location.

10 Ensure also that the new bearing does not come into contact with any solvents. Solvent will degrade and dissolve the grease in the bearing and drastically shorten its useful life.

11 Having fitted the new bearing on its holder/sleeve, refit the assembly to the forked arm. Secure with the special wire clip.

12 Insert the clutch actuating lever and shaft, locate the torsion spring and apply the required preload before fitting the thrust bearing assembly to the central end of the actuating shaft.

13 Insert the forked arm fixing bolt, together with its tab washer. Tighten the bolt and lock by bending the tabs on the lock-washer around the bolt head flats and forked arm boss flat.

14 Finally check that the thrust bearing turns smoothly and freely, before refitting the transmission to the engine.

9 Fault diagnosis - clutch

1 Provided the clutch is not intentionally slipped excessively, or the pedal used as a footrest, which will cause rapid wear of the clutch thrust bearing: the only malfunction one would expect would be routine wear of the friction plate. This normal wear will become obvious as the clutch starts to slip; that is the engine turns normally but the car fails to accelerate properly or slows down unaccountably on hills. In such cases the clutch must be examined and repaired if necessary, immediately. Delay will be costly.

2 Squealing noises from the clutch (and make sure they are from the clutch and not the fanbelt or water pump) are most likely to come from a worn out clutch release bearing. The actual efficiency of the clutch may not be immediately affected but damage could be caused to the thrust boss on the driving plate if no action is taken. Another reason for squealing could be a worn out or oil contaminated friction plate. In such instances the next symptom one could expect would be clutch slip. Do not wait for that however, as the friction plate rivets could be scoring the flywheel or pressure plate surfaces. Once again inspection and repair involves gearbox removal.

3 Failure to disengage the clutch (sometimes referred to as 'clutch spin') when the pedal is fully depressed, can be caused by one or more of several factors. Symptoms are the total inability or considerable difficulty in engaging any gear at rest - and when

a gear is engaged it will be accompanied by a nasty crunch and the car bucking forward (or backwards). First check that the cable is moving the actuating lever when the pedal is depressed. It could be a broken or frayed (stretched) clutch cable. If the cable is alright, then the fault may be due to the friction plate sticking to the pressure plate or flywheel due to rusted splines which prevent it from floating fore-and-aft on the gearbox input shaft. This is not unusual if the car has been standing unused for a long time. Try engaging a gear, with the engine stopped and handbrake on; then depress the clutch and try starting the engine. If the clutch is seized solid the engine will not turn over but if you are lucky and the engine starts and the clutch can be slipped, it should be possible to get it back to normal operation after using it a few times.

Rust on the friction faces as well as on the splines will have the same effect and can be cured by the same treatment. If the clutch spin does not eventually disappear completely, then some other defect such as distortion on the pressure faces may be the cause and this will involve dismantling. Thirdly, the cause could be a worn out thrust bearing allied to a well worn clutch plate. Squealing noises each time the clutch is operated, will be an indication of this and dismantling will be necessary.

4 Another fault is judder - particularly to be noticed when the clutch is taking up the drive. Although the symptom is noticed when the clutch is operated, the clutch is not necessarily the culprit. Check the condition of the engine mountings (two forward and one at the end of the gearbox). If the engine vibrates and rocks excessively when started up it would indicate that they are spongy or broken. Then check that the universal joints on the driveshafts are not worn and that the front suspension is secure and free fron excessive backlash. Defective front dampers can also cause drive judder. If diagnosis finally indicates that the fault lies in the clutch it will be caused by wear, contamination or distortion in one or other of the components, and dismantling will be needed to ascertain for sure what is causing it.

Chapter 6
Manual gearbox and Hondamatic transmission

Contents

Specifications

	Manual gearbox	Hondamatic
Number of gears	4 forward 1 reverse	2 forward 1 reverse with torque converter

Ratios
	Manual gearbox	Hondamatic
1st	3.00 : 1	"1" 1.521 : 1
2nd	1.789 : 1	
3rd	1.182 : 1	"2" 1.034 : 1
4th	0.846 : 1	
Reverse	2.916 : 1	Reverse 2.045 : 1

Manual gearbox

Mainshaft
Axial movement ... ...   0.09 mm (0.0035 inches)
Service limit ... ...   0.30 mm (0.0118 inches)
End roller bearing journal diameter ... ...   31.98 mm -0.01 mm (1.2587 to 1.2598 inches)
                                                   +0.02
Shaft runout ... ...   0.03 mm (0.0012 inches)
Limit ... ...   0.07 mm (0.0028 inches)

1st and 4th gears
Bore ... ...   37.00 - 37.02 mm (1.4567 - 1.4574 inches) assembly standard
     37.05 mm (1.4587 in) service limit

2nd and 3rd gears
Gear axial play ... ...   0.03 mm (0.0019 inches)
     0.18 mm (0.007 in) service limit

Reverse gear shaft
Outside diameter ... ...   14.98 to 14.97 mm (0.5898 to 0.5894 inches)
     Service limit 14.94 mm (0.5882 in)

Reverse idle gear
Bore ... ...   15.04 to 15.01 mm (0.5921 to 0.5909 inches)
     Service limit 15.08 mm (0.5937 inches)

Synchronising mechanism
Fork to synchronising ring slot clearance ... ...   0.45 to 0.65 mm (0.0177 to 0.0256 inches)
     Service limit 1.0 mm (0.039 inches)
Blocking ring to gear clearance ... ...   1.00 mm (0.039 inches) assembly std
     Service limit 0.5 mm (0.0197 inches)

Input shaft (Counter)
Axial movement ... ...   0.09 mm (0.0035 inches) assembly
     0.3 mm (0.0118 inches) service limit
Needle roller bearing journal diameter ... ...   20 to 19.98 mm (0.7874 to 0.7866 inches)
Ball bearing (6304) journal diameter ... ...   22 to 21.98 mm (0.8661 to 0.8654 inches)

Hondamatic transmission

Stall rpm (all gears) ... ... 2200 to 2600 rpm

Oil pressures at 1000 rpm
(in Main Delivery Line, "L" clutch line and "D" clutch line) ... 71 to 114 lbs sq in
Service limit 57 lbs sq in

Torque converter
Turbine (thickness of washer surface in centre of turbine) ... 11.3 to 11.4 mm (0.4449 to 0.4482 inches)
Service limit 11.00 mm (0.4331 inch)

Stator side plate (thickness) ... ... 5.95 to 6.00 mm (0.2343 to 0.2362 inches)
Service limit 5.90 mm (0.2323 inch)

Thrust washer nominal 54 mm dia/37 mm bore thickness ... 1.95 mm to 2.05 mm (0.0768 to 0.0807 inches)
Service limit 1.90 mm (0.0784 inches)

Thrust washer nominal 66 mm dia/38 mm bore thickness ... 1.95 mm to 2.05 mm (0.0768 to 0.0807 inches)
Service limit 1.90 (0.0784 inches)

Thrust washer nominal 45 mm dia/17 mm bore thickness ... 2.45 mm to 2.55 mm (0.0965 to 0.1004 inches)
Service limit 2.40 mm (0.0945 inches)

Wet clutch assemblies
"L" and "D" clutch clearance between plates ... ... 0.5 to 0.8 mm (0.0197 to 0.0315 inches)
Clutch return springs free-length ... ... 39.7 mm (1.563 inches) new
Service limit 36.0 mm (1.4173 inches)

Clutch disc thickness ... ... 1.95 to 2.05 mm (0.0768 to 0.0807 inches)
Limit: when oil grooves have worn away

Clutch plate thickness ... ... 1.95 to 2.05 mm (0.0768 to 0.0807 inch)
Limit: flaking and discoloured surface

Clutch end plate ... ... 1.7 to 1.8 mm (0.0670 to 0.0710 inches) and 2.0 to 2.1mm
(0.0787 to 0.0827 inches)
Limit: flaking and discoloured surface

Thrust washers associated with "L" clutch:
Nominal 45 mm dia/22 mm bore thickness ... ... 1.95 to 2.05 mm (0.0768 to 0.0807 inches)
Service limit 1.90 inches (0.0748 inches)

Nominal 46 mm dia/33 mm bore thickness ... ... 1.15 mm to 1.25 mm (0.0453 to 0.0492 inches)
Service limit 1.10 mm (0.0433 inches)

Nominal 46 mm dia/20 mm bore thickness ... ... 2.95 to 3.05 mm (0.1161 to 0.1201 inches)
Service limit 2.90 mm (0.1142 inches)

Hydraulic system
Oil pump:
Gear to housing axial clearance ... ... 0.03 to 0.06 mm (0.0012 to 0.0024 inches)
Gear to housing radial clearance ... ... 0.05 to 0.09 mm (0.0020 to 0.0035 inches)
Clutch oil feed sleeve bore - in End Cover and Cast Iron
stator shaft retainer ... ... 52.05 to 52.08 mm (2.049 to 2.050 inches)

Stator shaft
Bush bore ... ... 17.0 to 17.018 mm (0.6693 to 0.6701 inches)
Service limit 17.1 mm (0.6732 inches)

Diameter of needle roller journal surface ... ... 24 to 24.018 mm (0.9449 to 0.9454 inches)

Gear selection system
Reverse gear shift fork (thickness)
Internal mechanisms ... ... 5.8 mm (0.2284 inches) new
Service limit 5.2 mm (0.2047 inches)

Parking lock mechanism:
Pawl release spring free-length ... ... 30 - 33 mm (1.18 to 1.30 inches)
Parking brake shaft run out (max) ... ... 0.1 mm (0.004 inches)
Servo valve:
Check valve spring free-length ... ... 34 to 38 mm (1.338 to 1.496 inches)
Shift fork shaft bore ... ... 14.00 to 14.025 mm (0.551 to 0.552 inches)
Shift fork shaft valve bore ... ... 37 to 37.045 mm (1.4567 to 1.4585 inches)
External mechanisms
Lever push knob spring free-length ... ... 41 to 43 mm (1.61 to 1.70 inches)
Lever pivot assembly:
Lock pin spring free-length ... ... 90 to 92.5 mm (3.54 to 3.64 inches)
Selector stop spring free-length ... ... 27 to 28.5 mm (1.06 to 1.12 inches)
Lever pivot bushing bore ... ... 9.75 to 9.98 mm (0.384 to 0.393 inches)

Torque wrench settings

Manual gearbox	kg f m	lbs f ft
Mainshaft locknut (L.H. thread)	4.0 - 5.0	29 - 36
Countershaft locknut	6.0 - 7.0	43 - 51
Engine mount bracket	3.1 - 3.9	22 - 28
Transmission drain plug	3.5 - 4.5	25 - 33
Transmission case to clutch housing	2.3 - 3.1	17 - 22
Transmission end cover	1.0 - 1.4	7 - 10
Reversing light switch	2.3 - 2.7	17 - 20

								kg fm	lbs f ft
Low shift fork	...	...	...	...	...	...	...	1.0 - 1.4	7 - 10
Top shift fork	...	...	...	...	...	...	...	1.0 - 1.4	7 - 10
Reverse shift fork	...	...	...	...	...	...	...	1.0 - 1.4	7 - 10
Shift arm ...	...	...	...	...	...	...	...	2.0 - 2.8	14 - 20
Gearshift lever and rod ...	...	...	...	...	...	...	...	1.9 - 2.5	14 - 18
Gearshift extension mount	...	...	...	...	...	...	...	0.7 - 1.2	5 - 9

Hondamatic transmission

								kg fm	lbs f ft
Driveplate to crankshaft	...	...	...	...	...			4.7 - 5.3	34 - 38
Driveplate to torque converter	...	...	...	...				1.0 - 1.4	7 - 10
Torque converter	...	...	...	...	...	...		1.0 - 1.4	7 - 10
Mainshaft nut	...	...	...	...	...	...	...	4.7 - 5.3	34 - 38
Countershaft	...	...	...	...	...	...	...	8.0 - 10	58 - 72
Final driven gear	...	...	...	...	...	...		9.0 - 9.5	65 - 69
Bearing retainer:									
Pan head screw	...	...	...	...	...	...		0.8 - 1.2	6 - 9
Hex bolt	...	...	...	...	...	...	...	1.0 - 1.4	7 - 10
Main valve body ...	...	...	...	...	...	...		1.0 - 1.4	7 - 10
Servo valve body	...	...	...	...	...	...		1.0 - 1.4	7 - 10
Seal ring guide	...	...	...	...	...	...		1.0 - 1.4	7 - 10
Oil strainer	...	...	...	...	...	...		1.0 - 1.4	7 - 10
Inhibitor switch ...	...	...	...	...	...	...		0.8 - 1.2	6 - 9
Turnbuckle	...	...	...	...	...	...	...	0.8 - 1.2	6 - 9
Selector lever	...	...	...	...	...	...	...	0.8 - 1.2	6 - 9
Control cable clamp	...	...	...	...	...	...		0.8 - 1.2	6 - 9
Oil pressure senser point plugs	...	...	...	...				1.0 - 1.4	7 - 10

1 Manual gearbox - general description

The gearbox is positioned on the end of the engine and forms part of a geartrain to the differential unit which is held in the same housing.

The drive is taken from the engine by the clutch/gearbox input shaft. This shaft runs in three bearings: the flywheel centre bearing, the first gearbox bearing and the end bearing in the gearbox case. The input shaft has 4 fixed gears machined onto it, and these are in constant mesh with the synchronised gears on the output shaft. The output shaft runs in two bearings, and includes the gear which meshes with the differential crownwheel. The speedometer drive is taken from the outer end of the gearbox output shaft.

For those familiar with the layout of a gearbox of a conventional rear wheel drive car, this Honda gearbox will present one essential change: the drive is always across the gearbox. The input shaft has the familiar shape of a layshaft and serves the same purpose; it drives the synchronised gears on the output shaft. The Honda output shaft has the shape of a mainshaft, except for the gear cut at one end to drive the final drive directly.

There is no direct line from input to output shaft in the gearbox as found in the conventional rear wheel drive car. This layout affords the designer the freedom of choosing all the gear ratios - including top gear, which has been chosen to be an 'overdrive'.

The gearbox construction allows good and easy access to the geartrains, and does not present any task which is difficult. All bearings and shafts are exposed. It should prove to be a very easy gearbox to work on.

2 Manual gearbox/transmission - removal and refitting

1 The gearbox/transmission unit is removed from the car, without the engine. The basic procedure is to remove connections to the gearbox and final drive, then support the engine and detach the transmission, which can then be lowered from the car.

2 Commence the gearbox removal by raising the front of the car and supporting it with chassis stands placed beneath the suspension subframe. Chock the rear wheels and apply the handbrake.

3 Next, remove the front wheels and detach the positive and negative leads from the battery.

4 Remove the electrical leads from the starter motor and solenoid, and unbolt the starter motor from the engine. Note that the lower bolt passes right through the converter casing and is secured by a nut on the engine end.

5 Now disconnect the following from the transmission unit: reversing light switch leads, clutch actuating cable (from the actuating lever), the speedometer cable, and lastly the engine temperature sensor leads.

6 The gearshift mechanism should be uncoupled from the gearbox. There is a pin (8 mm) which connects the gearshift rod to the member projecting from the transmission case; this pin needs to be driven out of the rod with a suitable drift.

7 Next remove the left and right lower control arm ball joints in the front suspension. Chapter 8, details the technique for the ball joint removal.

8 Now grasp the wheel hub/disc assembly and pull outwards to draw the front driveshafts out of the differential unit. Plug the holes exposed in the differential with clean non-fluffy rag to prevent the ingress of foreign matter.

9 The next task is to support the engine in readiness for the gearbox and transmission to be removed. Honda supply a special lifting hanger and bolt (07966 - 6340100; 07966 - 6340200) which can be attached to the engine just to the left of the distributor and at the engine torque reaction rod fixing.

10 Alternatively, the engine may be jacked-up from beneath the car, just sufficient to unload the engine's flexible mountings.

11 The two nuts which secure the lower engine mount to the beam which passes beneath the engine and transmission should now be undone and removed. Next remove the support beam itself and then the lower flexible mounting from the engine.

12 Refit the support beam, now without the flexible mount, beneath the engine; and then lower the engine down so that it rests on the beam.

13 Move the jack so that it is positioned squarely beneath the gearbox/transmission unit. Take the weight of the unit on the jack and proceed to loosen the four bolts which secure the transmission case to the engine.

14 Using the jack to support the transmission, move the unit away from the engine horizontally - until the clutch shaft has disengaged the clutch unit and flywheel. Then lower the unit to the floor and remove to a bench.

Refitting the transmission

15 As to be expected the refitting procedure is basically the reversal of the removal procedure, but pay particular attention to the following points:

i) Ensure that the joint surfaces of the transmission case and engine are perfectly clean before refitting so that there is no misalignment of the two units when assembled.

ii) When offering the transmission unit back onto the engine, make sure that the clutch shaft engages the friction disc in the clutch, and the bearing in the centre of the flywheel, smoothly. The friction plate and the flywheel centre bearing can easily be damaged if any force is used to introduce the transmission shaft into the clutch or if it is not introduced squarely.

iii) It is essential that the transmission case/engine bolts, engine support nuts and bolts, and the suspension ball joint nuts and bolts are tightened to the correct torque.

iv) Remember to check that the all electrical connections have been refitted and are working, and check the play on the clutch pedal and actuating linkage. Lastly do not forget to refill the transmission unit with Castrol EP90 gear oil or the equivalent.

3 Gearbox (manual) - dismantling

1 Liberally coat the unit with a solvent such as Gunk, and wash the unit down with a strong jet of water. Dry the exterior thoroughly with a clean non-fluffy rag; the unit should now be completely clean and ready for dismantling.

2 Always work on a clean bench, and store each component as it is removed in a clean bin or on a clean shelf. It is particularly important with items such as bearings that no foreign matter be introduced into the bearing at any stage of the work on the transmission.

3 Begin the dismantling of the gearbox by undoing and removing the six bolts which secure the rear cover to the gearbox. Recover the gasket.

4 Now measure the end play on each of the mainshaft (output) and countershaft (input) of the gearbox.

5 The amount of end-play is an indication of the condition of the respective shaft bearings; therefore if the end-play is close to,

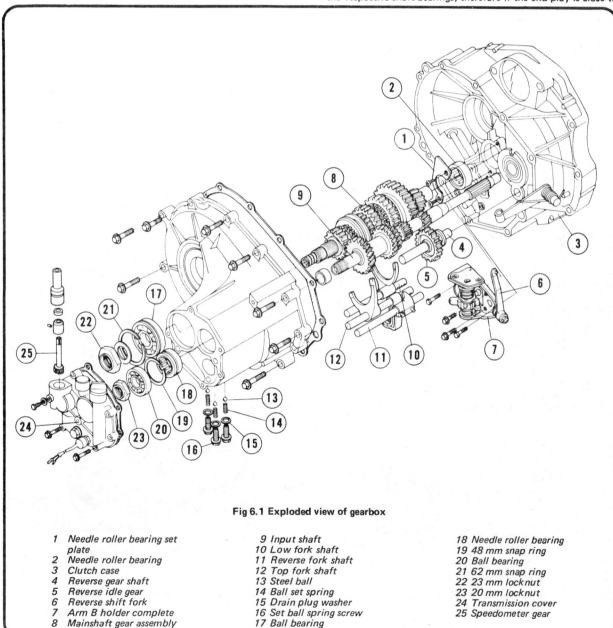

Fig 6.1 Exploded view of gearbox

1 Needle roller bearing set plate	9 Input shaft	18 Needle roller bearing
2 Needle roller bearing	10 Low fork shaft	19 48 mm snap ring
3 Clutch case	11 Reverse fork shaft	20 Ball bearing
4 Reverse gear shaft	12 Top fork shaft	21 62 mm snap ring
5 Reverse idle gear	13 Steel ball	22 23 mm locknut
6 Reverse shift fork	14 Ball set spring	23 20 mm locknut
7 Arm B holder complete	15 Drain plug washer	24 Transmission cover
8 Mainshaft gear assembly	16 Set ball spring screw	25 Speedometer gear
	17 Ball bearing	

or exceeds, the limit stated in the Specifications at the beginning of this Chapter, the bearings will need particular examination.

6 Check the end-play with a dial gauge mounted on the transmission case and with its probe resting co-axially on the end of the respective shaft.

7 Bend back the locking tab on the mainshaft locknut, and undo and remove the nut. The mainshaft nut has left-hand threads, and it will be necessary to engage a gear and hold the countershaft locknut, to enable the mainshaft nut to be undone (Fig. 6.2). Do not remove the countershaft nut at this time.

8 Next remove the ball bearing race on the end of the mainshaft, with a standard puller or sprocket puller.

9 Now undo and remove the three gearshift detent locking ball retaining bolts, and recover the springs and balls from the gearbox casing (Fig. 6.3).

10 Undo and remove the bolts which secure the gearbox casing to the clutch/differential housing. Lightly tap the clutch/differential housing with a soft mallet and drift, in the locations indicated in Fig. 6.4, to separate the casing and housing. **Do not prise apart with a screwdriver.**

11 The geartrains are now exposed and are quite accessible.

They are 'free standing' in the clutch/differential housing.

12 Next remove the reverse idler gear and shaft and then the reverse gearshift fork (Fig. 6.5).

13 The forward gearshift forks assembly should now be removed by undoing the fork retaining bolts and then pulling the shift rods up until they clear the housing. Finally remove the forks from the shafts (Fig. 6.6).

14 If it is intended to carry out some repair to the gear selector mechanism, it should be dismantled as follows:

15 Undo and remove the two retaining screws, and remove the retaining plate. Then push the shift arm against the large spring and release. Remove the pivot shaft.

16 Take care not to lose the detent ball and spring retained by the pivot shaft, when the pivot shaft is removed.

17 Finally remove the interlock bar and shaft arms.

18 The countershaft and mainshaft may be removed together by holding both shafts and lightly tapping the flywheel end of the mainshaft with a soft metal hammer (Fig. 6.7).

19 The gearshift arm can be withdrawn from the aluminium casing once the rubber lock washer and bolt have been removed (Fig. 6.8).

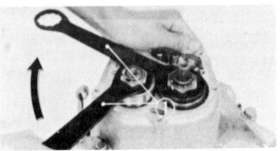

Fig 6.2 Undoing main and input shaft end nuts (Sec 3)
1 Locknut wrenches

Fig 6.3 Removing the gear fork shaft detent balls and springs (Sec 3)

Fig 6.4 Points where the transmission case is lightly tapped to free case and clutch/differential housing (Sec 3)

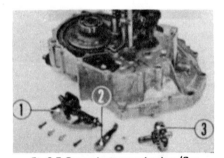

Fig 6.5 Gear selector mechanism (Sec 3)
1 Gearshaft arm pivot assembly
2 Reverse gear fork
3 Reverse idle gear

Fig 6.6 Removal of forward gear forks and shafts (Sec 3)

Fig 6.7 Removal of input shaft and mainshaft together (Sec 3)

Fig 6.8 Gearshift rod components in the clutch/differential housing (Sec 3)
1 Gearshift rod end protect-   2 Shift arm
    ion boot   3 Shift rod

4 Mainshaft (manual gearbox) - examination and renovation

Measuring clearances

1 Before the mainshaft is dismantled further, it is necessary to determine the side clearance of the gears on the mainshaft. Use a feeler gauge to check the axial of clearance between the differential drive-gear and the synchronised gear cluster and each gear on the mainshaft (Fig. 6.9).

2 If any side clearance is greater than that given in the Specifications at the beginning of this Chapter, it will be necessary to dismantle the mainshaft in order to adjust the clearances or replace gears. Check the clearance between selector forks and sliding rings. Check with the specification to determine limits (Fig. 6.10).

Dismantling the mainshaft

3 Begin by temporarily refitting the mainshaft assembly into the clutch/differential casing, so that the differential crownwheel meshes with the mainshaft output gear. Lock the differential crownwheel - and hence the mainshaft, in position by either fitting Honda tool '07924 - 6340200', or a short strip of metal between the crownwheel gear teeth and casing.

4 Having locked the differential gear and mainshaft, loosen the

Fig 6.9 Checking end-play of mainshaft gear assemblies (Sec 4)

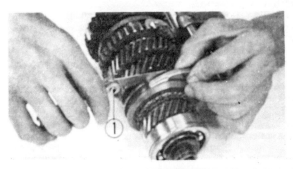

Fig 6.10 Checking clearance between shift fork and synchroniser ring (Sec 4)   1   Feeler gauge

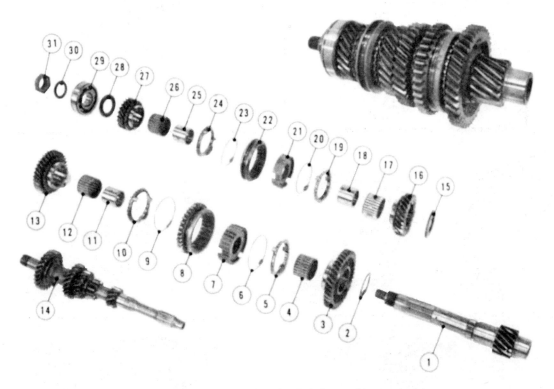

Fig 6.11 Countershaft and mainshaft assembly components

1 Mainshaft	9 Synchronizer spring	17 Needle roller bearing	24 Blocking ring
2 Thrust plate	10 Blocking ring	18 Distance collar	25 Distance collar
3 Mainshaft low gear	11 Distance collar	19 Blocking ring	26 Needle roller bearing
4 Needle roller bearing	12 Needle roller bearing	20 Synchronizer spring	27 Mainshaft top gear
5 Blocking ring	13 Mainshaft second gear	21 Synchronizer hub	28 Thrust plate
6 Synchronizer spring	14 Input shaft	22 Synchronizer sleeve	29 Ball bearing
7 Synchronizer hub	15 Distance plate	23 Synchronizer spring	30 Thrust plate
8 Mainshaft reverse gear	16 Mainshaft third gear		31 Locknut

main nut (right-hand thread) which retains all the bearings and gear assemblies on the mainshaft. Remove the nut and pull all the gears assemblies and bearings off the mainshaft.

5   The spacer bearing races for second, third and fourth gears are available in various lengths (as specified at the beginning of this Chapter), and are used to adjust the gear side clearances.

Inspection

6   Inspect the synchronising cone surfaces in each gear synchronising assembly, and measure the wear of the cone surface by determining the gap between the female ring and the male cone (Fig. 6.12). If the gap is smaller than the service limit indicated in the Specifications at the beginning of this Chapter, a new gear and cone should be fitted.

7   Next measure the gap between the selector fork and the synchroniser sleeve. Either or both the shift fork and the sleeve will need to be replaced if the clearance exceeds the service limit (Fig. 6.10).

8   Finally check the oil holes in each gear and in the mainshaft are free of obstructions, and check the gear internal diameters, bearing surfaces mainshaft mount (Fig. 6.13) and the splines on the mainshaft for signs of wear.

9   If any of the parts are worn and are outside service limits, they should be replaced. There is no provision for reworking any of the gearbox parts.

Reassembly of mainshaft

10 The procedure is basically the reversal of the dismantling sequence, but the following points should receive particular attention:

i)   When assembling the synchronising sleeve over the splined hub, ensure that the three pairs of larger teeth cut inside the sleeve, mate with the matching teeth cut in the hub.

ii)   The indexing pairs of teeth are 120º apart (Fig. 6.14 and 6.15).

iii) Ensure that each part is given a coat of gear oil before assembly.

iv) Ensure that each gear runs perfectly freely on the mainshaft, and that the synchronising sleeves slide smoothly on the hub.

5   Input shaft (manual gearbox) - examination and renovation

1   The input shaft is completely solid and requires only visual examination of the gearteeth, bearing seats and clutch disc teeth.

2   Again, if the input shaft shows signs of wear, particularly on the splines it should be replaced. There is no provision for rework.

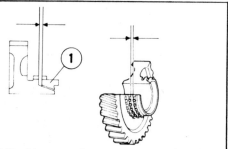

Fig 6.12 Checking wear of synchroniser cones (Sec 4)

1   Blocking ring

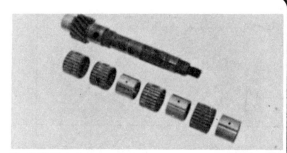

Fig 6.13 Mainshaft needle roller bearing assemblies (Sec 4)

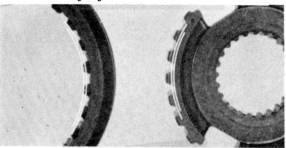

Fig 6.14 Mating of synchroniser hub and sliding ring (Sec 4)

Fig 6.15 Synchroniser system components (Sec 4)

Fig 6.16 Refitting mainshaft, input shaft and gearshift fork at the same time (Sec 6)

Fig 6.17 Lowering the transmission case into position (Sec 6)

6 Gearbox (manual) - reassembly

1 The reassembly procedure follows as can be expected, the reversal of the dismantling sequence.

2 Begin by refitting the ball bearing races into the clutch/differential housing, which accept the input shaft and mainshaft. It is advisable to use a soft metal drift, preferably tubular, acting on the outer race of the bearing to drive the bearing home on its seating. It is essential that the bearing is not driven askew into its position, because the surface of the seating in the housing can be damaged.

3 The mainshaft bearing is retained by a 'half-moon' plate and two screws. The input shaft centre bearing is an interference fit in the clutch/differential housing.

4 Having prepared the input shaft, mainshaft and clutch differential housing, bring the input shaft and mainshaft together and then lower them into position on the housing. Neither shaft can be removed or installed separately.

5 Once the mainshaft and input shaft are in position, the third/fourth gearshift fork and shaft, followed by the first/second shift fork and shaft can be installed.

6 If the mainshaft has been dismantled, it will now be possible to tighten the end nut to its appropriate torque. Again Honda tool '07924 - 6340200' can be used to lock the differential crownwheel gear and hence the mainshaft, or alternatively, the gear may be locked with a strip of metal passing between the gear and the housing. Do not attempt to lock the nut at this time.

7 Add the reverse gear and shaft assembly, followed by the reverse gear selector fork and shaft.

8 Next the shift fork selector assembly may be fitted. Note that two of the bolts which fix this assembly to the housing face are special and are used to locate the selector mechanism. These two bolts should be inserted first, followed by the remaining two.

9 Now prepare the gearbox casing and clutch/differential housing joint surfaces. They should be clean and smooth and clear of old gasket material.

10 Stick a new gasket in position on the housing after smearing both sides of the gasket with a little medium grease.

11 Fit the roller bearing outer race, rollers and cage into the gearbox casing ready to accept the input shaft. Locate the outer race of this bearing with the large circlip.

12 Carefully lower the gearbox casing down over the gear assembly. Do not use force, but ensure that the end bearing on the mainshaft, and the roller bearing sleeve on the end of the input shaft are guided into their respective positions on the gearbox casing. Light taps with a soft faced mallet should be all that is required to encourage the casing down to its proper position.

13 Once the casing is in position, secure it with the ten bolts which should be tightened evenly to the torque specified at the beginning of this Chapter.

14 Fit the end ball race bearing on the input shaft and screw on the end-nut. Tighten the nut to the torque specified at the beginning of this Chapter.

15 Lock both input shaft and mainshaft nuts by depressing the lip on the nut into the groove in the shaft with a centre punch.

16 The large circlip which fits around the mainshaft end bearing should now be installed.

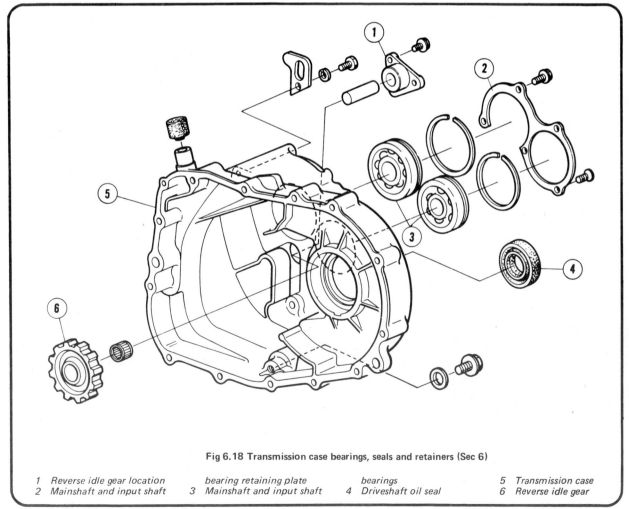

Fig 6.18 Transmission case bearings, seals and retainers (Sec 6)

1 Reverse idle gear location	bearing retaining plate	bearings	5 Transmission case
2 Mainshaft and input shaft	3 Mainshaft and input shaft	4 Driveshaft oil seal	6 Reverse idle gear

17 The three detent balls, their springs and locating screws can now be inserted into the gearbox casing to engage the three shift fork shafts. The balls springs and screws may be stuck together with grease to ease installation.

18 Finish the assembly of the gearbox by fitting the gearbox casing end cover. Again the joint surfaces should be smooth and clean, and a new gasket should be used.

19 The unit is now ready to be installed back into the car.

7 Gearshift mechanism and gearlever - general

1 The mechanism conveys an axial and rotational movement to the relay mechanism inside the gearbox, from a gearlever mounted on a gimbal arrangement. A radius rod links the gearlever pivot assembly to the transmission block to prevent possible relative movement between the pivot and transmission, affecting the gearshift mechanism.

2 It is essential that the pivot pins and joints are in good order to ensure that relatively large movements of the gearlever are not required in order to change gears.

3 The mechanism can be accessed once the front of the car has been raised onto chassis stands placed beneath the front suspension subframe. Remove the front centre carpets, inside the car, to reveal the lever boot and fixings. Remove the boot fixings and slide it up the gearlever.

4 The pivot assembly is now revealed and it can be removed once the fastenings have been undone from above and beneath the car floor.

5 The gearshift relay rod is retained to shaft through the gearbox casing by an 8 mm pin. The pin is driven out by a drift or Honda tool '07944 - 6110200'.

6 The gearshift lever pivot extension needs to be removed from the transmission casing if it is desired to remove the lever mechanism.

7 Refitting is simply the reversal of the removal procedure.

8 Fault diagnosis - manual gearbox

Symptom	Reason/s	Remedy
Weak or ineffective synchromesh	Synchronising cones worn, split or damaged	Dismantle and overhaul transmission unit. Fit new gearwheels and synchronising cones.
	Baulk ring synchromesh dogs worn, or damaged	Dismantle and overhaul transmission unit. Fit new baulk ring synchromesh.
Jumps out of gear	Broken gearchange fork rod spring	Dismantle and replace spring.
	Transmission unit coupling dogs badly worn	Dismantle transmission unit. Fit new coupling dogs.
	Selector fork rod groove badly worn	Fit new selector fork rod.
	Selector fork rod securing screw and locknut loose	Tighten securing screw and locknut.
Excessive noise	Incorrect grade of oil in transmission unit or oil level too low	Drain, refill or top-up transmission unit with correct grade of oil.
	Bush or needle roller bearings worn or damaged	Dismantle and overhaul transmission unit.
	Gear teeth excessively worn or damaged	Dismantle, overhaul transmission unit. Renew gearwheels.
	Laygear thrust washers worn allowing excessive end-play	Dismantle and overhaul transmission unit. Renew thrust washers.
Difficulty in engaging gears	Clutch faulty	Inspect and repair as necessary.

9 Hondamatic transmission - general description

The main components of the automatic transmission are the torque converter and a special gearbox enclosing two forward speeds and one reverse gear.

The torque converter is housed in an enlarged bellhousing between the engine and gearbox, and its appearance is that of a large almost hemispherical container with a ring gear for the starter motor attached to the face nearest the engine. The container encloses the torque converter system of vanes, and is kept full of oil under pressure by a pump mounted in the gearbox casing.

The transmission functions as follows: The engine delivers power to the torque converter which balances the speed and torque from the engine to the speed and torque 'required' by the gearbox. The converter has the characteristic that if the input speed from the engine is greater than the output speed to the gearbox, the output torque will be between 1 and 2 times greater than the input torque; depending on the difference of input and output speeds.

This torque characteristic is derived from the way the drive/impeller vanes in the converter are coupled to the output/turbine vanes. The impeller vanes are shaped so that as they rotate the oil in the impeller is flung radially outwards to the top tip of the vanes and forwards in the direction of the vanes rotation. The oil on leaving the impeller impinges onto the output turbine which is driven by the oil in the direction of rotation of the impeller. If the impeller is rotating faster than the turbine - typically when the engine is working to accelerate the car - the oil flung onto the turbine by the impeller creates a greater torque on the turbine than that exerted by the engine on the impeller. The stator in the converter serves to correct the direction of flow of oil from the turbine back to the impeller and improves the efficiency of the converter.

The power output from the converter is transmitted to the final drive via the two speed gearbox. The gears are changed manually; number 1 serves up to a speed of 50 mph and number 2 is the cruising gear. Multiplate wet clutches attached to each gear train connect the selected train to the gearbox mainshaft and final drive via the fixed gears on the countershaft.

The Hondamatic is therefore a semi-automatic system, because the driver must still select the appropriate gear for the particular road conditions at the time. The torque converter adds a degree of flexibility to the gear selected, and does not take the need for thought, regarding choice of gear, from the driver.

10 Hondamatic transmission - removal and refitting

Removal

1 The technique for removing the Hondamatic unit follows basically the procedure detailed for the removal of the engine and transmission in Chapter 1, of this manual. There are multiple splines to join the torque converter and gearbox: the difficulty in separating these splines prohibits the removal of the Hondamatic gearbox by itself.

2 In addition to those tasks detailed in Chapter 1 for the removal of the engine and transmission, the following tasks should be added to cater for the Hondamatic transmission.

3 The centre console trim needs to be removed to gain access to the gearshift cable length adjustment turnbuckle. (photo)

4 Once the car has been raised onto chassis stands at the front, the gearshift cable can be detached from the transmission once the centre engine support and support beam has been removed. (photo)

5 Undo the bolts securing the shift lever cover to the transmission housing: remove the cover. (photo)

6 Extract the pin which retains the cable to the shift lever, and undo the bolt and bracket which clamps the cable sleeve, to separate the cable from the transmission. (photo)

7 The transmission oil cooler hoses should now be disconnected from the unions on the transmission block. (photo)

8 Remove the transmission then as described for the engine and transmission, in Chapter 1.

9 Once the engine and Hondamatic transmission has been removed clear of the car, the engine and transmission should be separated. Four 8 mm bolts secure the transmission casing to the cylinder block.

Refitting

10 As usual, refitting follows the reversal of the removal sequence, as for manual transmission: but the following points must be taken into account.

11 Before offering-up the torque converter to the engine drive-plate, refill the torque converter - as far as possible - and fill the transmission with the specified oil.

12 As the transmission is brought up to the engine, be careful to ensure that the mating splines of the turbine and mainshaft, stator hub and stator shaft, and finally converter impeller and transmission oil pump drive gear, are engaged gently.

13 Secure the Hondamatic transmission to engine with four 8 mm bolts, **do not** put the starter motor back until the engine and gearbox has been refitted in the car.

14 Once the engine and transmission has been refitted, follow the procedures detailed in Chapter 1 for the installation of the engine ancillaries.

15 To improve the pick-up of oil in the transmission by the oil pump, prime the pump by pouring a little oil into the pump through its inlet line tapping. (photo)

16 Check the following, with the engine at normal running temperature, and transmission oil at the proper level:

Adjustment of gearshift cable length
Stall rpm in 1, 2 gears
Selector lever positions
Oil pressures in the L and D clutch supply lines

Procedures for these adjustments and tests are given later in this Chapter.

11 Torque converter (Hondamatic) - removal, renovation and refitting

Removal and dismantling

1 It will be necessary to remove the engine and gearbox as directed in Chapter 1, of this manual, and then separate the gearbox from the engine, in order to expose the torque converter

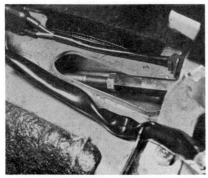

10.3 Hondamatic gearshift cable turnbuckle

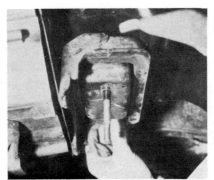

10.4 Removal of centre engine support

10.5 Removal of converter cover plate to reveal gearshift cable

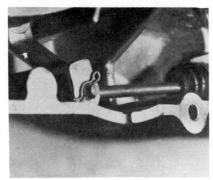

10.6 Hondamatic gearshift cable - transmission end

10.7 Transmission oil cooler lines

10.15 Priming oil pump through oil cooler port

which is attached to the engine. Do not attempt to separate the converter and engine before removing the transmission.

2 Once the torque converter has been exposed, remove the eight 6 mm bolts which secure the torque converter assembly to the driveplate on the end of the crankshaft. Lift off the torque converter.

3 Dismantling the torque converter: Remove the eight bolts which retain the converter pump cover to the pump housing (Fig. 6.19 and 6.20).

4 Once the cover bolts have been removed, the whole converter can be pulled apart, beginning with the separation of the cover from the converter assembly.

5 The next component to be removed is the converter turbine, followed by the stator assembly.

6 The stator assembly comprises the stator vane unit which runs on a ratchet mechanism which permits the vane unit to run in a clockwise direction relative to the stator hub which is splined to fit on the gearbox shaft sleeve.

7 The ratchet mechanism is retained in the stator by the two large circlips; once these have been removed the stator hub, stator ratchet cam complete with locking rollers, and the main thrust bearings, can be extracted from the stator body.

8 After the stator has been dismantled, only the converter pump body to cover joint seal ring needs to be prised from the seating in the pump body.

9 The converter is now completely dismantled and is ready for inspection. (photo)

Inspection

10 Thoroughly clean all parts in new oil, do not use wire brushes or abrasives. Wipe the oil off the parts with a clean, non-fluffy rag and space them out on a clean workbench. When dealing

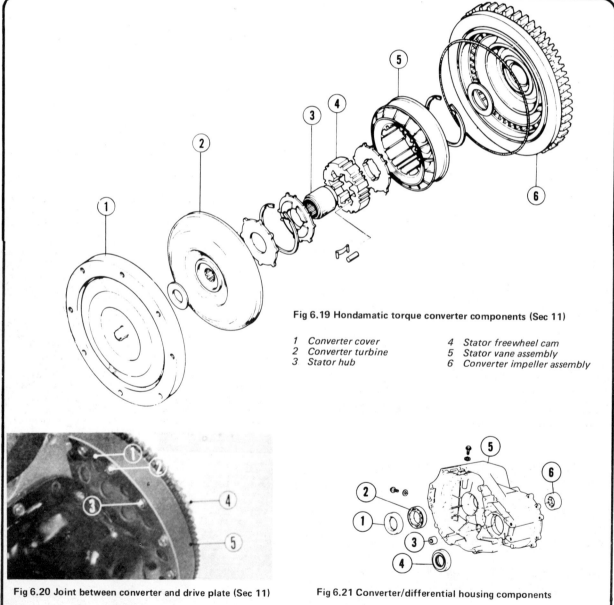

Fig 6.19 Hondamatic torque converter components (Sec 11)

1 Converter cover
2 Converter turbine
3 Stator hub
4 Stator freewheel cam
5 Stator vane assembly
6 Converter impeller assembly

Fig 6.20 Joint between converter and drive plate (Sec 11)

1 Driveplate
2 Bolt - torque converter assembly to drive plate
3 Bolt torque converter to ring gear
4 Ring gear
5 Torque converter assembly

Fig 6.21 Converter/differential housing components

1 Converter impeller shaft oil seal
2 Impeller shaft bearing
3 Gear selector shaft oil seal
4 Drive shaft oil seal
5 Torque converter case
6 Mainshaft pinion end roller bearing

with fine assemblies such as this torque converter, it is preferable to work on a soft metal (aluminium) surface. Parts could easily collect splinters from a wooden bench, which could later ruin the results of all your labours repairing the converter.

11 Pay particular attention to the following points when inspecting the converter components:

    i)   Wear or damage to the converter turbine surfaces especially the thrust washer face.
    ii) Wear or damage to any of the thrust washers.
    iii) Wear or damage to the interior and/or exterior surfaces of the stator hub.
    iv) Damage to the ratchet mechanism rollers and the mating surfaces on the stator cam.
    v) Wear or damage to the bush in the centre of the pump cover.

12 Check with the Specifications at the beginning of this Chapter for the service limits of wear of the pump cover centre bush: if the limit is exceeded, the torque converter cover will need to be replaced.

13 Measure the thickness of the centre of the turbine member, where the thrust washer is positioned and replace the impeller if either the vane surfaces are pitted and corroded or the thrust washer face has worn beyond its service limit.

Reassembly

14 Reassembly follows the reverse of the dismantling sequence.

15 Place the stator hub inside the cam, and slide the rollers and springs into position between the cam and hub. Insert the sub-assembly into the vane unit and then temporarily install the stator sleeve into the hub. Check that the sleeve can be turned **clockwise only** when the stator assembly is viewed from the pump side (the side with the thinner vane).

16 Once the ratchet mechanism is working properly, fit the thrust washers to each side and install the two large circlips.

17 Place the stator assembly, together with loose thrust washers into the pump body, coat the thrust washers with new oil. (photo) Fit the converter turbine over the stator, and place the last loose thrust washer on top of the turbine. (photo) Finally before placing the pump cover onto the body, fit the seal ring into its groove seat in the periphery of the pump body. (photos) Ensure that the cover and body alignment marks coincide.

18 Place the ring gear on the converter body so that the chamfered side of the gear faces towards the converter.

19 Insert the eight bolts which hold the converter assembly together. Tighten them to the torque specified at the beginning of this Chapter. (photo)

Installation of converter

20 Installation follows the reversal of the removal sequence. Offer the converter assembly up to the driveplate on the end of the crankshaft, and secure with eight 6 mm bolts. Tighten the bolts to the specified torque (Fig. 6.20).

21 Bring the transmission up to the engine, and gently insert the driveshaft and stator sleeve into the torque converter. Do not use force. Turn the transmission round to-and-fro if necessary, so that the splines on the driveshaft and stator sleeve mate with their respective splines in the torque converter.

22 Once the transmission is in position, secure it to the engine block with four 8 mm bolts. Tighten these bolts to the specified torque.

23 Refer to Section 10, of this Chapter for the instructions for refitting the transmission and engine into the car.

---

12 Transmission (Hondamatic) - dismantling

Removal

1 Follow the instructions detailed in Chapter 1, Section 10, of this manual, for the removal of the engine and automatic

11.9 Torque converter components

11.17(A) Installing stator assembly

11.17(B) Lowering turbine into position

11.17(C) Fitting cover seal 'O' ring

11.17(D) Fitting torque converter cover

11.19 Fully assembled converter

transmission. Separate the transmission from the engine by undoing the four 8 mm bolts around the torque converter bellhousing.

2 Carefully withdraw the automatic gearbox and converter bellhousing off the engine block. Remove the gearbox unit to a clean strong bench.

Dismantling the Hondamatic transmission

3 **Note:** Ensure that all tools are clean, before commencing work on the gearbox. It is advisable to work on a bench with a surface of soft metal (aluminium). Splinters or other foreign matter find their way into the fine mechanisms in this gearbox and can ruin the results of your efforts.

4 Begin by removing the nine bolts which retain the right side cover on the gearbox casing. Remove the automatic transmission fluid level dipstick.

5 The right side cover houses the speedometer driver gear, the gearbox input shaft end bearing oil seals, rings and seal sleeve. (photo)

6 If it is intended to gain access and inspect the cover and associated components only, then proceed to follow the inspection instructions given later in this Section.

7 Continuing with the dismantling, and having removed the cover, the 'L' clutch, gear and countershaft is now exposed.

8 Straighten the lock-washer on the end of the mainshaft and undo the nut on the end of the shaft. Make a tool from a piece of steel tube to undo this special nut which retains the 'L' clutch on the mainshaft. (photo)

9 Once the nut has been removed, pull the 'L' clutch assembly off the mainshaft, and then pull the 'L' gear together with its thrust washers and needle roller bearing off the mainshaft. (photos)

10 Move the gear selector lever into the 'P' position, straighten the lock-washer and undo the nut from the end of the countershaft.

11 Pull the 'L' gear bearings and thrust washer off the end of the countershaft. (photo)

Dismantling 'L' gear clutch

12 All the clutch plates are held in position by a single retaining ring (Fig. 6.22). Remove the ring and plates to reveal the actuating piston and its return spring. Use a spring compressor (Honda 07960 - 6120000) or an improvised tool (Fig. 6.23) to compress the return spring to allow the piston spring retaining ring to be released, so that piston, spring and ring can be removed.

13 Remove the spring compressor, and then proceed to extract the clutch actuating piston. The simplest way is to blow compressed air into the oil feed passage.

14 The 'L' gear clutch is now fully dismantled and is ready for inspection and reassembly as detailed later in this Section.

Removal of the transmission case

15 It will have been necessary to remove the transmission from the engine, the right end cover and the 'L' gear train and clutch, before the transmission case can be removed.

16 Commence removal of the casing by undoing the five screws and bolts which secure the plate retaining the main and countershaft bearings. Be careful not to damage the heads of the screws.

17 Fit a transmission case puller - Honda tool '07933 - 639000' - or an improvised puller which bears down on the end of the mainshaft and is bolted to the case.

18 Undo and remove the fourteen bolts which secure the transmission case to the converter bellhousing.

19 The case is now ready to be drawn off the counter and mainshaft assemblies. Use the puller, already fitted, and slowly remove the case, complete with the countershaft and mainshaft bearings, reverse idler gear and shaft oil seals. If you are fortunate just a few jerks will be required to free the cover from the converter case. (photo)

20 Large split rings are fitted in the outer race of both shaft bearings, to locate the bearings in the seats in the transmission.

12.5 Transmission end cover removed

12.8 Special nut and "special" tool on mainshaft

12.9A Removal of "L" clutch

12.9B Removal of "L" gear from mainshaft

12.11 Removal of "L" gear from input (counter) shaft

12.19 Removal of gearbox cover

Use a tubular drift to press the bearings out of the case.

21 The reverse idler gear runs on a needle bearing shaft and holder secured to the inside of the casing with three bolts.

22 Inspect the driveshaft oil seal, and if worn, prise out of the casing. Use a seal embossed with 639 only, as a replacement.

23 The casing components are now fully dismantled ready for inspection, as detailed later in this Section.

Mainshaft: countershaft, 'D' gear and clutch and gear mechanism

24 Continuing with the dismantling of the automatic transmission, and having exposed the mainshaft and countershaft assemblies, it now remains to extract the gearshift mechanism, together with the shaft assemblies as follows (Fig. 6.24):

25 Begin by removing the bolt which retains the reverse gear selector fork to the shaft. Recover the locking tag washer.

26 It will be necessary to draw the mainshaft and countershaft from the transmission/converter case together with the selector

fork. (photo)

27 Once the mainshaft is free, the 'D' gear and clutch assembly may be slid off the shaft. (photo) The 'D' clutch can be dismantled in the same manner as the 'L' clutch, described earlier.

28 Taking the countershaft, slide the thrust washers, reverse gear and reverse gear selector off the countershaft. (photo)

29 Using a tubular drift, press the reverse gear hub and 'D' gear off the shaft at the same time. Then remove the snap ring from the end of the countershaft and pull off the needle roller bearing.

Parking control gear

30 This assembly can be dismantled when the right side cover, transmission case and countershaft reverse gear have been removed.

31 Commence by moving the manual valve backwards, to the position marked '1' and then remove the 6 mm roller pin from the end of the manual valve rod (Fig. 6.25). (photo)

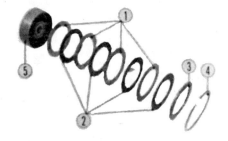

Fig 6.22 Wet clutch dismantled (Sec 12)

1 Clutch plates
2 Clutch discs
3 End plate
4 Clutch plate retaining ring
5 Clutch piston barrel

Fig 6.23 Installation of clutch piston spring compressor (Sec 12)

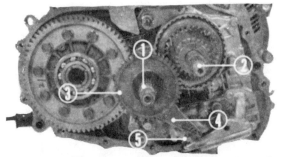

Fig 6.24 Position of countershaft and mainshaft (Sec 12)

1 Countershaft
2 Mainshaft
3 Reverse gear
4 Reverse gear shift fork
5 Shift fork to shaft set screw

Fig 6.25 Gearshift mechanism to valve assembly (Sec 12)

1 6 mm roller pin
2 Spool valve member
3 Valve body

12.26 Removal of mainshaft and input shaft together

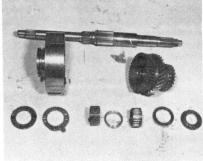

12.27 Mainshaft and "D" clutch and gear

12.28 Input (counter) shaft "D" and Reverse gears

12.31 Disengaging relay lever from servo valve spool

12.32 Removal of gearshift relay shaft and parking lock shaft together

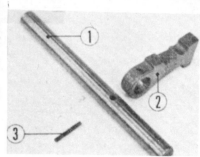

Fig 6.26 Parking mechanism lock pawl and shaft (Sec 12)

1 Shaft
2 Pawl
3 Spring pin (Pawl to shaft)

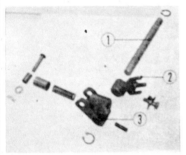

Fig 6.27 Gear selector relay shaft components (Sec 12)

1 Relay shaft
2 Spool valve shift lever
3 Parking mechanism lever

12.39 Servo valve body

12.40 Torque converter casing

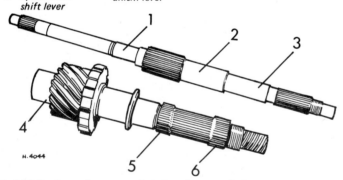

H.4044

Fig 6.28 Bearing surfaces on mainshaft and countershaft

1 Converter stator shaft needle bearing surface
2 "D" gear and clutch needle bearing surface
3 "L" gear and clutch
4 Countershaft pinion roller bearing surface
5 "D" gear splines
6 "L" gear splines

Fig 6.29 Clearance between clutch plates (Sec 13)

Fig 6.30 Checking oil pump gear axial clearance (Sec 13)

1 Oil pump drive gear
2 Oil pump driven gear
3 Valve body cover
4 Steel rule
5 Feeler gauge

Fig 6.31 Checking oil pump gear and housing (Sec 13) radial clearance

1 Oil pump drive gear
2 Oil pump driven gear
3 Pump body
4 Feeler gauge

32 Remove the manual change lever shaft and parking brake shaft together. (photo) A single tension pin retains the pawl to the parking brake shaft and should be removed only when absolutely necessary, with a small flat faced circular drift (Fig. 6.26).

33 Another tension pin retains the parking brake lever on the shift lever shaft. A bolt locked with a tab washer secures the manual valve lever to the shift lever shaft (Fig. 6.27).

34 Again the parking brake lever components should only be dismantled when absolutely necessary.

35 Details of the inspection required of the parking control gear are given later in this Section.

Servo body, valve body and oil pump

36 Having already removed the transmission case, mainshaft assemblies and countershaft assemblies, continue by undoing the two bolts which secure the transmission oil strainer to the pump and valve housing. Lift off the strainer.

37 Undo and remove the three bolts which secure the stator shaft seal ring guide to the servo body, to permit the guide and stator shaft member to be removed.

38 Then undo and remove the six bolts (2 long, 3 medium length and 1 short) which secure the servo body assembly to the casing. Recover the servo body gasket.

39 Now lift the valve body evenly off the transmission end casing. Be careful, do not drop the oil pump gear, orifice plug or torque converter check valve. Finally extract the oil pump drive and driven gears. (photo)

Torque converter casing

40 This assembly includes the countershaft roller bearing, mainshaft bearing and seal, differential oil seal, and the gearshift lever oil seal. These items cannot be removed from the converter casing until the transmission case, main and countershaft assemblies, servo valve body and parking controls have each been removed. (photo)

41 Continue by removing the differential gear assembly as detailed in Chapter 7, of this manual.

42 Next, remove the converter oil hose joint 'A' and the 8 mm sealing bolt.

43 The countershaft needle roller bearing, mounted in the converter casing needs Honda tool set '07936 - 6340000', or a tool improvised on those lines. Once the bearing is removed, **do not re-use it.**

44 The oil seals for the differential, mainshaft and gear selector shaft can all be prised out of the seatings with a broad screwdriver. Do not re-use oil seals once they have been removed, therefore inspect them in-situ.

---

13 Transmission components (Hondamatic) - inspection and renovation

---

1 The following paragraphs will detail the inspection of the transmission components, in the order that they were separated from the transmission assembly. Inspection should be carried out after the components have been cleaned in fresh transmission oil, and wiped dry with a non-fluffy rag. Lay the parts out on a perfectly clean soft metal surface. Cleanliness is absolutely essential when working on automatic transmissions; no foreign matter must find its way into the fine mechanism. Check your micrometer with standard slip gauges, and ensure your gauges and instruments are clean. All important dimensions, wear limits and inspection rules are given in the Specifications at the beginning of this Chapter.

2 Right side cover parts

i) Mainshaft end bearing: replace if bearing worn or felt to be rough when turned.

ii) Clear and clean transmission fluid pipes and drillings.

iii) Examine the journal surfaces on the 'L' clutch, and cover mating surfaces. Replace appropriate parts.

iv) Examine the speedometer drive gear, and replace it if the

teeth show signs of wear.

3 'L' clutch and gear

i) Examine the oil seal rings on the clutch and replace if broken.

ii) Check the dimensions of the clutch return spring and replace if its deformation exceeds the service limit.

iii) Check the thicknesses of the clutch plates and replace any that have worn beyond the service limit.

iv) Examine the gear teeth and clutch plate splines for wear or deformation. Replace those members on which teeth have worn beyond service limits.

v) Check the thickness of thrust washers, and replace any that have worn beyond service limits specified at the beginning of this Chapter.

vi) Check the axial play of the 'L' gear on the countershaft and replace the gear if this play exceeds the service limits.

vii) Finally rotate the needle roller bearing on which the 'L' gear and clutch runs and if found to be rough, replace the bearing.

4 Transmission case

i)   Examine the aluminium sealing washers, case joint surfaces, and oil seal seatings for scratches and deformation as appropriate.

ii)   Examine the oil seals; pay attention to the lip of the seals. If a seal edge is worn flat, discard the seal.

iii)   Rotate the bearings in the casing, if axial movement and/or roughness is detected discard the bearings and fit new ones.

iv)   Check the outside diameter of the reverse idler gear shaft, and then the inside diameter of the idler gear and shaft holder. Replace the appropriate item if wear exceeds service limits.

v)   Finally check the axial play of the reverse idler gear when in position on its shaft.

5 Mainshaft and countershaft assemblies

i)   Examine the oil seal rings on the 'D' clutch, and replace broken rings.

ii)   Check the dimensions of the 'D' clutch return spring, and replace it if it has deformed beyond service limits.

iii)   Check the thicknesses of the clutch plates, thrust washers and the reverse gearshift fork fingers. Replace items that have worn beyond service limits.

iv)   Examine the gearteeth and surfaces of the 'D' clutch and gear. Replace items if worn.

v)   Check for wear on the needle roller journals on the main and countershaft. Replace the shafts if the journals have worn excessively.

6 Parking control

i)   Examine the parking brake pawl; if the edges of the pawl tooth are rounded and there are signs of abrasive wear - replace the pawl.

ii)   Inspect the parking brake shaft, for bend of that shaft. If it is deformed beyond the limits given at the beginning of this Chapter - replace the shaft.

iii)   Check the free-length of the parking brake spring; if the free length does not meet with the Specifications at the beginning of this Chapter - replace the spring.

iv)   Examine the pawl release spring; if the spring arms are worn thin and polished - replace the spring.

7 Servo body, valve body and oil pump

i)   Examine the mating surfaces of the servo body, valve body, servo body and gasket, and finally gasket plate and converter case. If any part has an imperfect joint surface, then that part should be replaced. Any surface defects can result in oil leakage from pressure fed devices - the 'L' and 'D' clutches and the torque converter.

ii)   Examine the oil pump parts: check the pump gear to housing clearance, and the pump gear to housing thrust clearance. See Figs. 6.30 and 6.31 which illustrate the use of feeler gauges and steel rulers in checking the gear clearances.

iii)   Check the bore of the bushing in the stator shaft; if it has

worn beyond service limits, replace the bushing.
iv)   Check the oil pressure check valve spring free-length, and
replace it if it fails to match the Specifications given at the
beginning of this Chapter.
v)   Finally examine all the oil passages and galleries; clean them
carefully with clean oil. Do not use solvents.

8   Torque converter casing

i)   Inspect all the oil seals and if the lip edges have been worn
flat, or there are other signs of wear - replace the seals.
ii)   Rotate the bearings held in the casing, and if the movement
is rough or sloppy, the bearings should be replaced.
iii)   Examine aluminium washers used to seal the oil pressure
tappings on the torque converter casing and gearbox casing; if
these washers are deformed or cracked, replace the washers.

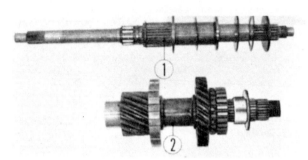

Fig 6.32 Mainshaft (1) and countershaft (2) (Sec 14)

---

14   Transmission (Hondamatic) - reassembly

1   The assembly of the transmission is detailed assuming that
it has been dismantled right down to the converter casing. The
sequence is to fit the oil seals and bearings into the converter
casing, then proceed to fit the servo body and stator shaft.
2   The assembly is then ready to receive the mainshaft and
countershaft assemblies which are installed together with the
reverse selector fork. Once the mainshaft and countershaft have
been installed the parking control should be fitted. Finally the
transmission case 'L' gear train and clutch, and lastly the right
end cover. As the assembly proceeds on the lines described,
watch for the following details:

Torque converter casing

3   If the countershaft end roller bearing has been removed from
the casing, it must not be re-used. Insert the new bearing carefully using a soft round drift - and take care not to drive the
bearing askew into its seating. The same precautions must be
taken when fitting oil seals. The seatings are machined from the
aluminium alloy and are easily marked and damaged. Prime the
bearings and seals with a little new transmission oil before proceeding to the next stage of assembly.

Servo body, valve body and oil pump

4   Begin by mounting the servo body to the valve body. Use a
new gasket - do not use gasket paste. Ensure that the orifice plug
in the valve body is clean. Next mount the oil pump gears and
converter check valve into the valve body. Coat the gears
liberally with new oil, and keep them in place by putting the
steel gasket plate in position on the joint side of the valve body.
(photo) Carefully lower the valve assembly down onto the converter casing. Insert the six valve body fixing bolts and tighten
them to the torque specified at the beginning of this Chapter.
5   After the valve assembly has been fitted, lower the stator
shaft into position. (photo) Make sure the shaft arm is properly
located on the converter pressure regulating valve and the gate
spigot. Secure the shaft by fitting the 'D' clutch sleeve member.
This is made of steel and is located over the arm of the stator
shaft. Tighten the fixing bolts to the specified torque. (photo)

Mainshaft

6   Slide the 'D' clutch assembly onto the central splines on the
mainshaft, then place the thrust washer, roller bearings with
spacer onto the shaft, next to the 'D' clutch. The bevel on the
inside edge of the thrust washer should face towards the roller
bearings. Fit the roller thrust bearing into the 'D' gear, and then
slide the gear onto the roller bearings on the mainshaft. Finally
fit the thrust washer and spacer onto the right-hand end of the
'D' gear. (photo)
7   Put the mainshaft assembly aside, ready for installation into
the converter casing with the countershaft. (photo)

Countershaft

8   Slide the 'D' gear into position on the splines next to the
shoulder machined on the countershaft, then fit the reverse gear

selector sleeve onto the 'D' gear. The reverse gear bearing should
now be assembled onto the shaft and then the roller bearing
itself. Once the bearing is in place, slide the reverse gear into
position followed by the end thrust washer (Fig. 6.32).

Mainshaft and countershaft installation

9   Bring the mainshaft and countershaft together so that the 'D'
gears are meshing. Place the reverse gear selector fork onto the
selector sleeve on the countershaft. Make sure the fork is the
correct way round, with the curved edge towards the mainshaft.
10   Take hold of the mainshaft and countershaft, with the
reverse fork in position, and lower them together, still with 'D'
gears in mesh, into the converter casing. (photo)
11   It will be as well to have some assistance when installing the
mainshaft/countershaft assembly as there may be too much for
one pair of hands to do! When the shaft assemblies are in
position, bolt the reverse selector fork to the fork shaft. Lock
the bolt with the tab washer. (photo)

Parking control

12   Once the mainshaft and countershaft have been installed,
proceed to fit the parking control. This task requires the rod
assemblies to be held in their correct relative positions, whilst
they are installed.
13   Begin by assembling the parking shift lever assembly. The
manual valve lever is bolted in position on the lever pivot shaft.
The bolt is locked with a tab washer. Then fit the spring and
plunger into the brake lever and retain by fitting the clevis pin
and roller.
14   Slide the lever assembly onto the shift lever shaft and secure
into position with the tension pin. Finally fit the two circlips
onto their respective seatings on the shaft.
15   The parking brake pawl is secured to its shaft by another
tension pin. Do not use a pointed drift to drive the tension pins
into position. The drift should be round with a flat face to
contact the pin.
16   Bring the pawl shaft and brake lever shaft together so that
the lever engages the pawl. Fit the torsion spring onto the pawl
shaft so that it acts on the lever shaft and pawl.
17   Now whilst holding the two shafts together in the correct
relative positions, lower them into the converter casing. Ensure
that both shafts are properly seated and then engage the manual
valve with the manual valve lever on the shift lever shaft. Retain
the manual valve in the lever by fitting the 6 mm roller pin and
rollers. (photo)

Transmission casing

18   Having fitted the parking control, mainshaft and countershaft
assemblies it is time to fit the transmission casing. Insert the 'L'
clutch oil feed tube into the valve housing. (photo) If you
haven't already done so, fit the oil pump pick-up and strainer to
the oil pump housing.
19   Fit the reverse idler gear and shaft into the transmission
casing. (photo) Clean the casing joint surfaces of old gasket
material and stick a new gasket to the joint face with medium

14.4 Servo valve assembly with gasket plate

14.5A Stator shaft and torque reaction arm

14.5B "D" clutch oil feed sleeve

14.6 Mainshaft components

14.7 "D" gear, reverse gear and "D" clutch on mainshaft

14.10 Reverse gear selector fork

14.11 Fork retainer screw

14.17 Connecting gearshift relay lever to the servo valve

14.18 Fitting "L" clutch oil feed tube

14.19 Reverse idle gear in position

14.21 Installation of mainshaft bearing

14.23A Installation of "L" gear onto mainshaft

grease or a soft joint compound.

20 The casing can now be lowered around the gear and control assemblies and secured with fourteen bolts. Tighten these bolts to the recommended torque, noting that one is smaller than the rest and requires a lower tightening torque.

21 Complete the assembly of the casing by inserting the ball race bearings around the mainshaft, and countershaft. They should not require any particular force to drive them into position: hand pressure or light taps with a soft faced mallet should suffice. (photo) The bearings are retained by a circlip mounted in a groove in the periphery of the outer race being captured by a steel plate fixed to the top face of the transmission casing. The steel plate is fixed by small bolts and screws. After tightening the screws they should be staked to the steel plate with a centre punch.

'L' gear assembly

22 Having the transmission assembly complete to the point where the transmission casing is fitted and the countershaft and mainshaft end bearings are in position complete with retaining plate; slide the countershaft 'L' gear onto the countershaft splines: fix the gear in place with the 20 mm hexagon nut. Select 'Park' to lock the countershaft, and then tighten that nut to its specified torque. Once tightened stake the lip of the nut with a

centre punch to lock it to the countershaft.

23 Now place a space and thrust washer next to the mainshaft bearing, bevelled side towards the end of the shaft. Next slide the 'L' gear bearing sleeve onto the mainshaft, and follow by sliding the needle roller bearing assembly onto the sleeve. Coat the bearing with clean gear oil. (photo) Place the 'L' gear onto the mainshaft and its bearing, and then position the taper roller thrust bearing inside, followed by a washer so that all is prepared for the 'L' clutch. (photo)

24 Lower the 'L' clutch into position onto the mainshaft and 'L' gear. If the clutch has been disturbed, make sure that the teeth on the clutch plates are aligned so that all plates mate readily with the teeth on the 'L' gear drum. Once you are sure that all four clutch plates which engage the 'L' gear have in fact been engaged, fit the special nut and its tab washer onto the end of the mainshaft. The recess in the nut should fit the splines on which the 'L' clutch is mounted. (photo)

25 Use the special tool Honda '07916 - 639000' or one improvised to fit the nut, to tighten it to its specified torque. Lock this nut by bending up one of the tabs on the lock-washer to fit into one of the slots in the nut.

End cover, right-hand end

26 This cover assembly includes a small bearing which fits the

14.23B Installation of "L" gear onto mainshaft

14.24 Fitting mainshaft end nut and lock washer

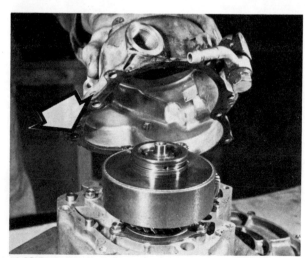
14.28 Fitting transmission end cover, arrow indicates "L" clutch oil feed seal ring

14.29 Gearshift lever in converter case

end of the mainshaft, and a steel 'L' clutch sleeve. The sleeve feeds oil to the 'L' gear clutch. Fit the small bearing first and when the sleeve is being fitted, take care not to damage the 'O' rings which seal the oil feed to the sleeve. Stake the sleeve fixing screws with a centre punch to lock them when they have been tightened.

27 Clean the mating surfaces of the cover and transmission casing: remove all traces of old gasket. Stick a new gasket to the cover with soft gasket paste. Use paste sparingly and do not use makes of paste which stiffen with time.

28 Finally before lowering the cover into position, check that the small 'O' ring which fits the 'L' clutch oil feed pipe, is in place and in good condition. (photo) The port in which this 'O' ring is fitted is to be found is shown in the photo. Fit the cover over the 'L' clutch and gear assembly onto the main casing. Nine bolts secure the cover to the casing and these should be tightened evenly to the torque specified at the beginning of this Chapter.

29 Insert the speedometer drive-gear and secure it to the cover with the specially extended bolt, and if you have not already done so, fit the gearshift relay lever to the end of the shift shaft in the gearbox. (photo)

30 The transmission is now ready for refitting to the engine.

15 Gearshift mechanism (Hondamatic) - general description

1 The mechanism comprises a selector lever pivoted so that the cable link to the transmission has a straightforward push-pull action. A number of system inhibit switches are mounted around the selector lever pivot and provide, for instance, prevention of the engine being started when a gear or park has been selected (Figs. 6.33; 6.34 and 6.35). Access needs to be gained to both

the underside of the centre of the car, as well as centre floor inside the car, whenever it is necessary to dismantle the shift mechanism.

2 The mechanism comprises a cable and sleeve which joints the shift lever in the transmission to the selector lever in the interior of the car. The lever is pivoted in a bracket secured by four nuts and bolts to the centre floor. Another metal housing serves to bring the cable through the floor to the car interior and selector lever, and is secured to the floor with four nuts and bolts. The cable length is adjusted by a turnbuckle at the selector lever end of the cable, and it is accessible from inside the car. The cable length needs to be adjusted to ensure that the selector lever position corresponds to the gear engaged (Fig. 6.36 and 6.37).

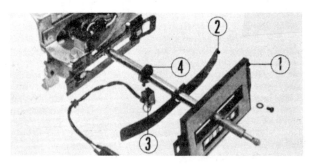

Fig 6.33 Gear selector components (Secs 15 & 18)

1 Console escutcheon   3 Light
2 Cover   4 Cover guide

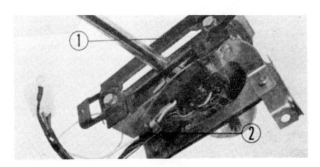

Fig 6.34 Position of the start inhibit and reversing light switch (Secs 15 & 18)

1 Selector cover holder   2 Inhibit and reverse light switch

Fig 6.35 Selector lever detent mechanism (Secs 15 & 18)

1 Switch contact holder

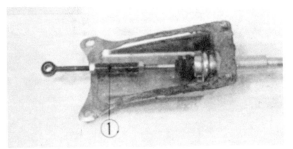

Fig 6.36 Selector cable length adjustment (Secs 15, 16 & 17)

1 Turnbuckle and locknuts

Fig 6.37 Selector cable termination - transmission (Secs 15 & 16)

1 Relay lever to shaft in the transmission   2 Cable

Finally, the micro-switches are mounted on the lever pivot bracket.

16 Gearshift cable (Hondamatic) - removal and refitting

1   This task is more involved than one might expect for a relatively small item: fortunately however, its individual removal and refitting is rarely necessary. Before starting work, raise the front of the car onto chassis stands placed beneath the reinforced underside of the body just rear of the front wheels. It will be necessary to raise the car sufficiently high to gain access to the centre of the underside of the car.
2   Begin by removing the screws which secure the centre console, and then lift the console up to reveal the selector lever pivot assembly. The clevis pin which secures the cable end fitting to the selector lever can then be removed. Lift up the centre carpet and undo the nuts and bolts securing cable sleeve end housing to the centre bodyshell.
3   It will be necessary to remove two nuts from underneath the car before the cable sleeve end housing can be lowered from the car. The housing, cable and sleeve will come away together and may be separated when the sleeve clamp is unbolted from the housing (Fig. 6.36).
4   To detach the cable from shift lever in the transmission is more difficult. Place a jack beneath the engine and take the weight. Then remove the middle engine support beam and the lowest engine mounting.
5   Next remove the cover plate which is secured on the base of the torque converter housing. Note that the plate extends over to the sump, where two bolts secure both plate and the sump. Once this cover plate has been removed, the clamp on the transmission end of the cable sleeve can be dismantled (Fig. 6.37).
6   Finally the clevis pin in the cable end fitting can be removed to detach the cable from the shift lever.

Refitting
7   This can proceed as the reverse sequence of the removal. Note that the sump bolts and clamp bolts have to be tightened to specific torques. Do not refit the centre console before the cable length has been adjusted.

17 Gearshift cable (Hondamatic) - length adjustment

1   The turnbuckle fitted on the selector lever end of the cable is used to adjust the cable length: to ensure that the selector lever positions correspond to the gears engaged in the transmission (Fig. 6.36).
2   Loosen the locknuts on the ends of the turnbuckle to allow it

to be turned to alter the effective length of the cable and hence the relative positions of the selector and shift levers.
3   Once the selector lever positions tally with the gears engaged in the transmission, hold the turnbuckle and tighten the locknuts. Fit the centre console.

18 Selector lever pivot assembly (Hondamatic) - removal, renovation and refitting

1   Detach the mechanism's cable from the selector lever, as detailed in Section 16, of this Chapter. Again raise the front of the car onto chassis stands placed beneath the reinforced sections of the bodyshell rearwards of the front wheels. It will be necessary to raise the car sufficiently high to gain access to the centre of the underside of the car.
2   Undo and remove the four nuts which secure the selector lever bracket to the bodyshell. Lift the lever and bracket assembly up into the interior of the car (Figs. 6.33; 6.34; 6.35).
3   Remove the two 4 mm screws which hold the 'T' handle on the end of the selector lever. Remove the handle complete with the push knob and spring.
4   Undo and remove the 5 mm screws which hold the console escutcheon to the bracket assembly. Next undo and remove the screws retaining the cover bracket and inhibitor/backlight switch to the lever pivot bracket unit. The lever itself can be removed when the control bracket and the pivot bolt itself have been removed.
5   The selector lever can be dismantled, but always check that spares are available.

Reassembly
6   Reassembly follows the reversal of the removal/diamantling procedure which has been detailed.
7   Apply a little medium grease to the lever pivot bushing, collar and lock pin collar. Once the selector lever has been fitted, the reverse light and starter inhibit switch can be installed.
8   Move the switch contact holder to a central position in the switch base. Now move the selector lever to its central 'N' position, screw the lever pin in the groove in the contact holder and tighten.
9   Next fit the selector lever cover holder so that the notched side is facing the inhibitor/reversing light switch. At this point it will be as well to check the movement of the selector lever, and the operation of the inhibit/reverse switch.
10 Fit the selector lever escutcheon to the pivot bracket assembly and then the 'T' handle to the selector lever. Refit the cable, adjust its length so that the selector lever positions correspond to gears selected.
11 When all is reassembled and working satisfactorily, refit the centre console.

19 Fault diagnosis - Hondamatic transmission

Due to the fairly complex nature of the Hondamatic system, the fault diagnosis involves quite a variety of test routines before faults can be isolated, therefore the chart shows basic faults followed by tests and respective fault identification. As usual check all lubricant levels and engine tuning before testing the transmission.

Symptom	Test	Test Result	Fault
Degraded	Check stall	Stall normal	Possible malfunction of stator ratchet in torque converter.
Acceleration	RPM in '1' and '2'	Stall '1' and '2' too high	Malfunction in high pressure oil feed system in the gearbox. Examine oil pump, pick up and regulator.
		Stall '2' is high '1' is normal	Malfunction of 'D' clutch.
		Stall '1' high '2' normal	Malfunction of 'L' clutch.

Symptom	Test	Test result	Fault
Car does not move when '1' is selected, but does move when '2' and 'R' are selected	Check stall rpm in '1'	Stall rpm '1' too high	Malfunction of 'L' clutch
Car does not move when '2' or 'R' is selected, but moves when '1' is selected	Check stall RPM in '2' and 'R'	Stall rpm '2' and 'R'	Malfunction of 'D' clutch.
		Stall rpm normal	Jammed reverse gear selection.
Car does not move when 'R' is selected but moves when	Check stall rpm when 'R' is selected	Stall rpm normal or low	Incorrect adjustment of control cable length - Parking lock pawl still engaged.
'I' and '2' are selected		Stall rpm high or no stall at all	Jammed reverse gear selector mechanism.
Car does not move when any gear is selected	Check transmission oil pressure at 'L' clutch tapping	Pressure in 'L' line normal	Malfunction in Servo valve or gear selector mechanism.
		Pressure in 'L' line is nil	Malfunction of pump.
		Pressure in 'L' low and fluctuates	Malfunction of pump system.
		Pressure in 'L' low and steady	Malfunction of pressure regulating valve.
Stall rpm is high in all gears	Check for fluid level in transmission. Check oil delivery pressure in transmission.		
Stall rpm is high in '2' and 'R' only	Malfunction of 'D' clutch - typical of slipping clutch.		
Stall rpm is high in '1' only	Malfunction of 'L' clutch.		
Stall rpm is low in all gears	Check tuning and power of engine. Malfunction of stator ratchet in torque converter.		

20 Stall and oil pressure checks - Hondamatic transmission

1 Check stall rpm in each gear as follows, and **do not allow the test to proceed in any gear for longer than 10 seconds.** Serious overheating of the transmission will result if this warning is not heeded, and will invalidate any test results.
2 Park the car on level ground and apply the handbrake. Chock the front wheels.
3 Warm up the engine to its normal running temperature and attach a tachometer to the engine. An electrical tachometer - connected to the ignition system is the easiest to fit.
4 Restart the engine and select gear '2'. Press the brake pedal to hold the car stationary and then press the accelerator pedal. Record the maximum steady engine rpm indicated by the tachometer.
5 Repeat the test detailed in paragraph 4 when gear '1' and finally 'R' is selected.

6 Check the stall rpm recorded with those given in the Specification at the beginning of this Chapter, and refer to Section 19 for fault identification as necessary.

Oil pressure checks
7 The specification shows oil pressure data as a function of engine rpm. It will be necessary therefore to raise the car onto chassis stands at the front and fit a tachometer to the engine to allow for the necessary test conditions.
8 There are three oil pressure tapping points in the transmission casing, one on the 'L' clutch line, one on the 'D' clutch line, and one on the main delivery line.
9 The 'L' line pressure sense tapping can be found on the end cover of the gearbox. (photo)
10 The 'D' line pressure sense point can be found near the front of the transmission and torque converter case joint. (photo)
11 The main delivery line pressure point is adjacent to the transmission case vent. (photo)

20.9 "L" clutch oil pressure sensing point

20.10 "D" clutch, oil pressure sensing point

20.11 Main delivery oil pressure sensing point

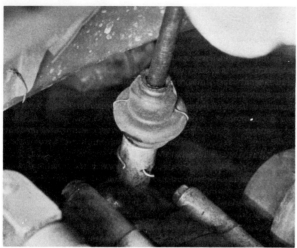

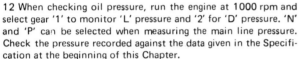
21.3 Speedometer cable termination at transmission end

21.10 Speedometer cable drive components

12 When checking oil pressure, run the engine at 1000 rpm and select gear '1' to monitor 'L' pressure and '2' for 'D' pressure. 'N' and 'P' can be selected when measuring the main line pressure. Check the pressure recorded against the data given in the Specification at the beginning of this Chapter.

13 Always use new aluminium washers when refitting pressure line plugs, and tighten those plugs to the recommended torque given in the Specification at the beginning of this Chapter.

14 Refer to Section 19, of this Chapter, to identify faults.

21 Speedometer cable (all models) - removal and fitting

1 The speedometer cable runs from the end of the transmission casing to the rear of the speedometer. It is driven by a gear machined on the end of the mainshaft in the gearbox.

2 Removal of the cable and its drive components is straightforward and proceeds as follows:

3 Begin by removing the wire clip which retains the cable and sleeve assembly to the cable drive on the end of the gearbox. Extract the cable/sleeve from the drive. (photo)

4 From inside the car, it is now necessary to move the speedometer panel assembly. Remove both positive and negative connections to the battery as a safety measure, in case wires shorted during the cable removal task.

5 Reach behind the minor panel and undo and remove the three wing nuts which secure the instrument panel to the facia.

6 Move the instrument panel away from the facia, in order to access the rear of the speedometer, to permit the cable assembly to be detached.

7 Extract the cable from the car. It is not repairable, and therefore once deemed faulty, should be replaced.

8 As usual, refitting follows the reversal of the removal procedure.

9 The cable drive components can be extracted from the transmission end cover once the special spigot bolt has been unscrewed from the cover boss.

10 The drive can be split into its three main parts: the drive body, bearing housing and driven gear. (photo)

11 The drive assembly seats in a bore machined in the transmission end cover, and a single 'O' ring provides a seal for the transmission oil.

Chapter 7 Final drive, driveshafts and wheels

Contents

Specifications

Final drive

Reduction:
    Hondamatic 4.117:1
    Manual transmission 4.933:1
Final driven gear backlash:
    Assembled standard ... ... 0.03 mm (0.0012 inch)
    Service limit ... ... 0.18 mm (0.0071 inch)
Differential bevel pinion shaft (outside diameter) ... ... 17.96 to 17.98 mm (0.7071 to 0.7079 inch)
Differential case:
    Bevel pinion shaft hole ... ... 18.04 to 18.01 mm (0.7102 to 0.7091 inch)
    Bevel pinion side clearance ... ... 0.15 mm (0.006 inch)

Tyres

Size ... ... 600S 12 - 4PR
Pressure ... ... 24 psi all round

Torque wrench settings

	kg f m	lb f ft
Front and rear wheel nuts	7.0 - 9.0	51 - 65
Front spindle nut	12.0 - 18.0	87 - 130
Rear spindle nut	10.0 - 13.0	72 - 94
Rear wheel bearing cap	0.4 - 0.7	3 - 5
Rear hub carrier and shock absorber	3.5 - 5.0	25 - 36
Final driven gear to differential cage	9.0 - 9.5	65 - 69

1 Final drive - description and notes

The final drive and differential is housed in part of the transmission casing, and is the same design in manual and Hondamatic transmissions. It comprises a drive pinion which is part of the mainshaft of the gearbox, a final driven gear, a differential assembly and lastly wheel driveshafts which fit into splines in the bevel output gears of the differential.

The final drive on the Civic presents fewer reassembly problems than conventional drives on rear wheel drive cars. The drive pinion and differential crownwheel mesh is not adjustable, because it is set by the bearing seatings in the transmission casing. However, the differential bevel gear adjustment remains, and the differential cage float adjustment.

2 Final drive - removal, dismantling and reassembly

1 Separate and remove the transmission assembly from the car, as detailed in Chapter 5, Section 5, of this manual. Clean the exterior of the transmission to ensure that foreign matter is not subsequently transferred into the gearbox and final drive mechanisms.

2 Refer to Chapter 6, and dismantle the transmission to the point when the transmission casing can be lifted off the clutch and final drive housing.

3 Again referring to Chapter 6, remove the mainshaft and countershaft assemblies from the clutch/final drive housing.

4 The differential and crown gear assembly should now be the only major item left in the final drive and clutch housing.

5 The differential assembly can be jolted out of the casing, or forced out using a tubular drift acting on the differential case bearing in the final drive housing. (photo)

6 Once the differential assembly is separated, the ball race bearings on each side of the differential can be pulled off the differential cage using a conventional puller.

7 Next hold the differential cage in a vice and undo and remove the bolts which secure the crown gear wheel on the cage. Loosen the bolts in a criss-cross pattern, or else the gear and cage may be distorted.

8 After the crown gear has been removed, drive out the small 4 mm pin which holds the differential bevel drive pinion shaft in place in the differential unit. Force the pin out with the drift acting from the side of the cage opposite to the differential cage. Then extract that shaft and the drive bevel pinions.

9 Once the drive bevels and their shaft have been removed, the driven bevels can then be extracted by moving into the centre of the cage and finally out of the large apertures in the side of the cage.

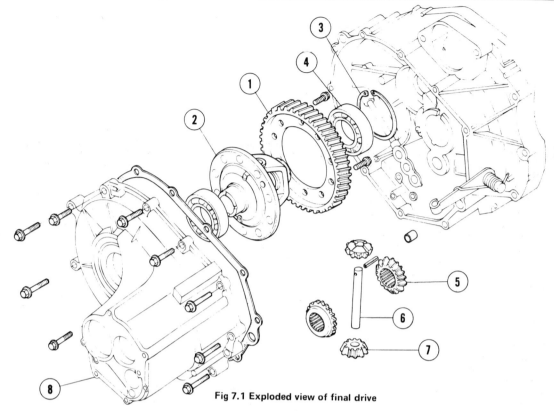

Fig 7.1 Exploded view of final drive

| 1 Final driven gear | 3 72 mm set ring | 5 Drive pinion | 7 Differential pinion |
| 2 Differential case | 4 Ball bearing | 6 Pinion shaft | 8 Transmission case |

2.5 Differential removed

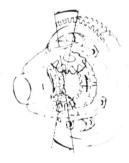

Fig 7.2 insertion of bevel gears into differential cage (Sec 2)

3.3 Front wheel hub nut and lockpin

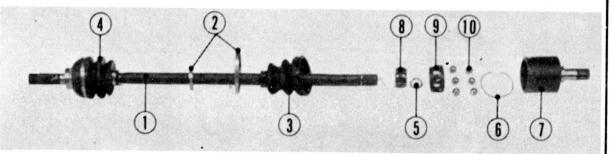

Fig 7.3 Driveshaft components (Sec 3)

1 Driveshaft	4 Boot A	7 Inboard joint	9 Cage
2 Boot bands	5 Snap ring	8 Inner retainer	10 Ball
3 Boot B	6 Stopper ring		

10 The differential and final drive is now fully dismantled, and the parts should be wiped clean with a non-fluffy rag and laid out on a clean bench for inspection.
11 Now examine the following items:

i) *The bearing seatings in both differential casing and the transmission casing. If seen to be scored and worn, replacement of the transmission is the only answer. The bearings must be an interference fit in those seatings.*

ii) *The differential cage bearings should be checked for rough movement, sloppiness and wear. If wear or roughness is detected, replacement is the only course of action.*

iii) *Examine the oil seals in each of the final drive housing and transmission casing.*

iv) *Finally closely examine the gear teeth on the final drive pinion, crown gear wheel, differential bevel gears and the splines inside the differential output bevel gears.*

There should be no pitting or scoring marks on the gear teeth. A smooth polished surface should be seen. Check with the Specifications at the beginning of this Chapter for major dimensions and service limits.

Reassembly of the differential and final drive
12 As usual the reassembly task follows the reversal of the dismantling procedure which has been detailed. The following tasks are in addition:
13 Apply a coat of new gear oil or molybdenum disulphide to each component as it is installed.
14 Install the differential driven/output bevel gears into the differential cage first and then insert the drive bevel gears between the output bevels. Rotate the output bevels to feed the drive bevel gears into position in the differential cage (Fig. 7.2). Once the drive bevels are in position, insert the gear shaft. Do not fit the retaining pin yet, but go on to measure the backlash of the bevel gears. Backlash can be varied by changing the thrust washers behind the drive bevels. These thrust washers are available in three thicknesses, and the thickness of washers used must be the same behind each drive bevel gear. If only one washer is changed the differential will be noisy.
15 Once the backlash has been adjusted to be within the specified limits, proceed to fit the crownwheel gear. Tighten the gear bolts in a criss-cross pattern to the specified torque. Then recheck the bevel gear backlash.
16 It is necessary to check the clearance between the differential cage bearings and the bearing seating spacers, before the final drive assembly can be completed.
17 Differential side clearance: Remove the large circlip which is inside the cage bearing seating in the clutch/final drive housing. Once the circlip has been removed, recover the spacers if any, and prise out the oil seal. If it is suitable for re-use, use a large circular drift, ease the seal out - it can easily be distorted.
18 Once the seal is out, refit the circlip and spacers, then reinstall the differential assembly and fit the transmission case onto the clutch/final drive housing using a new gasket. Tighten the fixing bolts to the recommended torque.
19 Next, with a soft metal tubular drift tap the differential cage and bearing from the transmission case side, so that it seats against the spacer and circlip on the engine side - in the clutch/final drive housing.
20 Then with the same tool, tap the differential and its bearings from the clutch/final drive housing side to force the differential cage and bearings against the shoulder in the seating on the transmission casing.
21 Now use a feeler gauge to measure the gap between the spacer and the differential cage bearing on the engine side. The gap can be brought to the specified dimension by fitting one of the spacers listed in the Specifications at the beginning of this Chapter. Repeat this check when the envisaged correct spacer has been fitted.
22 Once the right spacer has been selected and tried, separate the transmission case and clutch/final drive housing to

commence full assembly of final drive and transmission.

3 Driveshafts - removal, dismantling and refitting

1 The driveshafts are unequal length shafts with constant velocity joints incorporated at each end. The inside end of the shaft is splined and fits into the centre of the output bevels of the differential; the outer end is splined as well, to accept the front wheel mounting flange. Each constant velocity joint comprises 6 steel balls caged between conformal joint halves (Fig. 7.3).
2 This Section describes the removal and refitting of the driveshafts; it also covers dismantling, but if the joints on the shafts are known to be faulty, check the availability of spares before dismantling the shaft assemblies. Dismantling may be a waste of time. Replacement of boots necessitates dismantling of the inboard constant velocity joint.

Removal of driveshafts
3 Begin by removing the centre cap from the wheel hub, then extract the split pin and undo the driveshaft spindle nut. (photo)
4 Now jack-up the front of the car and support it on chassis stands placed beneath the strengthened areas of bodyshell just rearwards of the front wheels. Undo the wheelnuts and remove the wheels.
5 Next, drain the transmission oil, and whilst it is draining, remove the lower suspension arm ball joints from the front knuckle members. Extract the split pin which locks the nut on the ball joint pin, undo and remove the nut and finally press the tapered pin from the knuckle member. Insert a long lever into the suspension so that it reacts on the bodyshell near the arm pivot and bears onto the arm near the ball joint. Press onto the knuckle member, whilst tapping the pin receptacle with a hammer to unstick the taper.
6 Alternatively, of course, use a conventional puller to extract the ball joint pin.
7 The wheel hub is now free to move outwards, so take hold of the hub and driveshafts and pull the hub off the driveshaft outer spindle. After that pull the inboard end of the shaft out of the final drive.

Refitting driveshafts
8 As usual the refitting follows the reversal of the removal procedure, it will be necessary to take account of the following points:

i) *Coat the splines at each end of the driveshafts with molybdenum disulphide before refitting to the wheel hub and final drive.*

ii) *Tighten all nuts to the specified torque.*

iii) *Ensure that all boots are in perfect condition.*

Dismantling of driveshafts
9 Having removed the driveshafts from the car, begin dismantling the inboard joint as follows:
10 Undo and remove the boot retaining bands and then slide the boot along the shaft toward the outboard joint.
11 Now remove the large ring on the inside of the joint housing, so that the housing can be drawn off the joint.
12 Wipe the grease off the joint to reveal the circlip on the end of the driveshaft. Remove the circlip, to permit the joint cage to be withdrawn from the shaft. It will require an up and down motion to urge the joint balls out of the cage, and remove the inner joint retainer (Fig. 7.4).
13 It should now be possible to remove the inboard joint boot and then the outboard joint boot, once its retaining rings have been removed.
14 The outboard joint cannot be dismantled, and if worn or faulty the whole shaft assembly should be replaced.

Visual inspection
15 Examine the components, in particular the ball bearings inner

retainer, ball cage and joint housing. The boot on the outboard joint will need to be removed to permit the limited visual inspection of parts of that joint. Do not use solvents to clean any parts.

16 If there are any signs of scoring, pitting or corrosion, replace the affected parts.

17 If possible check the runout of the driveshafts, and check against the limits set on the Specifications at the beginning of this Chapter.

Assembly of driveshafts and inboard joint

18 The reassembly task follows the reversal of the dismantling sequence, but account must be taken of the following points: **Pack grease into both inboard and outboard joints, fill all gaps. When reassembling the inboard joint make sure the balls and cups in the retainer and cage are well greased (Fig. 7.5 and 7.6).**

4 Front wheel hub and bearings - removal, dismantling and refitting

1 The front wheel hub is held inside bearings in the knuckle member; the driveshaft spindle fits into the centre of the hub to transmit the engine power to the wheels. There are two ball race bearings which support the hub and there is no adjustment. Once wear is detected, the renewal of the bearings is the only course of action (Fig. 7.7).

Hub removal

2 Begin by jacking-up the front of the car, and support it on chassis stands placed beneath the strengthened bodyshell areas just rearward of the front wheels. Remove the front wheels.

3 Next remove the bolts which secure the front brake caliper to the knuckle, and lift the caliper aside. Tie it to the suspension, so

Fig 7.4 Removal of CV joint race circlip (Sec 3)

1 Circlip   2 Circlip pliers

Fig 7.5 Reassembly of CV joint (Sec 3)

1 Application of grease   2 Ball

Fig 7.6 Installation of CV joint boot (Sec 3)

1 Band fastener   2 Ring spanner

Fig 7.7 Checking for wheel bearing wear-any movement indicates wear (Sec 4)

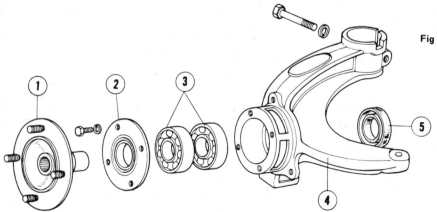

Fig 7.8 Front hub components (Sec 4)

1 Front hub
2 Front bearing dust seal B
3 Front wheel bearings
4 Knuckle
5 Front bearing dust seal A

that the flexible brake hose to the caliper is not strained.

4 Now remove the centre cap on the wheel hub to reveal the driveshaft spindle nut. Extract the split pin which locks the nut, and then remove the nut.

5 Attach a conventional puller to the wheel studs on the hub and pull the hub off the driveshaft spindle and out of the bearings in the suspension knuckle.

6 A puller can be improvised, the essentials are a member which is secured to the hub which can withstand a bolt which acts to force the spindle and hub apart.

7 Once the hub and disc have been removed, undo the four bolts which retain the disc to the hub and separate the two parts.

8 The bearings are an interference fit in the knuckle, and it will be necessary to remove the knuckle in order to press out the bearings.

9 **Note:** Do not attempt to press out old bearings until you have new ones in hand; bearings should not be re-used once they have been removed from the knuckle.

Knuckle removal

10 Use a conventional ball joint pin extractor to remove the steering rods from the knuckle: take care not to damage the joint seals.

11 Extract the split pin and undo and remove the nut which retains the lower suspension arm/knuckle ball joint pin in the knuckle. Lever the suspension arm from the knuckle, whilst tapping the knuckle near to the joint pin to loosen the taper and free the pin.

12 Next undo and remove the bolt which locks the lower end of the MacPherson strut to the knuckle. Once the bolt has been removed, tap the top of the knuckle with a hammer and slide it off the strut/shock absorber.

13 The knuckles can now be removed from the suspension. Support the driveshafts, so that they do not fall from the final drive, or else there will be a messy loss of oil.

14 Having transferred the knuckle assembly to the work bench, commence the removal of the front wheel bearings as follows:

15 Prise the oil/dust seal from the centre of the inboard side of the knuckle. Then undo and remove the three screws which secure the disc splash guard to the knuckle. Remove the splash guard.

16 Once the seal and guard have been removed, undo and remove the four bolts which secure the bearing retaining plate to the wheel side of the knuckle.

17 The two bearings are an interference fit in the knuckle, and it will require considerable effort to remove them. Ideally the knuckle should be supported beneath a hydraulic press and a cylindrical driver used to move the bearings out of the knuckle. Whatever method is used to remove the bearings, the knuckle should be supported as close to the periphery of the wheel bearings as possible.

18 Having removed the bearings, discard them because new bearings should be fitted on assembly.

19 Inspection is visual; the knuckles should be examined for

wear and damage. The seals should be renewed if the lips are worn or cracked.

Reassembly of knuckle and front wheel hub

20 Assembly follows the reversal of the dismantling procedure, except that the following tasks are included.

21 Pack each bearing with grease before pressing it into the knuckle, and ensure that the bearings are assembled so that the manufacturer's markings are facing inward, facing each other.

22 Assemble the front wheel hub into the bearings and knuckle before the knuckle assembly is refitted to the suspension.

23 When pressing the bearings into the knuckle use a tubular drift which acts only on the outer race of the bearings. It is important not to load the ball bearings during assembly.

24 Tighten all nuts and fasteners to the specified torques.

---

5 Rear wheel hubs and bearings - removal, dismantling and re-fitting

---

1 The rear wheel hub and bearings are incorporated with the brake drum. The bearings are an interference fit in the central boss on the brake drum, and run on a stub axle connected to the MacPherson strut on the rear suspension. The wheel studs fit through the side of the brake drum, to provide means for wheel attachment. Wear is detected as in Fig. 7.7; the bearings are not adjustable.

2 Removal of hub and bearings: Jack-up the rear of the car and support on chassis stands, then remove the rear wheels. Next undo and remove the three bolts which retain the bearing cap to the centre of the hub. (photo)

3 Now wipe the grease from the wheel axle nut, remove the split pin which locks the nut and then undo and remove the axle nut.

4 Pull the drum/hub and bearings from the stub axle. If it is reluctant to come off the stub axle, use a conventional puller which bolts to the drum and acts onto the stub axle to draw the drum/hub off the axle. (photo)

5 Once the drum/hub is off the car, transfer to a bench to start removal of the bearings. Begin by prising out the oil seal, and then insert a drift through larger inner bearing and pull the spacer off centre to drive out the smaller bearing. Once the smaller bearing has been removed and the spacer extracted, use the same drift to force the larger bearing from the hub. (photo)

6 Always rest the drift on the outer races to prevent applying shock loads to the ball bearings. Tap the periphery of the bearing evenly to avoid the bearing being driven askew in its seating.

7 The bearings are not adjustable, and therefore if wear and slack was felt on the hub and bearing assembly before removal, renewal of both bearings is the only course of action to be taken.

8 When installing new bearings, take every care to drive the bearings in evenly, not askew, and always apply the force necessary to the outer race - periphery of the bearing. It is essential not to apply shock loads to the balls in the new bearing.

5.2 Rear wheel hub nut and pin

5.4 Rear hub/drum removal

5.5 Rear hub bearing oil seals

9 Install the new oil seal so that its outer surface becomes flush with the drum/hub surface.

10 Grease the bearings generously before fitting to the stub axle, and once refitted, tighten the axle nut to the recommended torque. Lock the nut with a split pin.

11 Take care that no surplus grease finds its way to the friction surfaces on the drum.

6 Wheels - general

The wheels function in a harsh environment and are vital to the running of the car: it follows that the strength and trueness of the road wheels is critical.

A great deal of excessive wear on the wheel bearings and driveshaft joints can be attributed to buckled or deformed wheels. Carry out regular checks on the condition of the wheels; replace the wheels if they are deformed - do not re-work old wheels. Keep the wheels rust and corrosion free.

7 Tyres - general

In the same way that the condition of the wheels is critical, so it is perhaps more so with the tyres. It is good and essential practice to regularly - daily - inspect the tyres for cracks, cuts, blisters and foreign objects. The tyre walls and treads are highly strained items on the car and faults such as cracks and cuts can spread and become dangerous very quickly. Do not take any risks; once a fault has been discovered, remove the wheel, fit the spare and take the faulty tyre to a specialist garage so that it can be inspected and repaired.

Chapter 8 Suspension and steering

Contents

Specifications

Front suspension	Independent. MacPherson strut
	Coil spring and anti-roll bar
Rear suspension	Independent. MacPherson strut
	Coil spring
Shock absorbers	Telescopic, double acting incorporated into strut

Steering

Type	Rack and pinion
Steering gear backlash	0.15 mm (adjusting screw turned back 1/8th turn)
Overall ratio	16.91 : 1
Turns (lock-to-lock)	3.1
Steering wheel play	10 mm (0.4 inch) (maximum)
Steering column bushing bore:	
Upper	17.85 to 18.15 mm (0.703 to 0.714 inch
Lower	18.15 to 18.45 mm (0.714 to 0.726 inch)

Front wheel alignment

Castor	1° 45'
Camber	30' positive
Toe-in	Out 1 mm (0.04 inch)

Rear wheel alignment

Camber	30' positive
Toe-in	Zero

Torque wrench settings

	kg f m	lb f ft
Steering box mounting bolts	1.9 - 2.5	14 - 18
Rack end balljoint	5.0 - 6.0	36 - 43
Tie-rod end locknut	4.0 - 4.8	29 - 35
Tie-rod balljoint nut	4.0 - 4.8	29 - 35
Steering joint bolt	2.4 - 3.0	17 - 22
Steering wheel nut	3.0 - 4.5	22 - 33
Steering column support bolts	1.8 - 2.5	13 - 18
Rack guide locknut	4.0 - 5.0	29 - 36
Front backing plate mounting bolts	1.9 - 2.5	14 - 18
Rear backing plate mounting bolts	1.9 - 2.5	14 - 18
Front suspension member subframe	3.5 - 4.3	25 - 31
Engine mount beam and body	3.5 - 4.3	25 - 31
Front beam engine mount beam and centre beam	3.5 - 4.3	25 - 31
Lower arm balljoint nut	3.0 - 4.0	22 - 29
Radius rod	3.5 - 5.0	25 - 36
Lower arm mounting bolts	3.5 - 5.0	25 - 36
Front shock absorber and knuckle	5.0 - 6.0	36 - 43
Front shock absorber and bodyshell	1.0 - 1.6	7 - 12

							Kg f m	lb f ft
Anti-roll bar brackets	...	...	...	...	...	...	0.7 - 1.2	5 - 9
Front shock absorber centre nut	...	...	...	...	...		5.5 - 7.0	40 - 50
Rear shock absorber centre nut upper		...	...	...	...		5.5 - 7.0	40 - 50
Rear shock absorber centre nut lower		...	...	...	...		5.5 - 7.0	40 - 50
Rear shock absorber and bodyshell		...	...	...	...		1.0 - 1.6	7 - 12
Rear lower arm to bodyshell	...	...	...	...	...		3.5 - 5.0	25 - 36
Rear lower arm/shock absorber	...	...	...	...	...		5.0 - 6.5	36 - 47
Hub carrier to shock absorber	...	...	...	...	...		3.5 - 5.0	25 - 36
Rear radius rod to hub carrier	...	...	...	...	...		5.5 - 7.5	40 - 54
Rear radius rod to bodyshell	...	...	...	...	...		3.5 - 5.0	25 - 36

1 General notes

It is essential to maintain the suspension and steering systems in good order if the safety of your car is to be preserved. Even small amounts of wear in the suspension joints and steering system will affect the handling of the car to a dangerous extent. It is for that reason that the law requires checks to be made on the condition and serviceability of the suspension particularly, as well as the more obvious components such as the lights, tyres, and chassis.

The components that demand particular attention are as follows:

a) *Lower knuckle ball joint*
b) *Steering tie-rod ball joints*
c) *Top anchorage for the MacPherson struts*
d) *Anchorages and bushes for anti-roll bar*
e) *The shock absorbers*
f) *Lower control arm pivot bushes*

All of these points should be tested with a stout lever or screwdriver to see whether there is any movement between them and the fixed components. Checks on the suspension should always be made with the car jacked up and supported on chassis stands. It will be easier to detect small amounts of wear and movement when normal imposed loads are not acting on the suspension members. Together with the mechanical tests on the suspension and steering joints, the components themselves should be checked for serviceability, particularly:

a) *Steering rack mounting bolts, tightness*
b) *Steering column shaft couplings*
c) *Steering column retention bolts*
d) *Steering wheel retention*
e) *Front and rear wheel hub bearings (Chapter 7)*

There should be no play - or failure - in any single part of any of the aforementioned components. It is dangerous to use a vehicle in a doubtful condition of this kind.

Finally, all parts should be kept clean and rust free, and if rust is found, use rust proof and paint to restore the parts condition. Rust left can cause cracks and possibly failure of that suspension member.

2 General description - steering system

The steering system comprises a rack mechanism, tie-rods and an articulated steering column assembly. The rack is housed in the rear main suspension subframe, and the lower control arms of the front suspension are pivoted on the same subframe (Fig. 8.1).

Tie-rods on each end of the rack join the rack to the front suspension knuckle members. The steering column shaft has two universal joints at its lower end compatible with the rack/pinion box.

The system is simple and compact, and the following Sections describe the procedures for rack and tie-rod removal, renovation and refitting, and then the removal, renovation and refitting of the steering column shaft assembly.

Do not use anything but the correct Honda spare parts when repairing the steering system; the serviceability of the steering is vital.

3 Steering rack and tie-rods - removal and refitting

1 Begin by jacking-up the front of the car and support it on chassis stands placed beneath the strengthened areas of the bodyshell just rearward of the front wheels (see Chapter 11 for jacking strong points).
2 Once the behicle is safely supported, remove the roadwheels.
3 It is necessary to support the engine and transmission with jacks or a hoist so that the support members no longer take the engine and transmission weight. It will be preferable to use a hoist and chain, because there will then be less congestion beneath the car.
4 Undo and remove the nuts which hold the steering tie-rod-end ball joints to the knuckle members. Use a conventional ball joint puller to force the ball pin from the knuckle. Take care not to damage the ball pin threads and ball joint rubber boot.
5 Once the tie-rods have been disconnected from the knuckle, proceed to remove the exhaust pipe from the manifold, and the gearshift rod/cable at the transmission.
6 Next undo and remove the nuts and bolts which secure the engine centre support beam to the suspension subframe members. Leave the flexible support on the engine.
7 Return to inside the car and turn the steering wheel so that the bolt which secures the steering shaft universal joint to the rack/pinion shaft, can be undone and removed.
8 Again underneath the car, undo and remove the four bolts which secure the rack assembly to the suspension subframe. The rack assembly is now free for removal. The design of the subframe demands that the rack assembly be manoeuvered a little so that it can be extracted from the frame. (photos)
9 Raise the left-hand tie-rod so that the rack and pinion assembly can be lowered in the frame until the pinion shaft clears the bottom of the frame. Then rotate the rack until the pinion shaft is pointing downwards: now move the rack to the right until the left-hand side tie-rod comes out of the bottom of the subframe. Finally, extract the whole rack assembly through the ball joint from the end of the left-hand tie-rod, to allow the tie-rod and rack to be extracted from the subframe.

Refitting
10 As usual this proceeds as the reversal of the removal task detailed above. Particular attention should be paid to the following:
i)   *Tighten all nuts and bolts to their specified torques*
ii)   *Check the tracking and alignment of the front wheels*
iii) *Apply grease to mating spline members before reassembly*
iv)   *Take care not to damage the rack boots when the assembly is being inserted into the suspension subframe*

4 Steering rack and tie-rods - renovation

1 The dismantling of the rack and pinion assembly proceeds as follows: (Fig. 8.2).

2 Remove the rack boot balance air line, and then undo the boot clamps so that the boots can be moved along the tie-rods to expose the tie-rod/rack joint.

3 Use a screwdriver to straighten the lock-washer which secures the tie-rod/rack joint.

4 Unscrew the tie-rods from the end of the rack and recover the rack travel stop washers, and the lock-washers (Fig. 8.3).

5 Turning your attention now to the pinion/rack box, undo and remove the rack pressure pad retaining plug; the plug is locked by a large thin nut and this will have to be loosened

before the plug can be unscrewed from the rack housing (Fig. 8.4).

6 Recover the rack guide spring, and the guide itself if necessary. Use circlip pliers to pull the guide out by gripping the holes in the top of the guide.

7 The pinion assembly can be removed as follows: begin by prising out the pinion shaft oil seal, and then extract the larger snap-ring which retains the pinion shaft assembly in place (Fig. 8.5).

8 The pinion shaft can now be extracted, and once it is out, the

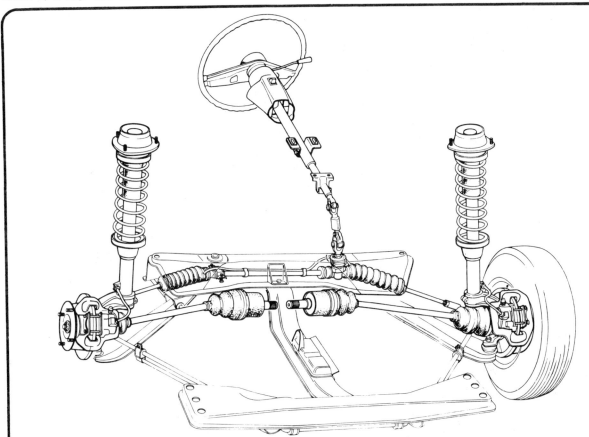

Fig 8.1 Layout of steering system (Sec 2)

3.8A Steering rack housing attachment

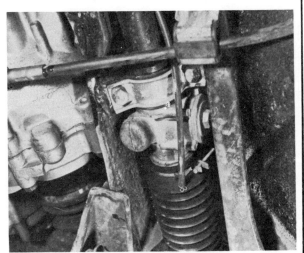

3.8B Rack housing attachment, steering gearbox end

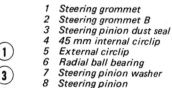

Fig 8.2 Steering rack - exploded view (Sec 4)

1 Steering grommet
2 Steering grommet B
3 Steering pinion dust seal
4 45 mm internal circlip
5 External circlip
6 Radial ball bearing
7 Steering pinion washer
8 Steering pinion
9 Gearbox
10 Grease fitting
11 Ball joint seal
12 Circlip
13 Tie-rod end
14 Tie-rod dust seal

15 Bellows band
16 Rack end
17 Air tube
18 Tie-rod lock washer
19 Tie-rod stopper washer
20 Tube clips
21 Gear box bracket
22 Gear box mount cushion
23 Rack screw locknut
24 Rack guide O-ring
25 Rack guide screw
26 Rack guide pressure spring
27 Steering rack guide
28 Steering rack

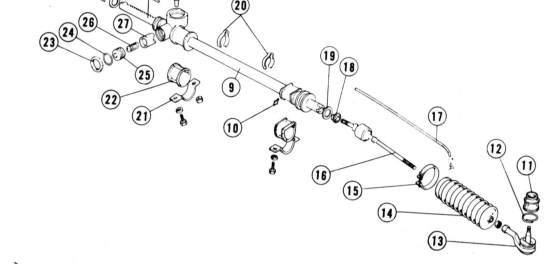

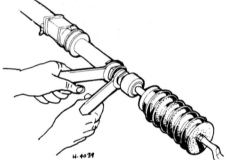

Fig 8.3 Removal of Tie-Rod from rack (Sec 4)

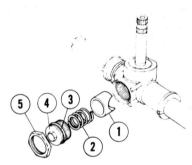

Fig 8.4 Steering rack block components (Sec 4)

1 Rack guide block
2 Guide block spring
3 Block 'O' ring
4 Screw plug
5 Plug locknut

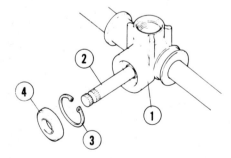

Fig 8.5 Steering pinion shaft components (Sec 4)

1 Steering gearbox
2 Pinion shaft
3 Circlip
4 Boot/grommet

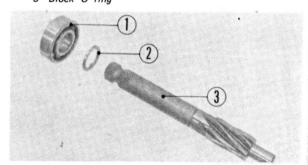

Fig 8.6 Steering pinion shaft components (Sec 4)

1 Ball bearing
2 Pinion washer
3 Pinion

small circlip on the shaft can be removed so that the ball bearing race can be slid off the shaft. Hold the bearing while lightly tapping the pinion with a light mallet to urge the shaft out of the bearing. Recover the pinion washer (Fig. 8.6).

9 Extract the rack from the rack housing.

10 Lay all the parts out on a clean bench for visual inspection.

11 Examine the teeth of the steering rack and pinion for wear, and if wear is seen, and if when previously in use, the rack movement was felt to be uneven, the only course of action is to renew the whole rack and pinion assembly.

12 Examine the bearing surfaces on the pinion shaft, the ball bearing assembly, and pinion washer - if wear or scoring is seen, replace the appropriate parts.

13 Lastly check the free-length of the rack guide backing spring and if the length does not match with the specification, replace the spring.

Reassembly of the rack and pinion assembly

14 The assembly procedure is the reversal of the dismantling sequence, except that the following tasks should be added:

15 Smear all sliding surfaces with grease before assembling in the following sequence. Insert the rack into the rack housing, then assemble the pinion shaft and refit into the rack housing. Once the pinion is engaged with the rack, fit the internal circlip which retains the pinion assembly in the rack/pinion housing. Finally install the grease/dust seal.

16 The next component to be refitted should be the rack guide. Insert it into the rack housing, opposite the pinion shaft; follow it with the backing spring and retaining plug. Remember to fit a new 'O' ring to the retaining plug, and tighten the plug until the rack cannot be moved, then turn the plug back 45° and hold it in that position while the locknut is tightened. The rack should now move smoothly when the steering system has been reassembled. The steering force should be measured at the steering wheel. See Section 5, of this Chapter for steering system checks.

17 Having assembled the rack and pinion, the tie-rods can be fitted to the rack ends. Fit the travel stop washers and new locking washers. Make sure that the lock-washer tags engage the slots at each end of the rack, once the tie-rod-ends have been screwed into the rack and tightened to the specified torque. Finally, the lock-washers should be bent over to lock the tie-rod screw.

18 Refit the boots over the rack and tie-rod joints and fasten into position, and remember the balance air line.

19 The rack and pinion assembly is now ready to be refitted to the car.

---

5 Steering system - checks

---

1 The following checks need to be made periodically on the steering system, and whenever the system has been reassembled after renovation:

i) Steering wheel axial and radial play
ii) Applied force to steering wheel to turn wheels
iii) Steering rack play
iv) Steering rack guide pressure
v) Front wheel alignment (toe-in)
vi) Steering wheel rotational play

Steering wheel axial and radial play

2 Hold the steering wheel firmly and try to move the wheel in and out of the column, and then left and right, and up and down. If there is any axial play check the following points

i) Steering wheel retaining nut torque
ii) Steering column assembly mounting bolts
iii) Steering column shaft bushings
iv) Steering column universal joints

If there is radial play of the steering wheels, check the steering column shaft bushes.

Applied force to steering wheel to move the wheels

3 Jack-up the front of the car, and support it on chassis stands placed beneath the suspension subframe. Move the wheels to the 'straight-ahead' position and then, inside the car, attach a spring balance to the steering wheel at the end of the spokes. Pull the spring balance downwards to measure the force necessary to move the steering system. Check the force reading with that given in the Specifications at the beginning of this Chapter. If the force exceeds specification check the following:

i) The adjustment of the steering rack guide
ii) Lubrication of all ball joints
iii) Steering column shaft universal joints
iv) Steering column shaft bushes

Steering rack play

Raise the car onto chassis stands placed beneath reinforced bodyshell areas rearward of the front wheels then from underneath the car, undo the rack boot restraining bands at the pinion end of the rack housing, move the bellows down the tie-rod to expose the rack (Fig. 8.7).

Grasp the rack and attempt to move it up, and down, and to-and-fro: check for movement when the steering is set fully-right, mid-right, straight-ahead, and left and finally full left. If any radial movement is detected proceed to the next check/adjustment which deals with the rack guide block.

Steering rack guide block pressure

Again from underneath the car, having supported it on chassis stands; undo the large locknut on the guide retaining plug. Then tighten the guide plug until the force exerted by the guide onto the rack, just prevents the front wheels from being turned by hand (Fig. 8.8). Then back off the plug some 45° and hold it in position whilst the locknut is tightened. Recheck

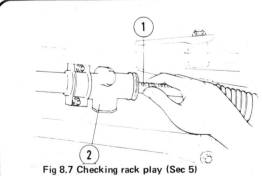

Fig 8.7 Checking rack play (Sec 5)

1 Rack   2 Gearbox

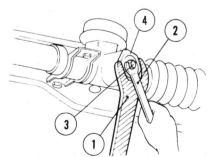

Fig 8.8 Adjusting rack guide block pressure (Sec 5)

1 Large spanner   3 Screw plug
2 Small spanner to turn   4 Locknut
  screw plug

the rack play, the applied force to the steering wheel, and the smoothness of rack movement as the wheels turn to lock.

Steering wheel rotational play

This is the play felt at the steering wheel when it is moved to turn the front wheels to the left and right. Check the play with the wheels pointing straight ahead, to the left and then to the right. If the play exceeds the specified limit, check for wear, looseness or adjustment of the following:

i)   *Steering shaft universal joints*
ii)   *Rack guide adjustment*
iii) *Tie-rod ball joints inboard and outboard*
iv)   *Lower suspension arm ball joint*

6 Front wheel alignment - checking and adjustment

1 Provided that reassembly of the steering and/or the front suspension involved only the renewal of joints and/or bushes and not disturbance of the lengths of any of the steering rods or suspension arm anchorages, then you should be able to drive carefully to your nearest Honda dealer or automobile workshop, where the wheels may be aligned with the specialist equipment that is absolutely essential for this task.
2 If on reassembly of the steering system, the tie-rod lengths and/or the suspension arm anchorages were altered, then it will be necessary to check the alignment with simple equipment, before driving the car to the local workshop for final accurate alignment.
3 The castor, camber and toe-in details are given in the Specifications at the beginning of this Chapter.
4 Of all the settings to be considered, only the toe-in is likely to be seriously affected during repair work on the car.
5 The toe-in of the front wheels may be checked as follows - move the car onto a flat level area, check the tyre pressures on all four wheels. The car should be unladen.
6 The toe-in figure is the difference in distance between the middle of the tyre treads when measured at hub level on the most forward tip and the most rearward tips of the tyres (Fig. 8.9).
7 The adjustment of the front wheel toe-in is effected by loosening the nuts on each of the tie-rods which lock against the outer ball joints. Loosen the bellows retaining strap so that the tie-rod may be rotated and alter its effective length (Fig. 8.10). Once the correct toe-in has been obtained, tighten the tie-rod ball joint locknuts, check toe-in again, and finally secure the rack/tie-rod bellows.

7 Tie-rod ball joints - renovation

1 The inboard ball joint cannot be separated from the tie-rod, and therefore if any wear or damage to that joint is found, the tie-rod assembly will need to be replaced.
2 The outboard ball joint can be separated from the tie-rod and is available individually as a spare. The joint between the ball joint and the tie-rod provides the facility to alter the effective length of the rod and hence the toe-in of the front wheels. The outer ball joint is not repairable and therefore once wear or damage has been found, the joint should be discarded and a new one fitted.
3 Begin removal of the tie-rod and ball joints as follows: Raise the front of the car onto chassis stands and remove the roadwheels.
4 Extract the split pin which locks the ball pin nut and then undo and remove the nut.
5 Use a conventional ball pin extractor to push the pin from the front suspension knuckle.
6 Once the joint is separated from the knuckle, undo the locknut which secures it on the tie-rod, and then unscrew the ball joint from the tie-rod.

7 Fitting a new joint follows the reversal of the removal procedure. Ensure the new joint is lightly greased, and once the new joint has been fitted, check the toe-in of the front wheels as detailed in Section 6, of this Chapter.
8 If wear or damage has been found on the inner ball joint, remove the tie-rod as follows. Raise the car onto chassis stands placed beneath strengthened bodyshell points by the front wheel arch.
9 Remove the outer ball joint from the knuckle as detailed before in this Section, and then again from underneath the car undo the rack/tie-rod boot retaining straps and slide the boots down the tie-rod to reveal the tie-rod/rack joint.
10 Straighten the inner joint locking tag washer with a screwdriver so that the ball joint and the tie-rod can be unscrewed from the rack. If you are unlucky, it might not be possible to gain access to the lock-washer tag, or to the boot retaining strap, and in that unfortunate instance it will be necessary to remove the rack and pinion assembly from the suspension subframe.
11 Fitting a new tie-rod follows the reversal of the removal procedure. Ensure that the joint is lightly greased, and once the tie-rod has been fitted, check the alignment of the front wheels as detailed in Section 6, of this Chapter.

8 Front suspension - general description

1 The front suspension is designed on the MacPherson strut principle. The strut comprises the shock absorber and coil spring and the wheel knuckle is rigidly attached to its lower end. The movement of the knuckle in the vertical sense is controlled by the strut and in the lateral and fore and rear directions, by the lower control arm and radius arm.

The lower control arm is angled rearwards from the base of the knuckle to an anchorage on the suspension subframe. The lower arm accepts the greater horizontal loads from the knuckle.

The radius arm gives the final restraint to the knuckle and is anchored on the forward suspension frame. To inhibit roll at the front of the vehicle, a continuous crooked bar couples the radius arms on left and right front suspensions. The anti-roll bar is retained to the forward subframe by two clamps and rubber bushes.

The whole design is simple and effective and is very easy to maintain. All vital components are easily accessed and because there are only three load paths, there is a minimum of components liable to wear and necessitating inspection.

As mentioned earlier in this Chapter, the surface condition of suspension members is very important. Rust can lead to cracks into the material and structural failure. It is good policy to keep suspension members as clean and rust free as possible.

9 Front suspension shock absorbers and springs - removal and refitting

1 The front shock absorbers are part of the MacPherson strut in the front suspension. Removal is straightforward and proceeds as follows:
2 Raise the front of the car onto chassis stands placed beneath the suspension subframe, and then remove the front roadwheels.
3 Refer to Chapter 9, and seal the brake system fluid reservoir so that liquid loss is minimised when the fixed brake pipe is detached from the base of the shock absorber/strut, and the flexible brake hose is also detached from the same strut.
4 Undo and remove the bolt which locks the knuckle to the base of the strut. Then hold the knuckle assembly whilst giving the top of the knuckle taps with a medium hammer. The knuckle is to be urged off the base of the strut (Fig. 8.11).
5 Once the strut has been freed from the knuckle, undo the three nuts which retain the upper end of the strut/absorber to the bodyshell. Lower the strut/absorber from the car.
6 It is necessary to have special equipment to separate the shock absorber, spring and upper strut members (Fig. 8.12). The tools required are Honda No. 07959 and 6340000.

7 The task should really be entrusted to your nearest Honda dealer.

8 It is also necessary to renew shock absorbers and/or the springs in pairs; that is the front pair or the rear pair. The car's handling may be dangerously affected if the shock absorbers have slightly different characteristics due to their different states of wear.

9 Refitting follows the reversal of the removal procedure. Remember to bleed the brakes when it has all been assembled. Ensure that fasteners are tightened to the correct torques.

10 Front suspension lower control arm, radius arm and anti-roll bar - removal, renovation and refitting

1 The lower control arm comprises a major member which is retained on the rearward front suspension subframe, and a minor arm - stabiliser (radius arm) - which is retained on the forward subframe. The two members are not separable, and the rubbers built into the ends of the two arms at the anchored ends are not removable.

2 Removal of the lower control arm proceeds as follows: Raise the car onto chassis stands placed beneath the suspension subframes. Remove the roadwheels.

3 Support the front wheel hub, whilst removing the control arm ball joint from the base of the knuckle member.

4 Extract the split pin which locks the nut on the ball joint pin, then undo and remove the pin. (photo)

5 Use special tool No. 07941 - 6340000 to remove the ball pin and remove the pin from the knuckle.

6 Next remove the anti-roll bar, by undoing the bolts which retain the middle brackets to the front subframe and then the

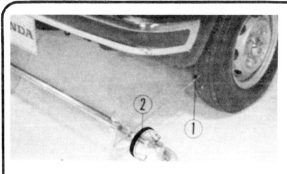

Fig 8.9 Measuring Toe-in of wheels (Sec 6)

1 Tyre centre at hub height   2 Measuring probe

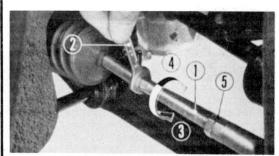

Fig 8.10 Adjustment of Toe-in on tie-rod (Sec 6)

1 Tie-rod
2 Spanner
3 Increase Toe-in
4 Decrease
5 Outer ball joint lock-nut

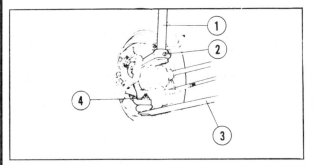

Fig 8.11 Front suspension detail (Sec 9)

1 Shock absorber
2 Lock bolt
3 Lower arm
4 Ball joint nut

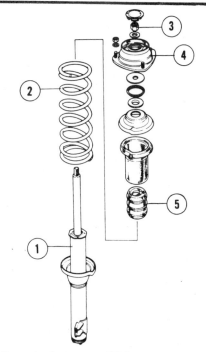

Fig 8.12 Front shock absorber - MacPherson strut detail (Sec 9)

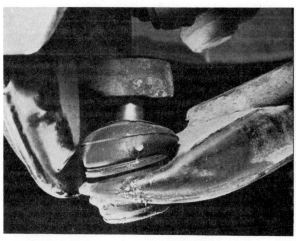

10.4 Removal of lower arm ball pin from knuckle

band and bushing to the radius arm between the front subframe and major lower control arm.

7   Once the anti-roll bar has been removed, undo and remove the nut and rubber bushes which secure the radius rods to brackets on the front subframe.

8   Finally undo and remove the pivot bolt at the anchorage of the major lower control arm.

Lower control arm ball joint and pivot bushing

9   The ball joint cannot be separated from the arm, so that when wear is found the arm/ball joint assembly should be replaced.

10 The pivot bushing is an interference fit in the end of the control arm. Use a broad cylindrical drift to force the bushing from the arm if its condition is suspect.

11 Reassembly follows the reversal of the removal procedure. Pay particular attention to the following:

    i)   The condition of the lower arm ball joint seal
    ii) The tightening torques of the pivot bolts, anti-roll bar bolts, radius arm nut and the ball joint pin nut
    iii) Use a new split pin to lock the ball pin hub

11 Rear suspension - general description

The rear suspension is conceptually the same as the front. The wheel hub is held on the base of the MacPherson strut which incorporates the shock absorber and spring. The movement of the base strut and hence the wheel is controlled by a lower control arm and a radius rod (Fig. 8.13).

The construction of the strut is very similar to that used in the front suspension, and as with the front struts the dismantling of the strut requires special tools and should really be entrusted to the nearest Honda dealer.

12 Rear strut shock absorber - removal and refitting

1   The removal of the strut shock absorber proceeds as follows: raise the rear of the car onto chassis stands and remove the roadwheels.

2   Seal the brake system fluid reservoir, as described in Chapter 9, to minimise liquid loss when the fixed brake pipe and brake hose are detached from the lower end of the MacPherson strut.

3   Once the brake pipes have been detached, disconnect the parking brake cable from the rear drum brake.

4   Next undo and remove the bolts which secure the absorber/strut to the wheel axle member and lower control arm. Note that the nut on the bolt which retains the axle member and strut in the lower control arm is locked by a split pin.

5   Lower the wheel axle member and drum so that the absorber strut is extracted upwards. Then undo the two nuts which secure the top of the strut to the bodyshell.

6   Remove the absorber/strut assembly from the car.

7   Dismantling the strut requires the same tool detailed for the front strut - and the same advice applies. The dismantling task should only be attempted with the special tool, preferably the job should be entrusted to the nearest Honda dealer (Fig. 8.14).

8   Refitting the strut assembly follows the reversal of the removal procedures, and the following tasks should be included:

9   The brake system should be bled, when the shock absorber/strut has been installed, ensure all fastenings have been tightened to the correct torques, and locked with split pins as necessary. Tighten the lower bolts to their specified torque when the car is standing on level ground.

13 Rear suspension control arm and radius arm - removal and refitting

1   The removal of the lower control arm and radius rod proceeds as follows: Raise the rear of the car onto chassis stands

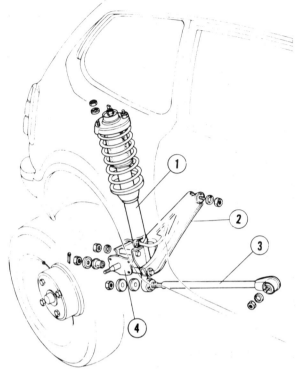

Fig 8.13 Rear suspension (Sec 11)

1   Rear shock absorber - Mac-   3   Radius arm
    Pherson strut   4   Rear hub carrier
2   Lower control arm

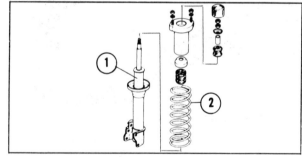

Fig 8.14 Rear shock absorber - MacPherson Strut detail (Sec 12)

1   Shock absorber   2   Spring

Fig 8.15 Adjustment of rear wheel Toe-in (Sec 14)

1   Rear radius rod   3   Nut
2   Self-locking nut

and remove the roadwheels.

2 Remove the split-pin which locks the lower arm outer pivot bolt, undo and remove the nut and extract the pivot bolt from the base of the strut and control arm bushes. Support the wheel hub assembly.

3 Now undo and remove the inner control arm pivot nut and bolt.

4 The control arm can now be removed from the car, and transferred to a bench for cleaning and inspection.

5 The radius arm can be removed after the anchorage pivot bolt has been removed and the self-lock nut removed from the hub end of the radius arm. Note that the effective length of the radius arm is adjustable to allow the toe-in of the rear wheels to be adjusted. The radius arm should not be removed therefore, unless absolutely necessary.

6 Inspect the control arm bushings and radius rod rubbers; if any are cracked or show signs of deterioration they should be replaced. Clean away all rust and apply rust proofer and paint to affected parts. Take particular care to clean the radius rod end threads, it may be difficult otherwise to move the nuts on the radius rod to adjust the rear wheel toe-in.

7 Refitting the control arm and radius arm follows the reversal of the removal procedures, except that the following tasks are included:

  i)   Tighten the pivot nuts and bolts to their specified torques when the car is standing on level ground - un-laden.

  ii)   Check the alignment - toe-in - of the rear wheels.

14 Rear wheel alignment - checking and adjustment

1 It is only possible to check toe-in with simple equipment, and even then the standard of adjustment is only really good enough to allow the car to be driven to the nearest specialist automobile workshop who have the equipment to check and adjust the alignment accurately.

2 Toe-in is adjusted by turning the self-locking nuts on the hub end of the radius arm (Fig 8.15). The toe-in dimension is the difference in distance measured at hub level between the tread centres of the front edge of the tyres and then the rear edges of the tyre.

15 Fault diagnosis - shock absorbers

1 The shock absorbers can be reckoned to need renewal if any one or more of the following symptoms or characteristics are found when observations are made:

  i)   Wheel vibration even when the wheels have been balanced.

  ii)   The vehicle 'floats' on the suspension and pitches and/or rolls in an unrestrained manner.

  iii) When the car is pushed down systematically at each corner, the car rebounds on the suspension, or returns to its normal position very slowly. If the absorbers are in reasonable condition the car should return to its normal rest position swiftly with the minimum of over-shoot/rebound.

Chapter 9 Braking system

Contents

Specifications

Type	Disc brake; drum brake on early models
Front brakes	Drum brake on early models
Rear brakes	Drum brakes

Front disc brakes

Pad area	20 sq. cm (3.1 sq. in)
Pad thickness	10.33 mm (0.4 inches) new
Service limit	2 mm (0.080 inches)
Disc thickness	9.6 mm (0.378 inches)
Service limit	9.0 mm (0.354 inches)
Disc face runout (max.)	0.15 mm (0.0059 inches)
Disc face parallelism limit	0.07 mm (0.0028 inches)

Drum brakes

Brake lining thickness	5.0 mm (0.2 inches)
Limit	2.0 mm (0.08 inches)
Brake drum internal diameter	180 mm (7.086 inches)
Limit	181 mm (7.126 inches)
Slave cylinders - bore to piston clearance (maximum) ...	0.13 mm (0.005 inches)

Master cylinder

Bore to piston clearance (maximum)	0.13 mm (0.005 inches)

Handbrake system

Correct operating point	1 to 5 notches on lever

Brake pedal

Height from floor	134.6 mm (5.3 inches)
Free-play	1 to 5 mm (0.004 to 0.2 inches)

Hydraulic fluid type	SAE J1703 or DOT 3, 4.
Brake servo unit	Actuated by Inlet Manifold Vacuum Pressure

Torque wrench settings

	kg f m	lbs f ft
Brake/clutch pedal bracket	4.0 - 5.0	29 - 36
Master cylinder to bulkhead	1.5 - 2.0	11 - 14
Parking brake lever	1.9 - 2.5	14 - 18
Caliper set bolt	5.0 - 6.0	36 - 43
Bleed screw	0.5 - 0.7	4 - 5
Parking brake equaliser	1.9 - 2.5	14 - 18
Two-way joint	0.7 - 1.2	5 - 9
Three-way joint	0.7 - 1.2	5 - 9
Brake pedal 'stop' switch	0.7 - 1.2	5 - 9
Brake pipe flare nut	1.3 - 1.5	9 - 11

1 General description

The braking system on the Honda Civic is a dual servo assisted hydraulic system acting on disc brakes at the front and drum brakes at the rear.

Some early models of the Civic were fitted with a single, non-assisted hydraulic system acting on drum brakes at both front and rear. Maintenance and repair tasks on both systems are described in this Chapter.

On all models of the Civic the parking handbrake operates the rear brakes only by an independent mechanical linkage.

Manual adjustment of the friction shoe positions in each rear drum brake and front drum brake is necessary to compensate for wear of the shoe linings. The adjustment of the rear brakes also affects the adjustment of the handbrake, although there is a separate adjustment on the parking brake system to accommodate wear in the mechanical linkage.

Disc brakes compensate for wear of friction material automatically.

Finally the brake light switch is attached to a bracket adjacent to the brake pedal and registers any movement of the pedal.

2 Routine maintenance

1 It cannot be emphasised too much that diligent inspection and maintenance of the braking system is essential to retain your safety in the car.

2 *Every week* remove the hydraulic fluid cap(s) and check the level of fluid which should be just in the 'max' mark on the side of the reservoir. Check that the vent hole in the cap is clear. Any need for regular topping-up, regardless of quantity. should be viewed with suspicion, and the whole braking hydraulic system should be inspected for signs of leakage.

3 *Every 3,000 miles or 3 months, whichever sooner, closely* examine all the flexible brake hoses, and hose connections. Use a mirror to inspect all parts of the hose, and remember to move the flexible hose so that cracks or other surface deterioration will be revealed. Replace any hoses which are not in anything but perfect condition, immediately. There is no way of knowing how dangerous a crack in a hose is.

Inspect all fixed metal brake pipes for corrosion and surface deterioration. These pipes are stressed by the fluid pressure in the braking system. Any corrosion on the outer surface can generate and propagate cracks in the metal which will lead ultimately to the sudden failure of the pipe.

Finally check the adjustment of the rear drum brakes and lubricate the adjuster **every time.**

4 *Every 6,000 miles, the thickness of friction material on both front and rear brake mechanisms should be checked.* The capability of the friction material to withstand heat is dependent on the thickness of the friction material on the brake pad or shoe. If the material has worn too thin, there is a risk that the material will disintegrate when hot with the consequent loss of braking

On the front disc brake pads, the thickness of the friction material should not fall below 2mm.

On the front drum brakes if fitted, and on all rear drum brakes, the thickness of the friction material on the brake shoes should not fall below 2mm if the shoe linings are bonded.

Alternatively, if the linings are rivetted to the shoes, the friction material thickness should not be allowed to fall below the point when the rivet heads begin to be worn.

Never interchange worn shoes or pads to even out wear, try and determine the reason for the uneven wear.

Lubricate and examine the parking brake linkage.

5 *Every 18 months to 2 years (24,000 miles)* it is necessary to renew the hydraulic fluid in the braking system. The fluid should prevent corrosion within the braking system and withstand the high temperatures experienced in the slave cylinders in the brake mechanisms. The condition of the fluid in the brake pipes and slave cylinders deteriorates in time and old fluid is liable to boil when the brakes are in hard usage. The vapour in the brake lines will lead to inconsistency of braking effort.

6 It is good practice every 24,000 miles to replace seals and hoses in the brake system as a 'preventative' maintenance.

7 If you have just acquired a secondhand car, it is strongly recommended that the whole brake system, drums, shoes, discs, pads, hoses, pipes, slave and master cylinders, are thoroughly examined. Even though the effectiveness of the braking system may be excellent, the friction materials may be near the end of their useful life, and it will be as well to know this without delay.

The hydraulic lines, cylinders and flexible pipes should be carefully examined for leaks and chafing. Faults should be rectified immediately.

3 Brake adjustment - front and rear drums

1 It should be appreciated that the state of adjustment of the brakes affects the amount of movement of the brake pedal when they are applied. Whenever the pedal travel becomes excessive, adjust the brakes as follows:

Front drums
2 The front brakes are fitted with two slave cylinders - one for each shoe. Shoe position adjustment is facilitated by pivot screws on each slave cylinder. Access to these two screws is gained through a hole in the side of the brake drum.

3 Jack the front wheels off the ground, and chock the rear wheels so that it is safe to operate the brakes inside the car. Depress the brake pedal several times.

4 Then reaching through the wheel and drum holes, turn the adjuster screws clockwise equally until the wheel will no longer turn.

5 Now back off the adjuster by 4 clicks and press the brake pedal down two or three times.

6 Turn the drum/wheel again and feel for any drag of brake shoes - if there is drag, turn back the adjuster screw one more click.

7 Repeat the above procedure for both front brakes and then proceed to check the adjustment of the rear brakes.

Rear drums
8 The rear brakes operate from a single slave cylinder and the shoe position adjustment is accomplished at the lower common pivot point. Both shoes pivot in a block at the base of the brake mechanism, the pivot geometry is altered by a tapered head bolt.

9 Jack-up the rear wheels and chock the front wheels so that it is safe to operate the brakes inside the car. Press the brake pedal several times and then check that the wheels are free to turn.

10 Use a standard adjuster screw socket to turn the screw clockwise until the wheels no longer turn, and then back off the adjuster by two clicks. Press the brake pedals several times, and then check that the wheels are free to turn. (photo)

If the brake shoes are felt to be dragging on the drum, turn the adjuster screw back by one more 'click'.

11 Once the brakes have been adjusted, the brake pedal and handbrake should require only a relatively small movement to operate the brakes.

4 Disc brake pads - removal, inspection and refitting

1 The front brake disc pads can easily be seen, once the road-wheel is removed. There is sufficient space to check the friction material thickness without having to remove the pads. Generally the pads should only need to be renewed if either the existing ones have worn too thin, or have become contaminated with oil or grease.

2 The procedure for the removal of the disc brake pads is as follows:

Jack-up the appropriate suspension and remove the road-wheel.

3.10 The rear brake adjustment tool

4.3 Removal of pad pin retaining clip

4.4 Removal of pad pin

4.5 Removal of pad and shim

4.10 Disc pads properly installed

Fig 9.1 Rear piston and piston guide removed from the slave cylinder block (Secs 5 & 6)

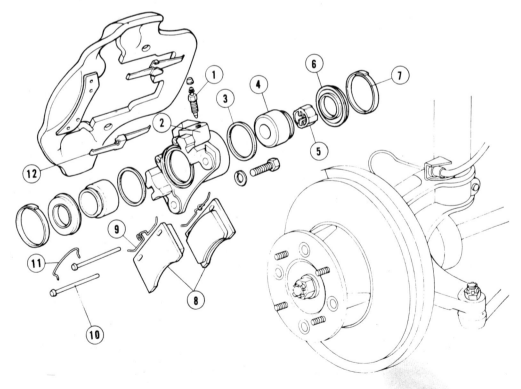

Fig 9.2 Exploded view of the front disc brake components (Secs 5 & 6)

1 Bleeder screw	4 Piston	7 Retaining ring	10 Pad retaining pin
2 Cylinder	5 Bias ring	8 Pad set	11 Pad retaining clip
3 Piston seal	6 Boot	9 Pad spring	12 Yoke spring

3 Then remove the brake pad retaining clip with a pair of pliers. (photo)
4 Extract the two pad retaining pins and recover the two pad springs. (photo)
5 Once the retaining pins have been removed, the two pads can be pulled from between the disc and caliper. Recover the backing shims and note the position from which they came: it is essential that they are refitted in their proper positions. (photo)
6 Now measure the thickness of the friction material on the pads, and examine the surfaces of the pad, looking for black polished areas which betray oil contamination.
7 If the pads need replacing - replace all four pads on the front brakes.
8 While you have the brake disc exposed it is a good opportunity to inspect the disc for scores and excessive wear.
9 Check the thickness of the disc and replace the disc if it has worn below the service limit given in Specification at the beginning of this Chapter.
10 Refitting of the disc pads follows the reversal of the removal sequence. (photo)
11 If new brake pads are being fitted, the slave pistons will need to be pushed *gently* back into its cylinder in the caliper block, to provide a sufficient gap between the pistons and the disc to accommodate the new pads.

It is as well to remember that as the pistons are moved back into the caliper block, brake fluid will be displaced and returned to the master cylinder reservoir.

The reservoir will overflow, unless fluid is taken out with a device such as a pipette, as the slave pistons are moved.

5 Disc brake slave cylinder and yoke - removal and refitting

1 The front disc brake comprises the following main components:

(i) The slave cylinder block, which has a single bore housing two opposing pistons
(ii) A pressed steel yoke
(iii) Brake pads and retaining systems (Fig. 9.2)

2 The slave cylinder block is bolted to the knuckle on the front suspension. The pistons move in opposite directions, but the one furthest from the brake disc acts on to the yoke plate to effect the required 'pinching' action of the friction pads on the brake disc.
3 Proceed to remove the cylinder and yoke assembly as follows:

Jack-up the appropriate lower suspension arm and remove the roadwheel. Remove the disc pads as detailed in Section 4, of this Chapter.
4 Working inside the engine compartment, remove the cap on the appropriate brake fluid reservoir and stretch a thin sheet of polythene over the top of the reservoir. Refit the cap. This measure will prevent excessive loss of brake fluid when brake pipe connections are subsequently undone.
5 Returning to the disc brake assembly, hold the lower end of the flexible brake hose so that the fixed pipe fitting can be unscrewed. Remove the steel clip which retains the flexible hose in the bracket on the base of the MacPherson strut, and extract the flexible pipe from the bracket.
6 It is not necessary, but it is possible at this stage, to remove the fixed brake pipe from the slave cylinder block. If you do remove it, plug the threaded orifice to prevent ingress of foreign matter into the slave cylinder.
7 Once the brake pipe connections have been undone, proceed to undo and remove the two bolts which secure the slave cylinder and yoke to the knuckle member of the front suspension.
8 Once the two bolts have been removed, the cylinder/yoke assembly may be lifted clear to a bench for further work if necessary.
9 Refitting the cylinder and yoke assembly follows the exact

reversal of the removal procedure, except that the following tasks are added:
10 Once the cylinder/yoke assembly has been refitted, the pads refitted and brake pipes reconnected - the brake system should be bled as detailed in Section 16, of this Chapter.
11 Remember to tighten the slave cylinder/knuckle bolts to the torque recommended at the beginning of this Chapter.

6 Disc brake slave cylinder and yoke - dismantling, inspection renovation and reassembly

1 Once the slave cylinder and yoke assembly has been removed as detailed in the previous Section (5) of this Chapter, place the assembly on a clean bench for overhaul.
2 The first task is to remove the yoke plate from around the slave cylinder. Move the yoke plate towards the rear - that is inboard side of the slave cylinder - so that the cylinder block can be extracted from the aperture usually occupied by the disc and brake pads.
The rear of the yoke should have disengaged from the piston guide inside the rear piston
3 Now, very gently, prise the piston/cylinder dust covers off each end of the cylinder assembly. Use a wooden or plastic spatula to unseat the seal, a screwdriver will most probably break and damage the seal.
4 All that remains now is to pull the two pistons from the slave cylinder with your fingers. Do not use pliers or similar metal tools or else the surface of the piston will be damaged. If the pistons are tough to remove, temporarily reconnect the slave cylinder to the vehicle brake hydraulic system. Then remove the polythene from the reservoir, so that the pistons may be pumped or forced out by hydraulic pressure.
5 Alternatively, blow compressed air into the hydraulic inlet port in the slave cylinder to impell the pistons out of the cylinder.
6 Once the pistons have been removed - all that remains is to remove the seals from insdie the cylinder bore. Again use a wooden or plastic spatula to unseat the seals: a metal tool will damage the surface of the bore. The seals should not be re-used once the slave pistons have been extracted from the cylinder.
7 Now that the slave cylinder assembly has been fully dismantled, wash all parts thoroughly in either methylated spirits or clean new brake fluid. Do not use any other solvents because any remains of non-recommended solvents could swell the piston seals and jam the piston in the cylinder.
8 Inspect the cylinder bores for scoring and wear, and replace the slave cylinder block if wear is found. Examine the surfaces of pistons, watch for corrosion and scoring; if any corrosion or scoring is found on the outer surfaces of the piston, the piston should be replaced.
9 Check the yoke springs and the various clips and springs; if any are corroded and pitted, the appropriate items should be replaced. The disc brake operates and creates a harsh environment and small metal components can easily break if they are in anything but good condition.
10 To reassemble the slave cylinder and yoke assembly, wet all seals in clean brake fluid. Insert the new 'O' ring seals into their grooves in the slave cylinder bore.
11 Then refit the new dust seals to each piston. Coat the exterior surfaces of the pistons and gently ease the pistons into the slave cylinder. When fully inserted refit the dust seals to the rims of the slave cylinder.
12 Insert the rear piston/yoke guide into the rear piston, and fit the yoke springs onto the edges which engage the slave cylinder block. (Fig. 9.2).
13 Insert the cylinder block into the yoke plate and slide into position into the rear end of the plate so that the plate tongue engages the rear piston guide.
14 The slave cylinder yoke assembly is now ready to be refitted to the front knuckle member on the suspension. Refer to Sections 4 and 5, for refitting details.

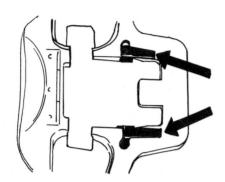

Fig 9.3 Yoke springs in position on the yoke plate (Secs 5 & 6)

Fig 9.4 Disc (1) and wheel hub (2) fastening arrangement (Sec 6)

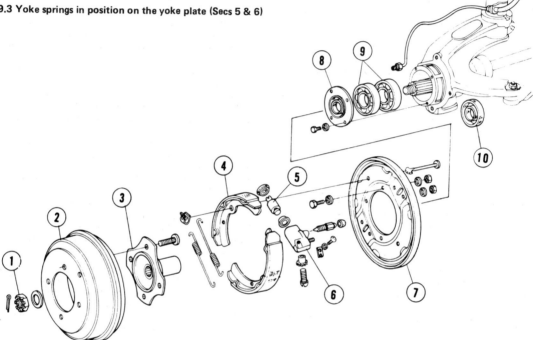

Fig 9.5 Exploded view of the front drum brake (Sec 7)

1 Spindle nut
2 Front brake drum
3 Front hub
4 Brake shoe
5 Front piston

6 Front cylinder
7 Front back plate
8 Front bearing dust seal B
9 Front wheel bearings
10 Front bearing dust seal A

Fig 9.6 Rear brake adjuster block components (Sec 7)

1 Brake adjuster
2 Adjuster bolt

3 Brake adjuster pin

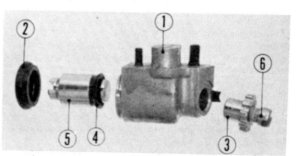

Fig 9.7 Front drum brake slave cylinder components (Sec 8)

1 Front wheel cylinder
2 Dust cover
3 Wheel adjuster

4 Front piston cup
5 Front piston
6 Adjusting screw

7 Drum brake shoes - removal, inspection and refitting

1   Jack-up the car and remove the roadwheel from the brake to be examined. Chock the wheels at the opposite end of the car, and release the handbrake if you are working on the rear brakes.
2   Remove the roadwheel, and then slacken off the adjusters on that brake.
3   *Rear drum brakes:* Remove the brake drum after removing the bearing cap, stub axle nut and split pin. A sharp tug should be all that is required to free the drum/hub unit from the brake assembly.
4   *Front drum brakes:* the drum is held on by the roadwheel and once the wheel has been removed, the drum can be removed without undoing any more fasteners.
5   Once the brake drum has been removed, the brake shoes are fully exposed and can be inspected. (photo - rear brakes)
    Examine the friction lines for signs of oil/grease contamination (black glazed areas), and check the thickness of the linings. Refer to the Specification at the beginning of this Chapter for the minimum thickness of brake shoe lining permitted.
6   Examine the inside surfaces of the brake drum and watch for scoring and excessive wear. Again refer to the Specification at the beginning of this Chapter for major dimensions and limits for wear.
7   Always brush all the braking dust from the drum and brake assembly before reassembly or shoe removal.

8   If a drum is badly worn, it should be renewed, and often a perfectly satisfactory replacement may be obtained from a breaker's yard. It is no use having drums turned up on a lathe, because the rubbing surface radius will be altered to an extent

7.5 The rear brake shoes and slave cylinder exposed

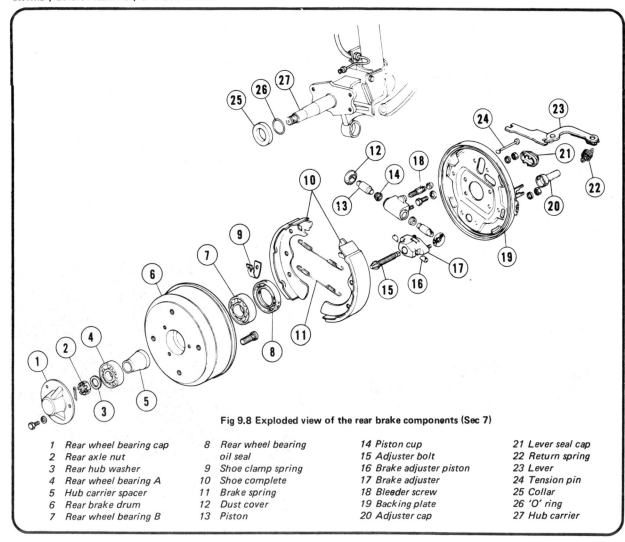

Fig 9.8 Exploded view of the rear brake components (Sec 7)

1 Rear wheel bearing cap	8 Rear wheel bearing oil seal	14 Piston cup	21 Lever seal cap
2 Rear axle nut	9 Shoe clamp spring	15 Adjuster bolt	22 Return spring
3 Rear hub washer	10 Shoe complete	16 Brake adjuster piston	23 Lever
4 Rear wheel bearing A	11 Brake spring	17 Brake adjuster	24 Tension pin
5 Hub carrier spacer	12 Dust cover	18 Bleeder screw	25 Collar
6 Rear brake drum	13 Piston	19 Backing plate	26 'O' ring
7 Rear wheel bearing B		20 Adjuster cap	27 Hub carrier

when standard shoes will not match properly.

Front and rear brake shoes - removal and refitting
9 Having inspected the brake shoes and decided on replacing the shoes, proceed as follows: (Fig. 9.5 and Fiq 9.8).

> a) *Remove the mid-shoe retaining pins. It will be necessary to compress the steel clip on the shoe to allow the 'T' ended pin to be turned through 90⁰ and permit removal of the pin.*
> b) *Take a particular note of the position and orientation of the two shoe return springs.*
> c) *Use a screwdriver to lever one of the shoes off the slave cylinder pistons, and once clear, remove both shoes with springs still in position.*

10 Before fitting new shoes check that the brake slave cylinder(s) is securely bolted to the brake backplate. Also check that the pistons in the brake cylinder move freely, and that there are no fluid leaks.
 The rubber boots on the ends of the cylinder should be clean and renewed if there are any breaks or splits in the rubber.
11 Finally, handle the new shoes with clean hands and tools to prevent contaminating the new linings.
12 The refitting of the brake shoes follows the reversal of the removal procedure. Be careful if you use a screwdriver or something similar to ease the shoes back around the actuating cylinders next to the backplate, so as not to damage the brake linings or the rubber boots on the slave cylinders.
13 The refitting procedure is as follows:

> a) *Turn the adjusters back to the minimum throw position.*
> b) *Couple the shoes with the lower spring first and position the shoes around the lower slave cylinder (front) or brake adjuster (rear).*
> c) *Fit the forward shoe into the slave cylinder and hold in position with the mid-position retainer clip and pin.*
> d) *On the rear brakes, ensure that the handbrake lever and push-plate is in position, and then refit the upper inter-shoe spring and pull or lever the rearward shoe into position on the slave cylinder.*
> e) *Secure the rear shoe with the mid-position retaining pin.*

14 Once the shoes are back into position, visually position the shoes so that the linings are concentric with the wheel axle and backing plate.
15 Refit the drum and in the case of the rear brake, the drum and hub are combined and hence it will be necessary to tighten the hub bearings nut to the recommended torque and lock it with a split pin.

16 In the case of the front drum it is necessary to fit the roadwheel as well. Ensure that the adjuster access holes in the drum and wheel are aligned to permit subsequent adjustment of the brakes.
17 Press the brake pedal a few times to align the shoes onto the drums and then adjust the brakes as detailed in Section 3, of this Chapter.
18 If the brake pedal feels spongy, bleed the brakes as detailed in Section 16, of this Chapter.
19 Check the adjustment of the brakes after several hundred miles motoring, because the shoe linings - particularly if rivetted to the shoe - need to bed in.

8 Drum brake slave cylinders - removal, inspection, renovation and reassembly

1 The wheel slave cylinders on the front and rear drum brakes dismantle and reassemble in the same manner. The cylinders in the rear brakes have two opposing pistons, whilst the front cylinders have single pistons. (Figs. 9.7 and 9.9).
2 If it is suspected that one, or more, of the wheel slave cylinders is malfunctioning, jack-up the suspected wheel and remove the brake drum as detailed in Section 7, of this Chapter.
3 Inspect for signs of fluid leakage around the wheel cylinder, and if there is any, proceed to paragraph 6, of this Section.
4 Next get someone to press the brake pedal very gently and a small distance (engine not running).
5 Watch the wheel slave cylinder and check whether the pistons move out a little. On no account let them come right out or the slave cylinder assembly will have to be reassembled and the brake system bled.
 On releasing the brake pedal, make sure that the retraction of springs on the shoes moves the pistons back without delay. If both pistons move, all is well; but if only one piston moves, only one shoe has been effective and repair is necessary.
6 If there is a hydraulic fluid leakage, or the piston does not move (or only moves a little under pressure), then the piston seals will need renewal at the very least.
7 Begin by removing the brake shoes as detailed in Section 7 of this Chapter, then remove the fluid reservoir cap(s) and stretch a thin sheet of polythene over the reservoir and refit the cap(s). This measure will prevent excessive loss of hydraulic fluid when hydraulic connections are subsequently undone.
8 Unscrew the fixed brake pipe from the rear of the brake slave cylinders, cover the end of the pipe to prevent ingress of foreign matter into the pipe. (photo)
9 Remove the cylinder from the backing plate by undoing the two screws from the rear side of the backing plate. Once the

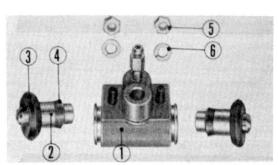

Fig 9.9 Rear brake slave cylinder components (Sec 8)

1 *Rear wheel cylinder*   4 *Piston cup*
2 *Piston*   5 *Attaching nut*
3 *Dust cover*   6 *Spring washer*

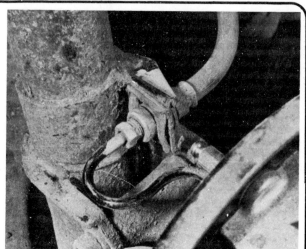

8.8 The fixed brake pipe from strut to slave cylinder on rear brakes

fixing screws have been removed, lift the cylinder assembly from the backing plate.

10 Work on a clean bench, and pull out the pistons from the cylinder, complete with seals (and springs if fitted). Discard the seals - they should not be reused.

11 Wash the pistons and cylinders in methylated spirits or clean brake fluid. Examine the piston and cylinder for signs of wear or scoring and if there are any, the whole assembly should be replaced. If the piston and cylinder are in good condition only new seals need be fitted.

12 Soak new seals in clean hydraulic fluid and refit the piston seals so that the lip faces away from the centre of the piston. Coat the piston with hydraulic fluid as it is eased back into the cylinder. Refit the dust seals and then bolt the cylinder back onto the backplate.

13 Recouple the fixed brake pipe to the slave cylinder then refit the brake shoes as detailed in Section 7, of this Chapter.

14 Fit the brake drum and bleed the brakes as detailed in Section 16, of this Chapter.

15 Finally check the adjustment of the brake shoes.

9 Master cylinder - removal and replacement

1 Two patterns of master cylinder have been fitted to the Honda Civic. On early models, fitted with drum brakes on all four wheels, a single piston master cylinder was fitted. It was coupled directly to the brake pedal and no servo unit was fitted. Later models were fitted with disc brakes at the front and drum brakes at the rear - a tandem piston master cylinder was fitted which was coupled to the brake pedal via a servo unit. (Figs. 9.10 and 9.11).

2 The technique for removing the master cylinder whether single or tandem is basically the same.

3 Remove the reservoir cap(s) and cover the reservoir with a thin sheet of polythene and refit the cap. This measure will prevent an excessive loss of fluid when the hydraulic connections are subsequently undone.

4 Unscrew the hydraulic pipe connections to the master cylinder and move the metal pipes away a little to permit removal of the master cylinder.

5 Finally undo the two nuts which secure the master cylinder to the servo or bulkhead as appropriate.

6 A single push rod protruding from the servo unit actuates the tandem master cylinder. Therefore, once the two nuts securing the tandem cylinder to the servo have been removed, the cylinder assembly can simply be lifted clear.

7 When the single master cylinder is fitted, it cannot be removed until the pin retaining the piston pushrod to the brake pedal has been removed. The pushrod is retained in the master cylinder by a plate and circlip, and cannot be removed until the master cylinder assembly is on the workbench.

8 Refitting the master cylinder follows the reversal of the removal procedure, except that the whole brake system must be bled before the car is taken on the road. (Section 16, of this Chapter).

10 Master cylinder - dismantling, inspection, renovation and reassembly

1 The overhaul of the tandem master cylinder is described here; the single piston version is very much simpler and is accomplished in the same manner. (Figs. 9.10 and 9.11).

2 Begin by draining the reservoirs and then remove the fluid reservoirs from the master cylinder. Then unscrew the primary piston travel stop bolt.

3 Once the travel stop bolt has been removed, remove the circlip in the end of the cylinder and lift the clip and piston plate out of the cylinder.

4 Shake out the secondary piston and then the primary piston. It may be necessary to feed a little compressed air into the cylinder fluid outlets to encourage the pistons out of the cylinder.

5 Finally unscrew the outlet union fittings and recover the check valves and springs.

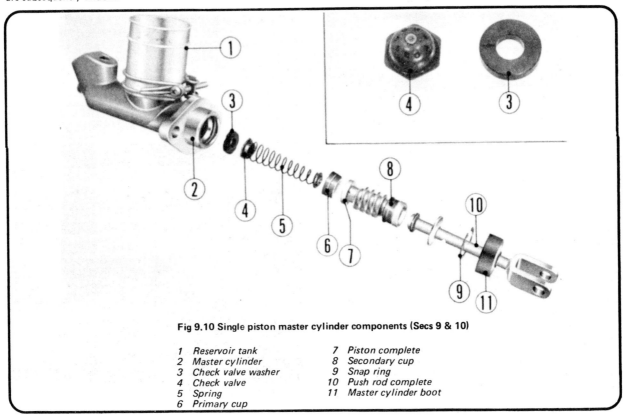

Fig 9.10 Single piston master cylinder components (Secs 9 & 10)

1 Reservoir tank	7 Piston complete
2 Master cylinder	8 Secondary cup
3 Check valve washer	9 Snap ring
4 Check valve	10 Push rod complete
5 Spring	11 Master cylinder boot
6 Primary cup	

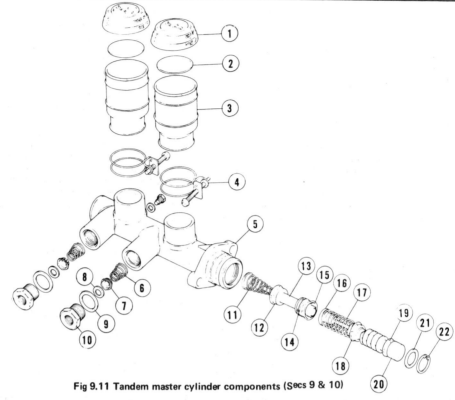

Fig 9.11 Tandem master cylinder components (Secs 9 & 10)

1 Cap	7 Check valve	13 Primary piston	19 Secondary cup
2 Float	8 Check valve washer	14 Wiper ring	20 Secondary piston
3 Reservoir tank	9 Packing	15 Piston cup	21 Stopper plate
4 Reservoir tank crip	10 Union cap	16 Secondary stopper	22 Snap ring
5 Master cylinder body	11 Primary spring	17 Secondary spring	
6 Check valve spring	12 Piston cup	18 Piston cup	

6 Now that the master cylinder has been dismantled, clean all parts in methylated spirits or clean hydraulic fluid.

7 Inspect the surfaces of the pistons and cylinder bores. Replace the whole assembly if wear or scores are found on any of the parts. Discard all seals, none should be re-used.

8 Once all parts have been cleaned and inspected, gather them together for reassembly.Soak the new seals in clean hydraulic fluid. Coat the pistons and cylinder bores in clean fluid.

9 Begin reassembly by slipping the seals onto the ends of the primary piston and secondary piston. Note the orientation of the seal cup lips. The primary piston cups face in opposite directions - away from the piston body. The secondary piston cups face towards the primary piston.

10 Now insert the primary piston into the master cylinder - take care not to damage the lips of the seals as the piston is introduced into the cylinder bore, Remember to fit the conical spring in front of the primary piston. Push the piston down into the cylinder and then introduce the secondary piston and the spacing spring and rod.

11 Again take care not to damage the seals as the piston is eased into the cylinder.

Once all the pistons have been inserted, push the stopper plate and fit the circlip to retain them all in the cylinder.

12 Screw the primary piston travel stop bolt, and then the hydraulic union fittings, check valves and springs. Finally fit the reservoirs to the master cylinder.

13 The master cylinder is now ready to be refitted to the servo unit.

14 The single piston master cylinder does not employ a spigot bolt to limit the movement of the piston, instead a circlip and washer is fitted in the end of the cylinder to retain the piston, and the pushrod which is connected to the brake pedal.

Note that the seal cups on the single piston face toward the cylinder end, away from the pushrod.

11 Brake servo unit - description

The vacuum servo unit is fitted into the brake system in series with the master cylinder and brake pedal to provide power assistance to the driver when the brake pedal is depressed. (photo)

The unit operates by vacuum obtained from the induction manifold, and comprises basically a booster diaphragm and a non- return valve.

The servo unit and hydraulic master cylinder are connected

11.1 The brake servo unit

together so that the servo unit push rod acts as the master cylinder pushrod. The driver's braking effort is transmitted through another pushrod to the servo unit piston and its built in control system. (Fig. 9.12)

The servo unit piston does not fit tightly into the cylinder but has a strong diaphragm to keep its periphery in contact with the cylinder wall so assuring an airtight seal between the two parts. The forward chamber is held under vacuum conditions created in the inlet manifold of the engine and during the period when the engine is not in use the controls open a passage to the rear chamber so placing it under vacuum. When the brake pedal is depressed, the vacuum passage to the rear chamber is cut off and the chamber is opened to atmospheric pressure. The consequent rush of air into the rear chamber pushes the servo piston forward into the vacuum chamber and operates the push rod to the master cylinder. The controls are designed so that assistance is given under all conditions. When the brakes are not required, vacuum is re-established in the rear chamber when the brake pedal is released.

Air from the atmosphere passes through a small filter before entering the control valves and rear chamber and it is only this filter that will require periodic attention.

12 Brake servo unit - removal and refitting

1 Refer to Section 9, of this Chapter, and remove the brake master cylinder.
2 Slacken the hose clip and remove the vacuum hose from the inlet manifold and from the union on the forward face of the servo unit.
3 Next remove the small pin that joins the servo pushrod to the pedal lever. Separate the pushrod and pedal lever.
4 The servo is held to the bulkhead by four nuts which are **screwed onto the studs attached to the servo projecting** through to the pedal side of the bulkhead.
5 Undo the four nuts, and lift the vacuum servo unit away. Take it to a clean bench for maintenance tasks.
6 Refitting the brake servo unit follows the reversal of the removal procedure. Remember to use new spring lock washers and tighten nuts and bolts to their appropriate torques.

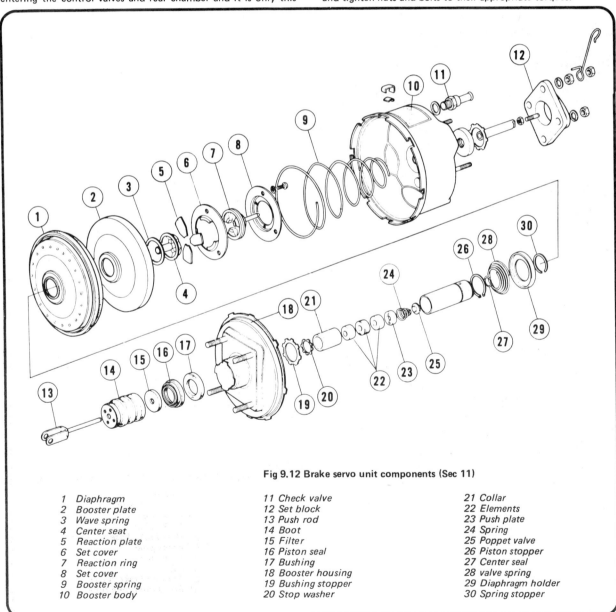

Fig 9.12 Brake servo unit components (Sec 11)

1 Diaphragm	11 Check valve	21 Collar
2 Booster plate	12 Set block	22 Elements
3 Wave spring	13 Push rod	23 Push plate
4 Center seat	14 Boot	24 Spring
5 Reaction plate	15 Filter	25 Poppet valve
6 Set cover	16 Piston seal	26 Piston stopper
7 Reaction ring	17 Bushing	27 Center seal
8 Set cover	18 Booster housing	28 valve spring
9 Booster spring	19 Bushing stopper	29 Diaphragm holder
10 Booster body	20 Stop washer	30 Spring stopper

13 Brake servo unit - maintenance

1 Under normal operating conditions the servo unit is very reliable and does not require overhaul except possibly at very high mileages. In this case it is better to obtain a service exchange unit, rather than repair the original.
2 However, the air filter may need renewal and fitting details are given below.
3 On LH drive cars, where the brake pedal effort is transferred to the servo unit on the right-hand side by a shaft and lever, there is just enough room to reach the air filter which is inside the bellows at the rear of the servo unit.
4 On RH drive cars the area around the servo is more cluttered, with the steering column, accelerator pedal and possibly the clutch pedal close by. Even so it should be possible to reach the filter.
5 In either case, removal of the servo unit will make for easier working and greater access to the unit.
6 Remove the pin jointing the servo pushrod to the brake pedal lever, then still working in the foot well, remove the pushrod, and ease the bellows off the air inlet of the booster.
7 The air filter is retained in the booster by a tag spring washer.

Ease that washer out and draw out the filter. (Fig. 9.13).
8 Replacement of a clean filter is the reversal of removal.

14 Brake effort proportioning valve assembly - general

1 The tandem master cylinder provides for extra reliability of the brake system. Each piston in the tandem master cylinder feeds an equaliser and then a proportioning valve assembly. (Fig 9.14).
2 The slave cylinders in the rear drum brakes and front disc brakes need different hydraulic fluid pressures because of the different forces required on the shoes and pads to effect the proper braking effort on the wheels.
3 The valve assembly is not repairable, and is fortunately simple in design and reliable.
4 Should ever it be necessary to remove the valve assembly, unbolt it from the bodyshell and undo the pipe connections. Make sure that the reservoir caps have been sealed with polythene to minimise loss of fluid when the connections are undone.
5 Refitting is straightforward but bleeding of the brakes will be necessary as detailed in Section 16, of this Chapter.

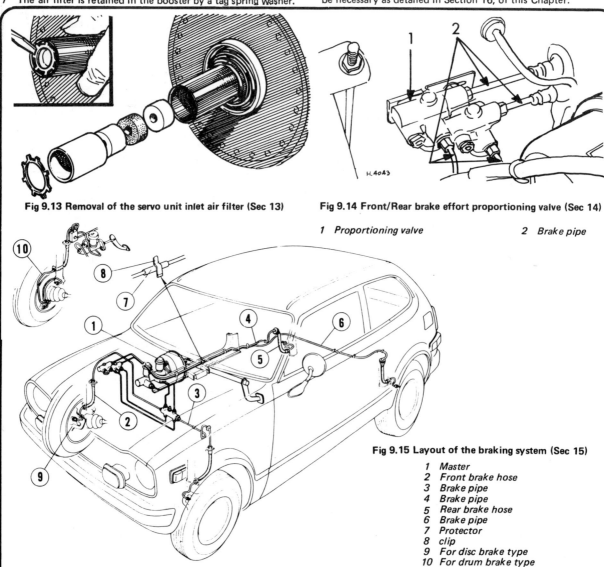

Fig 9.13 Removal of the servo unit inlet air filter (Sec 13)

H.4043

Fig 9.14 Front/Rear brake effort proportioning valve (Sec 14)

1 Proportioning valve　　　　2 Brake pipe

Fig 9.15 Layout of the braking system (Sec 15)

1 Master
2 Front brake hose
3 Brake pipe
4 Brake pipe
5 Rear brake hose
6 Brake pipe
7 Protector
8 clip
9 For disc brake type
10 For drum brake type

15 Hydraulic fluid pipes - inspection, removal and replacement

1 Periodically and certainly well in advance of the MOT Test, (UK) if due, all brake pipes, connections and unions, should be completely and carefully examined. Fig. 9.15 shows the composition of all such pipes and unions in the system.

2 Examine first all the unions for signs of leaks. Then look at the flexible hoses for signs of fraying and chafing (as well as for leaks). This is only a preliminary inspection of the flexible hoses, as exterior condition does not necessarily indicate interior condition which will be considered later.

3 The steel pipes must be examined equally carefully. They must be thoroughly cleaned and examined for signs of dents or other percussive damage, rust and corrosion. Rust and corrosion should be scraped off, and, if the depth of pitting in the pipes is significant, they will need replacement. This is most likely in those areas underneath the chassis and along the rear suspension arms where the pipes are exposed to the full force of road and weather conditions.

4 If any section of pipe is to be removed, first take off the fuel reservoir cap, line it with a piece of polythene film to make it airtight and screw it back on. This will minimise the amount of fluid dripping out of the system when the pipes are removed.

5 Rigid pipe removal is usually quite straightforward. The unions at each end are undone and the pipe drawn out of the connection. The clips which may hold it to the car body are bent back and it is then removed. Underneath the car the exposed union can be particularly stubborn, defying all efforts of an open ended spanner. As few people will have the special split ring spanner required, a self-grip wrench (mole) is the only answer. If the pipe is being renewed, new unions will be provided. If not, then one will have to put up with the possibility of burring over the flats on the union and of using a self-grip wrench for replacement also.

6 Flexible hoses are always fitted to a rigid support bracket where they join a rigid pipe, the bracket being fixed to the chassis or rear suspension arm. The rigid pipe unions must first be removed from the flexible union. Then the locknut securing the flexible pipe to the bracket must be unscrewed, releasing the end of the pipe from the bracket. As these connections are usually exposed they are, more often than not, rusted up and a penetrating fluid is virtually essential to aid removal (try Plus-Gas). When undoing them, both halves must be supported as the bracket is not strong enough to support the torque required to undo the nut and can be snapped off easily.

7 Once the flexible hose is removed, examine the internal bore. If clear of fluid it should be possible to see through it. Any specks of rubber which come out or signs of restriction in the bore, mean that the inner lining is breaking up and the pipe must be replaced.

8 Rigid pipes which need replacement can usually be purchased at your local garage where they have the pipe, unions and special tools to make them up. All that they need to know is the pipe length required and the type of flare used at the ends of the pipe. These may be different at each end of the same pipe. It is a good idea to take the old pipe along as a pattern.

9 Replacement of pipes is a straightforward reversal of the removal procedure. It is best to get all the sets (bends) in the pipe made preparatory to installation. Also any acute bends should be put in by the garage on a bending machine, otherwise there is the possibility of kinking the pipe and restricting the bore area and fluid flow.

10 With the pipes replaced, remove the polythene from the reservoir cap and bleed the system, as described in Section 16.

16 Bleeding the brake system

1 The system should need bleeding only when some part of it has been dismantled which would allow air into the fluid circuit; or if the reservoir level has been allowed to drop so far that air has entered the master cylinder.

2 Ensure that a supply of clean non-aerated fluid of the correct specification is to hand in order to replenish the reservoir during the bleeding process. It is advisable, if not essential, to have someone available to help, as one person has to pump the brake pedal while the other attends to each wheel. The reservoir level also has to be continuously watched and replenished. Fluid bled out should not be re-used. A clean glass jar and a 9 - 12 inch length of 1/8 inch internal diameter rubber tube that will fit tightly over the bleed nipples, is required.

3 Bleed the rear brakes first as these are furthest from the master cylinder.

4 Make sure the bleed nipple is clean and put a small quantity of fluid in the bottom of the jar. Fit the tube onto the nipple and place the other end in the jar under the surface of the liquid. Keep it under the surface throughout the bleeding operation.

5 Unscrew the bleed screw ½-turn and get the assistant to depress and release the brake pedal in short sharp bursts when you direct him. Short sharp jabs are better than long slow ones because they will force any air bubbles along the line ahead of the fluid rather than pump the fluid past them. It is not essential to remove all the air the first time. If the whole system is being bled, attend to each wheel for three to four complete pedal strikes and then repeat the process. On the second time around operate the pedal sharply in the same way until no more bubbles are apparent. The bleed screw should be tightened and closed with the brake pedal fully depressed which ensures that no aerated fluid can get back into the system. Do not forget to keep the reservoir topped-up throughout.

6 When all four wheels have been satisfactorily bled depress the foot pedal which should now offer a firmer resistance with no trace of 'sponginess'. The pedal should not continue to go down under sustained pressure. If it does there is a leak or the master cylinder seals are worn out.

7 Automatic brake bleed valves are available for these cars which will enable you to do this work unaided.

17 Stoplight switch and brake pedal free-play - adjustment

1 The stoplight switch is bolted to a bracket adjacent to the brake pedal lever. The stoplight acts as the pedal travel stop. (photo)

2 Removal of the stop light is quite straightforward - it is retained to the bracket by two nuts on the switch. Undo the nuts to remove the switch.

3 Once the switch is refitted it will be necessary to adjust the brake pedal free play.

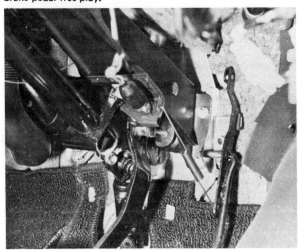

17.1 The brake stop light switch installation

18.3 The handbrake linkage adjustment mechanism

19.5 The termination of the transverse handbrake cable at the rear brake

Brake pedal free-play

4   Free-play is necessary to allow the master cylinder pistons to always return to a proper 'rest' position where the compensating valve ports are clear. The compensating valves allow fluid in the brake system to return to the reservoir when the brake pedal is released.

5   The free-play is a safety margin which ensures that the valve ports will be clear even when seals have swollen or metal parts have expanded or contracted due to adverse ambient conditions.

6   If there is no free-play of the pedal, the compensating valves are not likely to operate and the brakes will remain on - even thought the brake pedal has been 'released'.

7   Turn the two nuts on the brake light to obtain the specified pedal free-play - the distance the pedal moves between its 'rest' position and the point when the pushrod in the servo unit contacts the servo piston.

8   Once the desired pedal free-play has been obtained, check the tightness of the stoplight nuts.

9   Check the switches' operation using the continuity testing techniques detailed in Chapter 10, of this manual.

18 Handbrake - adjustment

1   The handbrake should operate the rear brakes within 5 notches of the rest position of the handbrake lever.

2   Whenever the handbrake needs to be raised by more than 5 notches to apply the rear brakes - check the adjustment of the rear brakes first. See Section 3, of this Chapter.

3   If it is found necessary to compensate for stretch and wear in the handbrake system, there is a single adjustment facility at the join of the lever cable and rear brake cable. (photo)

4   The lever cable has a threaded rod on the end, and a special nut fits on this rod and engages the rear brake cable equaliser.

5   Raise the rear of the car onto chassis stands to a sufficient height for you to reach the centre of the underside of the car -

where the handbrake adjuster is situated.

6   Turn the adjuster to effectively alter the length of the lever cable and compensate for stretch and wear in the linkage.

19 Handbrake cable - replacement

1   The handbrake system comprises a lever assembly inside the car, a single cable which connects the lever assembly to the equaliser lever mounted underneath the car between the rear wheels, and finally another cable which runs across between each rear brake and through the equaliser.

2   The single cable is retained to the handbrake lever by a single pin, and to the equaliser by the special adjusting nut. The whole removal and refitting task is accomplished from beneath the car.

3   The second cable which runs between rear brakes is the one most likely to stretch and wear. It operates in the worst environment, and undergoes a greater amount of flexing by the equaliser.

4   The equaliser comprises two pulleys around which the cable runs. The equaliser bracket is turned by the cable from the lever to effectively shorten and apply a tension to the transverse cable between rear brakes.

5   The equaliser is retained to its pivot on the underside of the bodyshell by a single nut locked by a split pin. The transverse cable is terminated in cylindrical blocks on the end of the shoe lever protruding from each rear brake. (photo)

6   Replacement of the transverse cable requires the removal of the equaliser and then the removal of the cable ends from the brake levers at each end.

Lift the cable from the pulleys in the equaliser. Refitting the cable follows the reversal of the removal procedure.

7   When either cable is replaced, re-adjust the brake cable linkage as per Section 18.

8   Give the cables liberal coatings of grease to prevent corrosion and reduce fretting between strands in the cables.

20 Fault diagnosis - braking system

Before diagnosing faults from the following chart, check that any braking irregularities are not caused by:

    1   *Uneven and incorrect tyre pressures*
    2   *Incorrect 'mix' of radial and crossply tyres*
    3   *Wear in the steering mechanism*
    4   *Defects in the suspension*
    5   *Misalignment of the chassis*

Symptom	Reason/s	Remedy
Stopping ability poor, even though pedal pressure is firm	Pads and/or discs badly worn or scored	Dismantle, inspect and renew as required.
	One or more wheel hydraulic cylinders seized, resulting in some brake pads not pressing against the discs	Dismantle and inspect wheel cylinders. Renew as necessary.
	Brake pads contaminated with oil	Renew pads and repair source of oil contamination.
	Wrong type of pads fitted (too hard)	Verify type of material which is correct for the car, and fit it.
	Brake pads wrongly assembled	Check for correct assembly.
Car veers to one side when the brakes are applied	Brake pads on one side are contaminated with oil	Renew pads and stop oil leak.
	Hydraulic wheel cylinder(s) on one side partially or fully seized	Inspect wheel cylinders for correct operation and renew as necessary.
	A mixture of pads materials fitted between sides.	Standardise on types of pads fitted.
	Unequal wear between sides caused by partially seized wheel cylinders	Check wheel cylinders and renew pads and discs as required.
Pedal feels "spongy" when the brakes are applied	Air is present in the hydraulic system	Bleed the hydraulic system and check for any signs of leakage.
Pedal feels "springy" when the brakes applied	Brake pads not bedded into the discs (after fitting new ones)	Allow time for new pads to bed in.
	Master cylinder or brake backplate mounting bolts loose	Retighten mounting bolts.
	Severe wear in brake discs causing distortion when brakes are applied	Renew discs and pads
Pedal travels right down with little or no resistance and brakes are virtually non-operative	Leak in hydraulic systems resulting in lack of pressure of operating wheel cylinders	Examine the whole of the hydraulic system and locate and repair source of leaks. Test after repairing each and every leak source.
	If no signs of leakage are apparent all the master cylinder internal seals are failing to sustain pressure	Overhaul master cylinder. If indications are that seals have failed for reasons other than wear all the wheel cylinder seals should be checked also and the system completely replenished with the correct fluid.
Binding, juddering, overheating	One or a combination of causes given in the foregoing sections	Complete and systematic inspection of the whole braking system.

Chapter 10 Electrical system

Contents

Specifications

Polarity	Negative (—) earth - all models
Battery	(20 hr rating) 32 or 45 amp hour

Alternator

Rating	Nominally 12 volts
Voltage/speed (no load)	14 volts 1200 rpm
If air conditioner fitted	820 rpm
Voltage/speed/load-amps	14 volts 5000 rpm 35 amps
If air conditioner fitted	40 amps
Rotor coil resistance	4.2 ± 0.1 ohms (4.5 ohms when air conditioner fitted)
Brush length	12.5 mm (0.49 inch) new
Service limit	5.5 mm (0.22 inch)
Diameter of rotor slip ring	32.5 to 32.1 mm (1.264 inch)
When air conditioner fitted	32 to 30 mm (1.165 inch)
Alternator to crankshaft speed ratio	2.24 : 1

Starter motor

Type	Solenoid operated, pre-engaged, D.C. Series wound
Power output	0.7 kw
Commutator:	
Outer diameter	33 to 32 mm (1.299 to 1.260 inches)
Out of round (max)	0.1 mm (0.004 inch)
Brush length:	
New	16 mm (0.62 inch)
Service limit	4 mm (0.16 inch)
Brush spring tension	1.6 kg, (3.5 lb.)
Pinion maximum travel point to pinion stop gap	0.3 - 1.5 mm (0.012 to 0.06 inch)

Voltage regulator
Voltage regulator coil:

Voltage		13.5 to 14.5 volts
Armature gap		0.3 mm (0.012 inch) minimum
Point gap		0.25 - 0.45 mm (0.010 to 0.018 inches)

Voltage relay coil)operating ignition warning light:

Operating voltage		4.5 to 5.8 volts
Relay point gap		0.4 to 1.2 mm (0.0016 to 0.050 inches)
Contact spring deflection (both coils)		0.2 to 0.6 mm (0.008 to 0.024 inches)

Fuses ... ...
4 off 15 amps,   4 off 10 amps

Main fuse ... ...   45 amps

Lights

Headlights	50 and 40 watts
Front turning/side light	21 watts/35 watts (32/3cp. USA)
Side turning repeater lights	4 watts (4 cp USA)
Rear stop/tail lights	21/5 watts (32/3 cp USA)
Rear turn lights	21 watts (32 cp USA)
Interior light	5 watts
Gauge lights	3 watts
Reversing light	21 watts (32 cp USA)
License number plate light	10 watts (4 cp USA)
Tailgate light	5 watts
Warning and indicator lights	1 watt
Turn indicator lights	3 watts

Switch checking routines

Ignition switch
Terminal continuity:

Switch 'OFF'	Nil
Position 'I'	White to white/red
Position 'II'	White to black yellow to white/red
Position 'III'	White to black/white to black yellow

Turn signal switch
Terminal continuity:

Left	Green/white to green/blue to green/blue to green/yellow to green
Right	Green/white to green/yellow to green/yellow and separately green/blue to green
Neutral	Green/blue to green/yellow to green

Hazard warning switch
Terminal continuity:

Off	Green to green and separately green/white to green/white
Hazard	Green/red to green/yellow to green/blue to green/yellow to green/blue

Lighting switch (USA type)
Terminal continuity:

Off	Nil
Side lights	Red/green to red/black
Head and side lights	Red/green to red/black to red to red/black

Lighting switch (UK type)
Terminal continuity:

Off	Nil
Side lights	Red/green to red/black and separately white to red/black
Head and side lights	Red/green to red/black and separately red to red/yellow and separately again white to red/black

Head light dipswitch
Terminal continuity:

Main beam	Red/yellow to red/blue
Dipped beam	Red/yellow to red/white
Mid-position	Red/yellow to red/blue to red/white

Windscreen wiper/washer switch
Terminal continuity:

Off	Blue/white to blue
Wiper (1)	Blue to black
Wiper (2)	Black to blue/yellow
Washer	Green/black to green/black

Voltage regulator continuity checks

Electrical resistance across terminals 'IG' and 'F'
    Nominal resistance ...   .   11 ohms
    If resistance recorded is zero, regulator coil contacts defective
    If resistance recorded is high or infinity, the coil is defective.

Electrical resistance across terminals 'L' and 'E'
    Nominal resistance ...   .   100 ohms
    If resistance recorded is low or zero, the contact points of the voltage relay are defective.
    If resistance recorded is high or infinity the relay coil is defective - open circuit.

Electrical resistance across terminals 'N' and 'E'
    Nominal resistance ...   .   23 ohms
    If resistance recorded is very low or zero, pressure coil is defective - short circuit.
    If resistance recorded is high or infinity, coil is open circuit.

Gauge and sensor systems
Voltage regulators are built into each gauge

1. Engine temperature sensor	Resistance 27.5 $\pm$ 1.5 ohms at 100°C
2. Fuel tank contents sensor	Resistance 32.5 $\pm$ 7 ohms half full
3. Oil pressure sensor turn off	Pressure 2.8 to 5.7 lbs ft in $^{-2}$

Torque wrench settings

	kg f m	lb f ft
Alternator	4.0 - 4.6	29 - 33
Alternator stay	2.0 - 2.5	14 - 18
Starter motor	4.0 - 5.0	29 - 36

1 General description

The electrical systems on the Honda Civic are divided into the following groups or sub-systems:

    (i)   *Ignition circuit (detailed fully in Chapter 4)*
    (ii) *Starter circuit*
    (iii) *The battery charging circuit*
    (iv) *The lighting circuits*
    (v) *Interior accessories*
    (vi) *Safety circuits*

The electrical components in each circuit are connected through switches and in some cases fuses, to the positive (+) terminal on the battery. The negative (−) terminal on the battery is connected to the bodyshell of the car, which now forms the earth return of each electrical circuit. This method of earthing reduces the possibility of disconnection, and simplifies fault finding because the circuit can be taken as a single discrete wire.

Each circuit wire can be identified by the colour of the insulation, and the circuit diagrams given in this Chapter show circuit and cable colour information.

Each circuit, as has been stated, is supplied with electricity by the battery. The battery is kept charged and its supply of electricity to the vehicle's electrical systems, is supplemented by the alternator on the engine. All electrical systems therefore operate on the battery voltage which is 12 volts. The alternator develops between 14 to 15 volts so that it can charge and replenish the battery with electricity, and supply the vehicle's electrical systems with power.

Since the operating voltage of each system on the car is 12 v, variable cable sizes are used throughout the electrical systems to cater for the variety of powers demand by those systems. The starter motor circuit for instance, has cables which are some ¼ inch diameter to take the nominal 70 amps to 380 amps that may flow through them.

In this Chapter, the major electrical devices are described first, and then the various systems.

2 Electrical system - repair notes

The electrical system on the Honda Civic reflects the trend to ever more profusion as is apparent on so many new cars.

Unfortunately the likelihood of failure increases with system complexity, and therefore whereas the mechanics of your car will be more reliable than in years past, electrical systems will most probably demand more attention than any others on the vehicle. However it should be appreciated that most electrical system faults are cheap to repair, because they are usually caused by broken connections, corroded mountings or worn insulation of electrical leads.

The number of electrical system faults that are bound to occur justifies the procurement of several items of electrical test gear:

    i)   *A multimeter:*
          Reading Volts   *0 − 20 v D.C.*
          Current   *0 − 3 amps*
          Resistance − up to 2,000 ohms
    ii) *Jumper Wires*
          5 amp rating, fitted with crocodile clips
    iii) *12 v bulb plus holder, connected to wires with clips.*
    iv) *A selection of fine point pliers, wire strippers, wire*
          cutters and small screwdrivers
    v) *A small soldering iron (12 watt)*

Having obtained a useful collection of tools for electrical system repair, the following codes of practice should be adhered to, to ensure reliable repairs.

Cleanliness

Corrosion is one of the most frequent causes of failure of electrical joints. Any foreign matter and particularly water, will cause corrosion, therefore ensure that:

a) *All surfaces which serve to conduct electricity must be clean and dry before reassembly.*
b) *All seals, boots and covers on electrical devices must be in first class condition and be properly assembled. Use soft silicone sealing compounds as well as rubber seals to ensure water tight seals on items such as side lights which are positioned in a harsh environment.*

Neatness

Most electrical cables contain insufficient metal, and have insufficient bulk of insulation to enable them to be unsupported over distances greater than 3 or 4 inches. Indeed if wires are allowed to flex, because of inadequate support, the copper conductor will inevitably fatigue and break. Such breaks can be difficult to find, and therefore prevention is better than cure.

Whenever repair wires are fitted or wires to new accessories are installed, ensure that they are properly routed and supported over the whole of their length.

Do not take wires and cables near any part (hinge, door, lid stay) which might rub and abrade the cable. The insulation material on automobile wiring has a relatively low abrasion resistance.

Insulation

Some electrical faults can be caused by electrical conductors (terminals, wires, bolts etc.) being inadequately covered with insulating material. In such cases there would be insufficient protection from metal objects coming into contact with the conductor and possibly shorting it out with an adjacent conductor.

When terminals or wires are repaired, fit insulative sleeving over joints or bare conductors to maintain insulation integrity.

---

3 Electrical system - continuity testing

1   As mentioned in Section 2, of this Chapter, it is essential to have certain items of electrical test equipment. Absolutely essential pieces of equipment are those used for continuity checking.

As a minimum you will require:

i)   a 5 amp wire, 3 or 4 ft long with crocodile clips
ii) a 12 volt bulb and bulb holder connected to wires with alligator/crocodile clips on their ends (Fig. 10.1)
iii) a 3 volt bulb and battery set with wires fitted with crocodile clips (Fig. 10.2))

2   The 12 volt bulb set is used for checking continuity of circuits when powered by the car's own battery. Fig. 10.3 illustrates such a test. In these tests the bulb can be connected in series with devices in circuits to check the availability of power, or across - in parallel with devices, to check the operation of switches etc.

3   The small voltage bulb and battery set is used to check the continuity of devices when isolated from their circuit. For instance it can be used to check the continuity of coil windings within relays, motors, or connections within switches etc.

The bulb and battery set can also be used to check insulation, but its low voltage does not allow a reliable indication of insulation quality to be given.

Fig. 10.4 illustrates tests that can be made with the bulb and battery set.

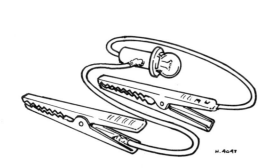

Fig 10.1 Continuity checking equipment (1) (Sec 3)

12 volt bulb, wires and crocodile clips

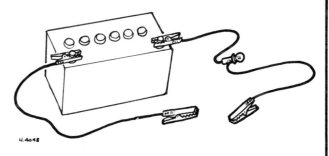

Fig 10.2 Continuity checking equipment (2) (Sec 3)

3 volt bulb, battery, wires and clips

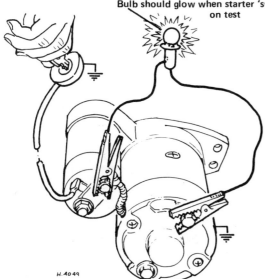

Fig 10.3 Continuity tests with 12 volt bulb (Solenoid Operation) (Secs 3 & 11)

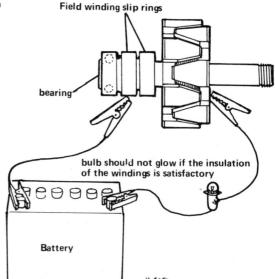

Fig 10.4 Continuity tests with bulb and battery (Insulation of alternator rotor windings) (Secs 3 & 9)

4 Battery - removal and replacement

The battery is situated on the left-hand side of the engine compartment when viewed from the front. It is held in place by two tie-rods and a pressed steel angle strip. It weighs in the region of 40 lbs and therefore should be handled with respect!

2 To remove the battery, begin by disconnecting the negative earth lead from the battery and bodyshell. Then disconnect the positive lead from the battery.

3 Once the leads have been removed, undo and remove the two wing nuts which tension the tie-rods onto the angle strip which secures the battery. Lift the angle strip aside once the rod nuts have been undone.

4 Lift the battery from its seating in the bodyshell, taking great care not to spill any of the highly corrosive electrolyte.

5 Replacement follows the reversal of the removal procedure. Replace the positive lead first and smear the clean terminal posts

and lead clamp assembly beforehand, with petroleum jelly (Vaseline) in order to prevent corrosion. **Do not use ordinary grease**, it does not prevent corrosion of the terminals.

5 Battery - maintenance and inspection

1 Check the battery electrolyte level weekly by lifting off the cover or removing the individual cell plugs. The tops of the plates should be just covered with the liquid. If not, add distilled water so that they are just covered. Do not add extra water with the idea of reducing the intervals of topping-up. This will merely dilute the electrolyte and reduce charging and current retention efficiency. On batteries fitted with patent covers, troughs, glass balls and so on, follow the instructions marked on the cover of the battery to ensure correct addition of water.

2 Keep the battery clean and dry all over by wiping it with a dry cloth. A damp top surface could cause tracking between the

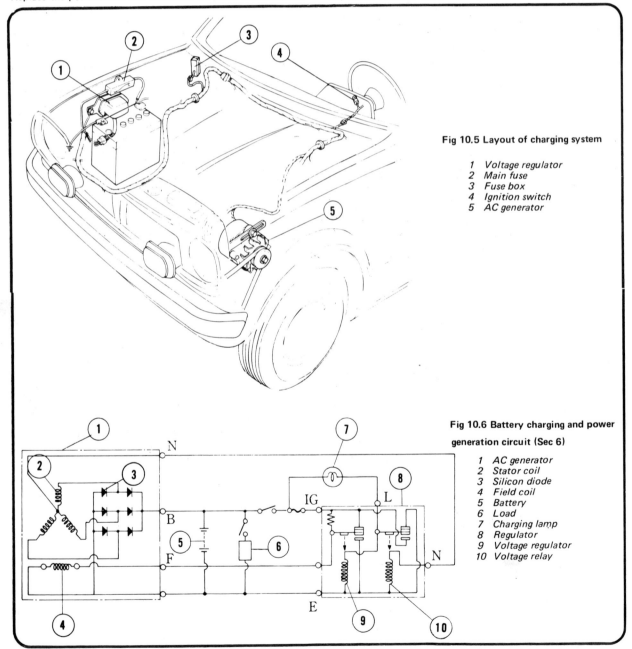

Fig 10.5 Layout of charging system

1 Voltage regulator
2 Main fuse
3 Fuse box
4 Ignition switch
5 AC generator

Fig 10.6 Battery charging and power generation circuit (Sec 6)

1 AC generator
2 Stator coil
3 Silicon diode
4 Field coil
5 Battery
6 Load
7 Charging lamp
8 Regulator
9 Voltage regulator
10 Voltage relay

two terminal posts with consequent draining of power.

3 Every three months remove the battery and check the support tray clamp and battery terminal connections for signs of corrosion - usually indicated by a whitish green crystalline deposit. Wash this off with clean water to which a little ammonia or washing soda has been added. Then treat the terminals with petroleum jelly and the battery mounting with suitable protective paint to prevent the metal being eaten away. Clean the battery thoroughly and repair any cracks with a proprietary sealer. If there has been any excessive leakage the appropriate cell may need an addition of electrolyte rather than just distilled water.

4 If the electrolyte level needs an excessive amount of replenishment but no leaks are apparent, it could be due to overcharging as a result of the battery having been run down and then left on recharge from the vehicle rather than an outside source. If the battery has been heavily discharged for one reason or another it is best to have it continuously charged at a low amperage for a period of many hours. If it is charged from the car's system under such conditions the charging will be intermittent and greatly varied in intensity. This does not do the battery any good at all. If the battery needs topping-up frequently, even when it is known to be in good condition and not too old, then the voltage regulator should be checked to ensure that the charging output is being correctly controlled. An elderly battery, however, may need topping-up more than a new one because it needs to take in more charging current. Do not worry about this provided it gives satisfactory service.

5 When checking a battery's condition a hydrometer should be used. On some batteries where the terminals of each of the six cells are exposed, a discharge tester can be used to check the condition of any one cell also. On modern batteries the use of a discharge tester is no longer regarded as useful as the replacement or repair of cells is not an economic proposition. The tables following gives the hydrometer readings for various states of charge. A further check can be made when the battery is undergoing a charge. If, towards the end of the charge, when the cells are meant to be 'gassing' (bubbling), one cell appears not to be, then it indicates that the cell or cells in question are probably breaking down and the life of the battery is limited.

6 Battery - charging and electrolyte replenishment

1 It is possible that in winter when the load on the battery cannot be recuperated quickly during normal driving time external charging is desirable. This is best done overnight at a 'trickle' rate of 1 - 1.5 amps. Alternatively a 3 - 4 amp rate can be used over a period of four hours or so. Check the specific gravity in the latter case and stop the charge when the reading is correct. Most modern charging sets reduce the rate automatically when the fully charged state is neared. Rapid boost charges of 30 - 60 amps or more may get you out of trouble or can be used on a battery that has seen batter days. They are not advisable for a good battery that may have run flat for some reason.

2 Electrolyte replenishment should not normally be necessary unless an accident or some other cause such as contamination arises. If it is necessary then it is best first to discharge the battery completely and then tip out all the remaining liquid from all cells. Then acquire a quantity of mixed electrolyte from a battery shop or garage according to the specifications in the table given next. The quantity required will depend on the type of battery but 3 - 4 pints should be more than enough for most. When the electrolyte has been put into the battery a slow charge not exceeding one amp - should be given for as long as is necessary to fully charge the battery. This could be up to 36 hours.

Specific gravities for hydrometer readings (check each cell) - 12 volt batteries:

	Climate below 80°F (26.7°C)	Climate above 80°F (26.7°C)
Fully charged	1.270 - 1.290	1.210 - 1.230
Half-charged	1.190 - 1.210	1.120 - 1.150
Discharged completely	1.110 - 1.130	1.050 - 1.070

Note: If the electrolyte temperature is significantly different from 60°F (15.6°C) then the specific gravity reading will be affected. For every 5°F (2.8°C) it will increase or decrease with the temperature by 0.002.

7 Alternator - general description

The main advantage of the alternator lies in its ability to provide a relatively high power output at low revolutions. Driving slowly in traffic with a dynamo means a very small charge or even no charge at all, reaching the battery.

In similar conditions even with wipers, heater, lights and perhaps radio switched on, the alternator will ensure a charge reaches the battery.

The alternator is of the rotating field, ventilated design and comprises principally a laminated stator on which is wound a 3 phase output winding, and a twelve pole rotor carrying the field windings.

Each end of the rotor shaft runs in ball race bearings which are lubricated for life. Aluminium end brackets hold the bearings and incorporate the alternator mounting lugs. The rear bracket supports the silicone diode rectifier pack which converts the A.C. output of the machine to a D.C. output, for battery charging and output to the voltage regulator (Fig. 10.7 and 10.9).

The rotor is belt driven from the engine through a pulley keyed to the rotor shaft. A special centrifugal action fan adjacent to the pulley, draws cool air through the machine. This fan forms an integral part of the alternator specification. It has been designed to provide adequate airflow with the minimum of

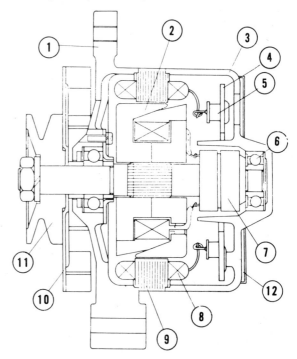

Fig 10.7 Section through the alternator

1 Drive end frame	7 Slip ring
2 Rotor	8 Stator coil
3 Rectifier end frame	9 Stator core
4 Rectifier holder fin	10 Fan
5 Rectifier	11 Pulley
6 Ball bearing	12 Protector cover

noise at all speeds of rotation of the machine - rotation is anti-clockwise when viewed from the drive end.

The rectifier pack of silicone diodes is mounted on the inside of the rear end casing, the same mounting is used by the brushes which contact slip rings on the rotor to supply the field current. The slip rings are carried on a small diameter moulded drum attached to the rotor. By keeping the circumference of the slip rings to a minimum, the contact speed and therefore the brush wear is minimised.

8 Alternator - maintenance, testing, removal and refitting

1 The alternator has been designed for the minimum amount of attention during service. The only items subject to wear are the brushes and bearings.

2 If the ignition warning light on the instrument panel lights up, indicating that the battery is no longer being charged, carry out the following checks:

i) *Examine the cables from the battery to the alternator and ensure all connections are clean, and tight, and that the cable is in good order. If proper working has not been restored proceed to the next check.*

ii) *This test will only determine whether there is a significant fault in the voltage regulator or the alternator.*
Unplug the connector from the voltage regulator and fix a jumper wire between the 'F' and 'I G' terminals (Fig. 10.8). These terminals are connected to the white/red and black/yellow leads respectively.
This effectively supplies a full field current directly to the alternator rotor. Refit the connector with jumper in position. Now start the engine and run gently for no longer than half a minute: if the ignition/battery warning light still glows, the

alternator system or warning light relay is suspect, and you should proceed to check iii, below.
If on the other hand, the ignition light did not glow when the jumper lead was in position, the voltage regulator is suspect and you should refer to Section 15, of this Chapter, for further details.

iii) *To distinguish between faults in the alternator or battery/ ignition warning light relay, test the relay as follows:*
Disconnect the large lead attached to terminal 'N' on the alternator. Switch the ignition on, but do not start the engine. Now touch the alternator lead onto the positive (+) terminal on the battery. This should now activate the warning light relay and the ignition light will go off. If the

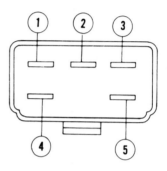

Fig 10.8 Voltage regulator terminals at connector (Sec 8)

1 Terminal E   4 Terminal IG
2 Terminal N   5 Terminal F
3 Terminal L

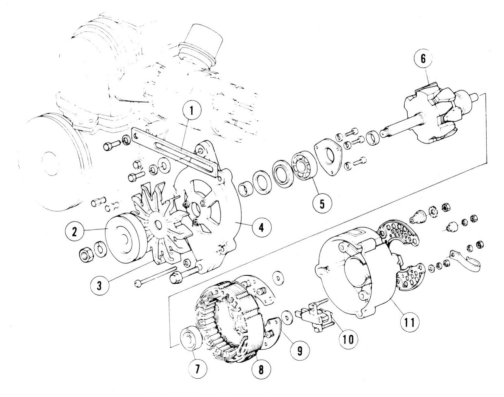

Fig 10.9 Exploded view of alternator components

1 Alternator   4 Drive end frame   7 Ball bearing   10 Brush holder
2 Pulley   5 Ball bearing   8 Stator   11 Rectifier end frame
3 Fan   6 Rotor   9 Rectifier

light does not go off, the relay is faulty and you should refer to Section 15, of this Chapter, for further details. If on the other hand the ignition light did go off, indicating that the relay is in reasonable order, the alternator is suspect and should be removed for inspection.

Alternator removal

3   Begin by removing both battery cable terminals and stow the cables carefully so that they do not inadvertantly come into contact with the battery posts. Detach the 'E', 'F' and 'N' plug from the alternator. Slacken the alternator mounting bolts and move the unit towards the engine; then remove the drivebelt which is now loose. Finally completely undo and remove the alternator mounting bolts so that the unit may be lifted clear.

Alternator refitting

4   The procedure for fitting the alternator is the reversal of the removal procedure, but the following tasks should also be completed:
i)   Clean electrical connections.
ii) Adjust drivebelt tension so that there is just half-an-inch lateral movement midway along the belt between the alternator and crankshaft pulleys.

9   Alternator - dismantling and reassembly

1   This task should only be attempted if specialist equipment and expertise is available.
2   Remove the end pulley by undoing the retaining nut whilst holding the shaft with a 6 mm Allen key.
3   Make alignment marks on the end members and centre part of the alternator with a centre punch, to ensure correct alignment on assembly.
4   Undo and remove the three long bolts which hold the alternator together. Separate the two ends and stator assembly gently, only use gentle taps with a light mallet to loosen the ends.
5   Watch the position of the washers and spacers, and insulators. it is essential to fit them back correctly.
6   Unsolder the brush holder lead and separate the brush holder from the stator. Label the leads with tags to ensure correct reassembly.

7   Unsolder the stator leads from the rectifier diodes; be careful not to overheat the diodes. Hold their terminals with long nose pliers to absorb the soldering iron heat.
8   Check the continuity of the rotor field windings and check for shorting to the rotor cone and shaft. (Fig. 10.4).
9   Measure the length of the brushes, they should not be less than 5.5 mm. New brushes may be fitted by unsoldering the worn ones, inserting the new brushes and soldering the wires to the new brushes.
10 Check the functioning of each diode. If any diodes show high resistance in both directions or low resistance in both directions, they are defective.
11 When resoldering leads to diodes, be as quick as possible, use a 100 to 120 watt iron, and sink the terminal heat into long nose pliers. Diodes on the plate have a red stripe and those on the negative earthed plate have a black stripe.
12 When installing the rotor into the rear casing, raise the brushes in the holders and hold raised by pushing a pin through the rear casing and brushes. The pin will hold the brushes so that there is little likelihood of them getting damaged as the rotor and slip rings pass into the rear casing.
    After installation, remove the pin to allow the brushes to rest on the slip rings.
13 Once assembled, tighten the pulley nut to its specified torque, and check the rotor for easy rotation.

10 Starter motor - general description

The starter motor fitted to the Honda Civic is a 12 volt pre-engaging machine. It comprises a D.C. series wound motor switched by a solenoid mounted on the motor casing. The solenoid also serves to move the motor pinion into engagement with the ring gear on the periphery of the flywheel, before the switch contacts are closed to supply electrical power to the starter motor (Fig. 10.10).

The motor pinion is mounted on a carriage which engages a spiral spline on the motor shaft. The carriage incorporates an overspeed clutch which allows the pinion gear to be driven at speeds greater than the starter motor speed when the engine starts.

Once the engine has started, and when the start switch is released, the solenoid cuts off the power from the motor and moves the pinion and carriage back from engagement with the flywheel ring gear.

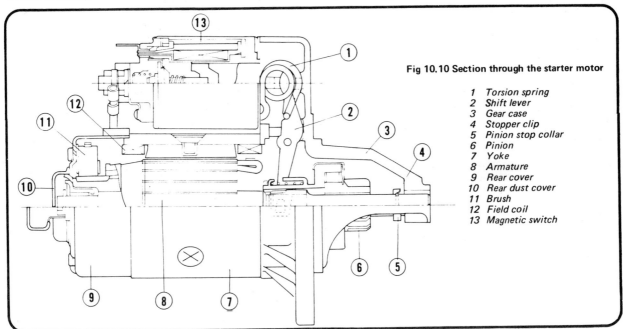

Fig 10.10 Section through the starter motor

1   Torsion spring
2   Shift lever
3   Gear case
4   Stopper clip
5   Pinion stop collar
6   Pinion
7   Yoke
8   Armature
9   Rear cover
10 Rear dust cover
11 Brush
12 Field coil
13 Magnetic switch

11 Starter motor - in-situ testing

1   If the starter motor fails to turn the engine, when the switch is operated, there are four possible reasons why:

a) *the battery is flat*
b) *the electrical connections between the switch, solenoid, battery and starter motor are failing somewhere to pass the necessary current from the battery through to the starter motor and earth.*
c) *the solenoid switch is defective*
d) *the starter motor is either jammed or electrically defective*

2   The test procedure for the starter system is as follows:
a) *Remove the battery connections, starter/solenoid power connections and the engine earth strap - and thoroughly clean them and refit them. Smear petroleum jelly (vaseline) around the battery connections to prevent corrosion. Corroded connections are the most frequent cause of electrical system malfunctions.*
b) *If the starter still doesn't work check the battery as follows: Switch on the headlights, if they go dim after a few seconds, the battery is definitely at fault. If the lights shine brightly, operate the starter switch and watch what happens to the lights. If they go dim, then you know that power is reaching the starter motor but failing to turn it. In this event check that the motor is not jammed. Place the car in gear and rock the car to-and-fro. If the starter system still does not operate properly, proceed to the next test.*
c) *Note whether a clicking noise is heard each time the starter switch is operated. This is the solenoid switch operating, but it doesn't necessarily follow that the main contacts are closing properly. If a click is not heard from the solenoid, it will most probably be defective. The solenoid contact can be checked by putting a voltmeter or bulb across the main cable connection on the starter side of the solenoid and earth. When the switch is operated there should be a reading of 12 volts or the bulb should light up.* **Do not put a bulb across the two solenoid power connections.** *If there is no reading or lighted bulb, the solenoid unit is faulty and should be replaced (Fig. 10.3). Finally, if it is established that the solenoid is not faulty, and 12 volts are getting to the starter, then the motor should be removed for inspection.*

12 Starter motor - removal and refitting

1   The starter motor is quite accessible with the engine in place in the car; it can be found on the transmission end of the engine, above the gearbox. It is held to the engine by two large bolts, one of which passes right through the clutch bell housing and cylinder block flange and is secured by a nut. The other bolt screws into the cylinder block. (photo)

2   Remove the earth (negative) lead from the battery and then proceed to disconnect the solenoid and motor electrical connections. Identify the leads as necessary to ensure correct refitment.

3   Then remove the two bolts (one secured by a nut) which secure the solenoid-motor assembly to the engine. The motor can now be lifted clear. (photo)

4   Refitting follows the reversal of the removal procedure, except that attention should be paid to the following points:

i) *Tighten the securing bolts to the specified torque.*
ii) *Ensure all electrical connections are tight and clean.*

13 Starter motor solenoid - removal and refitting

1   The solenoid is retained to the starter block by two bolts. Undo the electrical connection between the starter and solenoid

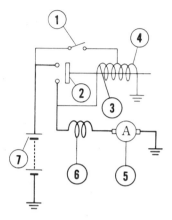

Fig 10.11 Starter motor electrical circuit (Sec 11)

1 *Starter switch*	4 *Magnetic switch*
2 *Magnetic switch*	*holding coil*
contact	5 *Armature coil*
3 *Magnetic switch*	6 *Field coil*
coil	7 *Battery*

switch from the solenoid. Then undo and remove the two solenoid retaining bolts, and lift the solenoid away. Take care to unhook the solenoid plunger from the pinion carriage lever. Recover the return spring retainer plate.

2   The solenoid is not repairable, and no attempt should be made to dismantle it: if it has been proven faulty, it should be renewed. If the solenoid only is suspected, the coiled resistance may be checked by connecting a multimeter across the 'S' and 'M' terminals on the solenoid. If an open circuit is found (infinite resistance) the solenoid is definitely faulty.

3   To refit the solenoid, ensure that the plunger is properly hooked onto the pinion carriage lever, and that the plate which retains the plunger and lever return spring is in position (Figs. 10.10 and 10.12).

4   Make sure that the electrical connections are clean and properly made.

14 Starter motor - dismantling and renovation

1   It will be necessary to dismantle the starter motor in order to complete the following tasks:

i) *Brush removal and replacement*
ii) *Armature and commutator inspection*
iii) *Pinion gear and overspeed clutch inspection*
iv) *Pinion gearshift mechanism inspection*

2   Begin the starter motor dismantling by removing the solenoid as detailed in the previous Section.

3   Prise off the rear dust cover the end-shaft bearing with a screwdriver, and then lever off the 'C' clip from the end of the motor shaft. Remove the thrust washers.

4   Continue then to undo the two small screws in the end cover which secure the brush holder plate to the inside of the end cover.

5   Next undo the two through bolts which hold the gear and shift lever case to the starter motor. Once the two bolts have been removed, tap the rear cover with a light mallet and lift it off the motor. The brush plate should remain in position around the commutator.

6   Finally dislodge the gear and shift lever case, and then extract the armature and brushes.

7   To remove the pinion gear from the armature, hold the armature shaft in a vice fitted with soft jaws, the pinion and carriage downwards to the armature. Near the end of the shaft there is

the travel stop ring which limits pinion movement.

8 Pull the ring out of its groove in the shaft with pliers, and then lift the gear and carriage off the shaft.

9 The motor is now dismantled and the parts should be laid out on a clean bench for inspection.

Brush removal, inspection and replacement

10 Having first dismantled the motor, proceed to remove the brushes as follows:

11 Extract the brushes from the holders mounted on the holder support plate.

12 Measure the length of the brushes and check the lengths against the limits quoted in the Specification at the beginning of this Chapter.

13 If possible check the brush spring load when deflected to an equivalent position to when the brush is installed.

14 Use a multimeter set to read electrical resistance, to check the insulation between brushes and brush holder support plate. Replace the holder if there is a low resistance recorded on any of the four brush holders.

15 If the brushes have worn too short, they are replaced as follows:

De-solder the brushes from the connecting wires: take care when soldering new wires not to allow the solder to flow up the wires and bind the individual strands.

16 Replacement is simply the reversal of removal.

Armature and commutator inspection

17 Clean the commutator with solvent and a non-fluffy cloth, scrape away any metal deposits from between the copper segments of the commutator. The commutator surface must be smooth and clean, free from scores and scratches.

18 The armature should then be checked for electrical insulation. Again use a multimeter to measure the electrical resistance between each segment of the commutator and the motor shaft. The resistance should be infinity. If a low resistance is measured the armature is faulty and should be replaced.

Motor pinion and overspeed clutch - inspection

20 Examine the pinion gearteeth; if any are damaged the pinion/clutch assembly should be replaced.

21 Check the freedom of movement of the gear and clutch assembly along the spiral spline on the motor shaft.

22 If any binding is felt, replace the pinion clutch unit, it is

12.1 Starter motor retaining nuts and bolts

12.3 Removal of starter motor

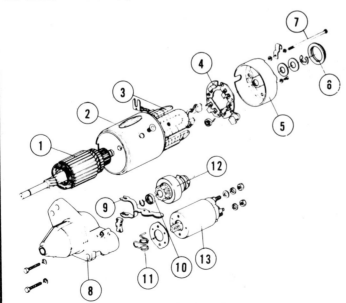

Fig 10.12 Exploded view of starter motor components

1 Armature complete
2 Yoke
3 Field coil
4 Brush holder
5 Rear cover
6 Dust cover
7 Through bolt
8 Gear case
9 Shift lever
10 Pinion stop collar
11 Torsion spring
12 Pinion complete
13 Magnetic switch

improbable that the fault lies with the spiral spline.

23 Finally check the operation of the overspeed clutch. Hold the pinion gear and turn the motor shaft clockwise when viewed from the pinion end. The clutch should not slip and the turning effort exerted on the shaft should be felt at the pinion.

However it should be possible to turn the pinion clockwise relative to the motor shaft. Renew the pinion/clutch assembly if it does not operate as required.

Starter - reassembly

24 The starter reassembly technique is basically the reversal of the dismantling procedure, except that the following points should be watched:

i) take care to assemble the pinion shaft correctly in the shaft casing.
ii) after assembly check the pinion carriage to travel stop clearance when the solenoid is excited to move the pinion into its engaged position. Apply 12 volts across the solenoid to activate it (Fig. 10.13).

15 Voltage regulator - description, removal, refitting and testing

1 The voltage regulator unit comprises two main devices, the voltage regulator and the ignition/battery warning light relay.

2 The voltage regulator governs the current that is fed into the alternator field coils. When the engine is not running or when it is running very slowly and the alternator is not developing more than 12 volts, the regulator relay coil remains weak and the field coils receive a full field current.

3 Once the alternator voltage reaches 14 volts, the regulator relay switches off the direct supply of full field current to the alternator, and switches the supply through a series resistor. This limits the field current, and hence the voltage developed by the alternator.

4 The battery charging lamp relay operates off the full return current to the alternator. It is connected directly to the centre point of the star wound output windings of the three phase alternator. The relay coil is therefore a low resistance device and functions to switch the ignition warning light return.

5 It is only possible with simple equipment to determine whether the voltage regulator is faulty.

6 Refer to the Specification at the beginning of this Chapter and measure the resistance across the coils in the regulator as detailed. Compare results with the data given.

7 Although it is possible to adjust the operation of both regulator relay and warning light relay, it is not a task that can be recommended without specialist knowledge and equipment.

8 If therefore the regulator has been found faulty, the unit should be removed, and a new one put in its place.

Removal and refitting

9 This task involves disconnecting the electrical leads from the regulator. Finally undo and remove the screws retaining the regulator to the bodyshell. Refitting as usual follows the reversal of the removal procedure.

16 Windscreen wipers - fault diagnosis

1 If the wipers fail to operate check the following:

i) All electrical connections to the wiper switch, fusebox, and wiper motor are clean and secure (Fig. 10.14).
ii) Check that the 10 amp fuse has not blown. If it has blown, do not fit a new fuse until the cause of the fuse failure is known.
iii) Remove the green and black wire from the motor terminals. Measure the voltage at the end of that wire. If 12 volts is recorded the power supply to the motor is satisfactory and if the motor still doesn't operate, proceed to next check.
If 12 volts is not recorded, there is a fault in the supply to the motor. Check the continuity of the wire between the motor and fuse.
iv) Next check the continuity of black and black-white wires to the motor when the wiper switch is in the off position. A bulb and battery can be used to check continuity. If there is no continuity (typical when the wiper parking device is inoperative), check the continuity of the individual black/white lead, black lead and 'Off' terminals on the wiper switch. Fit a bypass wire to any which are found to be faulty.
v) The next test is to connect a 12 volt bulb across the green/black and black wire terminals. Move the switch to the first stop position (slow). The bulb should glow when the wiper switch is operated. If the bulb does not glow, check the continuity of the slow speed terminals on the switch. If the bulb does glow, but when the wires are reconnected the motor still doesn't run, the wiper should be removed and replaced.
vi) The next test is to connect a bulb across the green/black and black/yellow wires when they have been disconnected from the motor. Turn the wiper switch to its last stop (fast). If the bulb glows when the switch is operated, and the motor still does not work when the wires are reconnected, the motor is faulty and should be removed.

2 If the wipers work slowly or with apparent difficulty, check the following:

i) All electrical connections to the wiper switch, fusebox and wiper motor should be clean and secure.
ii) Check the whole wiper linkage for obstruction or wear in components.

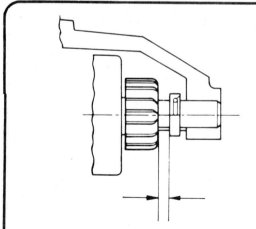

Fig 10.13 Pinion to Pinion travel stop clearance (Sec 14)

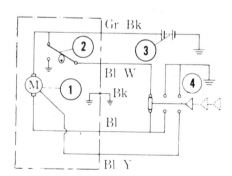

Fig 10.14 Windscreen wiper electrical circuit (Sec 16)

1 Wiper motor   3 Battery
2 Automatic stop switch   4 Wiper switch

iii) Disconnect the linkage from the motor and try the motor again. If it still does not operate, remove the motor for closer inspection.

3   The Specification at the beginning of this Chapter includes details of continuity and functioning checks on the windscreen wiper switch.

17 Windscreen wiper mechanism and motor - removal, renovation and refitting

1   Remove the wiper blades; they are a spring catch fit on the wiper arms (Fig. 10.15).
2   Remove the wiper arms from their spindles by undoing the special nut which secures them to the spindle.
3   Next remove the spindle bearing retaining nut, lift off the washer and cushion washer and then push the spindle and bearing down into the mechanism compartment.
4   Undo and remove the three motor retaining bolts, recover the spacers and washers. Then separate the two parts connector which serves the motor.
5   Finally remove the motor and wiper linkage complete.
6   Separate the motor and linkage after removing the split pin which secures the linkage arm to the motor crank.

Inspection of wiper linkage

7   Having removed the linkage from the car and separated it from the motor, check the following points:

i) Examine the wiper spindle bearing. if it is worn and sloppy on the spindle, replace it.
ii) Examine each joint of the wiper linkage, and replace the whole linkage if the joints are worn or sloppy.

Inspection of wiper motor

8   With a continuity tester or multimeter check the continuity of the wiper motor coil and its insulation. If there is a continuity between the green/black and blue terminals of the connector, and the green/black and blue/white terminal, the motor would seem in good order. Proceed to the next check.
9   Connect the motor across a 12 volt battery as indicated below; if the motor turns smoothly, it is in good order.

Low speed	*Green/Black wire to + terminal*
	Blue wire to − terminal
High speed	*Green/Black wire to + terminal*
	Blue/White wire to − terminal

10 If the motor is deemed faulty, replace it; it is not repairable.

Refitting the wiper assembly

11 As usual, reassembly and refitting of the wiper/motor assembly follows the reversal of the removal and dismantling procedure.

   Pay attention to the following points:

i) Install the motor in the 'park' position.
ii) Ensure that the linkage is assembled correctly and that it will not be cranked backwards.
iii) Use new cushion rubbers if the old ones are frayed.

18 Windscreen washer - removal, testing and refitting

1   Carry out continuity checks on the supply and earthing wires in the wiper washer circuit, if the washer does not operate.
2   If the connections are in order, and 12 volts is recorded at the green/black (+) and black (−) terminals of its connector to the washer motor when its switch is operated, the washer pump/motor unit should be connected directly to the battery to establish that it is faulty. Neither pump nor motor is repairable and therefore when found faulty should be renewed.

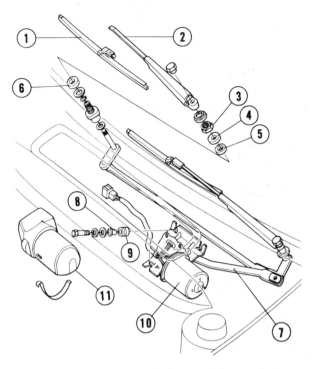

Fig 10.15 Exploded view of windscreen wiper mechanism components (Sec 17)

1	*Wiper blade*	*7*	*Link*
2	*Wiper arm*	*8*	*Mount collar*
3	*Pivol nut*	*9*	*Mount rubber*
4	*Cup washer*	*10*	*Wiper motor*
5	*Cushion rubber*	*11*	*Water seal cover*
6	*Cushion rubber*		

Removal of washer pump/motor

3   Commence by detaching the washer jet tube from the water sack. Then separate the electrical connector to the motor/pump unit.
4   Next remove the three clips from beneath washer sack, so that the motor can be removed. Take care not to damage the clips.
5   Refitting follows the reversal of the removal procedure.

19 Horn - in-situ testing, removal and refitting

1   The horns are operated by an earthing pushbutton switch on the steering column. Neither horns nor switch are repairable and therefore should be renewed complete if necessary.

In-situ testing

2   It will be necessary to check whether power is reaching the horns, and leaving them.
reaching the horns, and leaving them.
3   Remove the horn supply leads, and either connect a multimeter (volts) to the white/green supply lead and earth, or a 12 volt bulb. If there is no power, check the continuity of the supply wire.
4   Next separate the horns electrical connector, and connect a 12 volt bulb across the supply and return terminals. Depress the horn button. If the cabling and horn button are operative the test light should glow, and the horns are suspect.
5   The horns are wired in parallel and it is unlikely that they will fail simultaneously; therefore if both are suspected make a close examination of the wires between the connector and horns.

6 If the test light does not glow, and it has already been established that the supply is in order, check the operation of the
horn button with a continuity tester. It may be necessary to
dismantle the horn button assembly as detailed in Section 20, of
this Chapter.

7 Faults that render both horns inoperative are likely to be
either corroded or loose connections, or inadequate earthing of
the return lead from the horn button.

Removal and refitting of horns

8 Disconnect the negative (earth) lead from the battery, and
then separate the horn electrical connectors. Undo and remove
the attachment bolts and lift away the horn. Refitting follows
the reversal of the removal procedure.

20 Horn buttons - in-situ testing, removal and refitting

1 From beneath the instrument panel, separate the two part
connector which serves the horn buttons. The horn buttons act
to earth the horns when operated, and therefore only a single
wire (blue with red strip) serves the switches. This wire is
connected via the 8 way connector in the direction indicator
group.

2 Separate the eight way connector and attach a bulb/battery
continuity checker across the blue-red wire and earth. The bulb
should glow only when the button switches are operated. Refer
to Sections 2 and 3, of this Chapter, for details of electrical
circuit testing and repair.

Removal of horn buttons

3 Undo and remove the screws which secure the button switch
covers to the rear of the steering wheel spokes. Remove the
covers (Fig. 10.16).

4 Single wires connect to the switches and these pass to
connectors in the steering wheel hub. Separate the two single
connections, and detach the switches from the steering wheel
spokes.

Refitting the button switches

Follows the reversal of the removal procedure, except that
attention should be paid to the following points:

i) All electrical connections must be clean and secure.
ii) Ensure that wires are not pinched when covers have been
    refitted.

21 Turn signal and dipswitch - in-situ testing, removal and re-fitting

1 From beneath the instrument panel, separate the large eight
way connector (turn signal) and three way (light dip) connectors
on the steering column which serve the switch assembly at the
top of the column. Then carry out the continuity checks
detailed in the Specification at the beginning of this Chapter to
test the functioning of those switches. Use a bulb/battery set as
detailed in Section 3, of this Chapter.

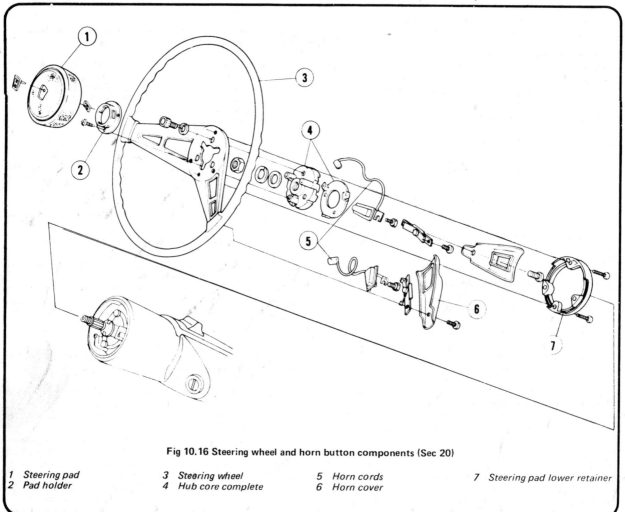

Fig 10.16 Steering wheel and horn button components (Sec 20)

1 Steering pad	3 Steering wheel	5 Horn cords	7 Steering pad lower retainer
2 Pad holder	4 Hub core complete	6 Horn cover	

Turn signal and light dipper switch removal

2 It is necessary to remove the steering wheel first as follows (Fig. 10.18).

3 Prise off the wheel centre pad and then use a socket spanner to reach the steering wheel retaining nut. Undo and remove the nut. Rub the rear side of the wheel with the palm of your hands to jolt the wheel off the steering column shaft. Finally disconnect the horn button switch wires.

4 Next undo the screws which secure the upper and lower covers at the top of the column assembly. Then turn and main light dipper switch unit and ignition switches are now fully revealed.

5 Undo the screw which is in the signal cancel cam, then tap the cam lightly to loosen it.

6 The turn signal and dipswitch is retained on the column by a wedge held in position by another screw. Undo this screw and then give the screw a light tap with a mallet to unlock the wedge (Fig. 10.17).

7 Remove the lock piece and switch; take care not to drop the cancel key and washers.

Refitting the switch assembly

8 Follows the reversal of the removal procedure, except that the tasks below are added:

i) Ensure that the wedge switch locking pieces are properly installed, and that the switch is registered into the recess in the top of the column.

ii) Ensure all electrical connections are clean and secure.

iii) Tighten the steering wheel retaining nut to its specified torque.

22 Ignition switch - in-situ testing, removal and refitting

In-situ testing

1 From beneath the instrument panel, next to the steering column, separate the electrical connector which serves the ignition switch.

Then carry out the continuity checks detailed in the Specification at the beginning of this Chapter, using a battery bulb set. Section 3, of this Chapter, described the continuity check technique. If the switch is found faulty, it is not repairable and therefore renewal is the only course of action.

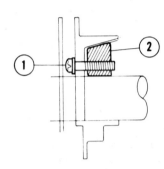

Fig 10.17 Steering column switch lock (Sec 21)

1 Lock screw
2 Lock wedge

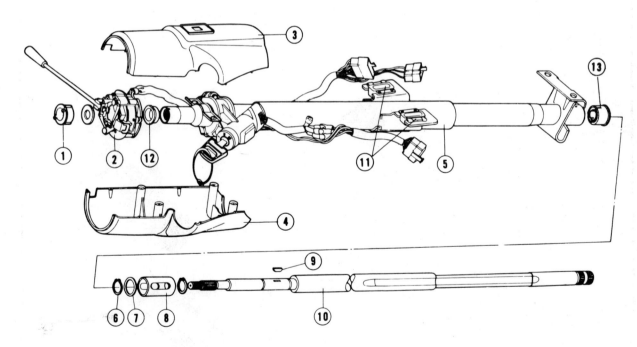

Fig 10.18 Steering column assembly (Sec 21)

1 Cancelling cam	6 Snap ring	10 Steering shaft
2 Turn signal switch	7 Spacer	11 Shear plates
3 Upper cover	8 Steering lock collar	12 Upper bushing
4 Lower cover	9 Lock collar key	13 Lower bushing
5 Steering column		

Ignition switch - removal and refitting

2 Remove the steering column covers as for the removal of the direction indicator switch. The ignition switch is held to the steering column by a clamp secured by two bolts. Undo and remove the clamp bolts and lift the switch from the column. Separate its cable two part connector if you have not already done so.

3 It will be as well to try and not move the front wheels, or it may be tedious to re-engage the steering column lock which is part of the switch.

4 Refitting is simply the reversal of the removal procedures, but make sure that the new switch and steering column lock is operative before refitting the column covers.

23 Instrument panel and switch panel - removal and refitting

1 The instrument panel incorporating the speedometer, fuel and engine temperature indicators, warning lights and tachometer if fitted, can be removed separately from the facia and switch panel.

Instrument panel

2 Remove the negative earth connection from the car battery, and then from behind the instrument panel, undo the three wing-nuts which secure the panel to the dashboard (Fig. 10.19).

3 Next disconnect the speedometer cable (and tachometer cables) at the transmission end, and then pull the instrument panel from the facia panel.

4 Once the panel is away from the facia, separate the electrical connectors which serve the instruments on the panel. Identify the connectors and cables with label tags to ensure correct re-connection.

5 Lift the meter case from the car.

6 Refitting follows the reversal of the removal procedure.

Switch panel

7 This too can be removed separately from the facia panel. Begin by removing the upper and lower covers from the top of the steering column, then undo the two bolts securing the steering column assembly to the underside of the dashboard (Fig. 10.20). Support the top of the column, whilst the two bolts securing the column assembly at its base are undone and

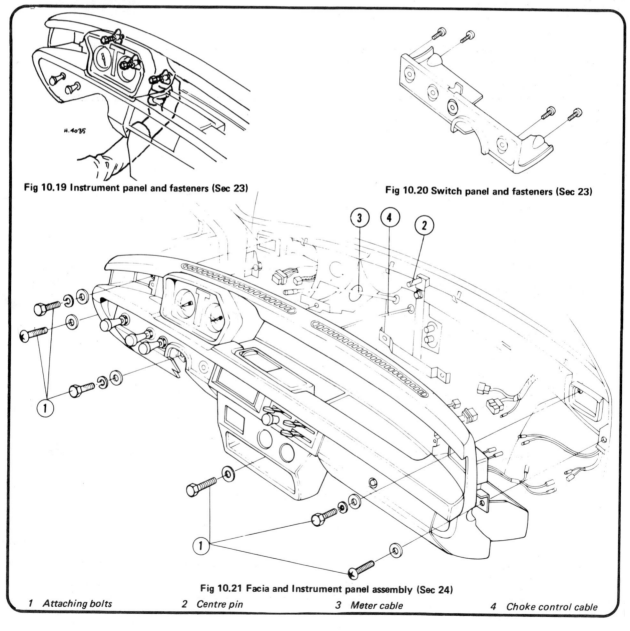

Fig 10.19 Instrument panel and fasteners (Sec 23)

Fig 10.20 Switch panel and fasteners (Sec 23)

Fig 10.21 Facia and Instrument panel assembly (Sec 24)

| 1   Attaching bolts | 2   Centre pin | 3   Meter cable | 4   Choke control cable |

removed. Once the steering column is free, lower it onto the floor and seat in the car.

8 Now that the rear of the switch panel is accessible, undo the four screws which secure the switch panel to the facia. Once the screws have been removed, the switch panel can be lifted from the facia.

9 Refitting as usual follows the reversal of the removal procedure.

24 Facia panel - removal and refitting

1 Begin by removing the steering column assembly and switch panel as detailed in the previous Section.
2 Remove the instrument panel as also detailed in the previous Section.
3 Now remove the heater fan switch connected from behind the heater control panel.
4 Disconnect the three heater control cables from the control levers on the heater.
5 Next undo and remove the screw on the outer edge of each fresh air inlet on the ends of the facia. Prise the vents from the facia.
6 Finally remove the six bolts which secure the panel to the dashboard. The whole panel can now be lifted from the car (Fig. 10.21).

Refitting
7 As usual this task follows the reversal of the removal procedure. The following points should be watched:

   i) *When refitting the facia, it should locate on the centre spigot in the middle of the dashboard. The spigot locates into a hole in the top centre of the rear side of the facia panel.*
   ii) *Tighten the securing bolts evenly working from the centre outwards.*
   iii) *Once installed check the operation of switches, levers and controls.*

25 Side and main light switch - In-situ testing, removal and refitting

1 In-situ testing involves separating the two part electrical connector serving the switch, and carrying out continuity checks (Section 3, of this Chapter) to investigate the functioning of the switch. Details of continuity requirements are given in the Specification at the beginning of this Chapter.
2 The switch is not repairable and therefore once found faulty should be renewed.
3 Remove the switch panel as detailed in Section 22, of this Chapter, and then remove the switch itself as follows:
4 Prise off the cover of the knob, then pinch the knob retaining the tabs together and pull the knob off (Fig. 10.22). Remove the switch.
5 Refitting follows the reversal of the removal procedure.

26 Headlights - removal and refitting

1 The headlights are sealed beam units, and are removed from the front of the car.
2 Begin by undoing and removing the two screws which retain the light retaining ring, then remove the ring.
3 Then remove the two adjusting screws and remove the mounting ring. Take care not to lose the springs.
4 Lastly remove the headlight housing once its three retaining screws have been undone and removed.
5 Once the headlight has been freed, lift it out from the front, and then separate the electrical connector serving the headlight.
6 As usual the refitting procedure is the reversal of removal except that the following tasks are necessary:

   i) *It is particularly essential that the join surfaces of the headlight assembly are clean on reassembly.*
   ii) *Ensure that the lens packing is in good condition and is correctly positioned on the mounting ring to prevent the ingress of water to the mounting.*

27 Headlights - alignment

1 Basic adjustments to headlight alignment may be made by turning the two spring loaded screws on the headlight mounting frame after removing the retaining ring (see previous Section).
2 During adjustment and alignment checks, the car should be loaded normally, that is with the usual amounts of petrol and luggage aboard. The tyres must be at their correct pressures. To be absolutely correct there should be a person in the driving seat and another in the passenger seat if two usually use the car.
3 Once the car is properly loaded, park it on level ground, some 33 ft or 10 metres from a vertical wall or screen.
4 Mark a horizontal line on the screen at a distance equal to the height of the headlight centre above the ground, minus 4 inches. Then mark two vertical lines which are directly in front of the headlights (Fig. 10.24).
5 Adjust the alignment of the headlights until the centre of the illumination of the main light beams are on the cross sections of the horizontal line and two vertical lines (Fig. 10.24).

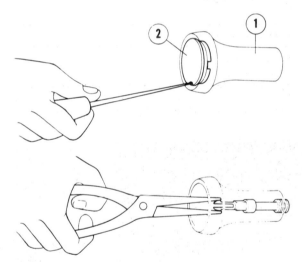

Fig 10.22 Removal of control knobs (Sec 25)

(above)   Removing mask plate (2)
(Below)   Squeezing clip to permit removal of knob (1)

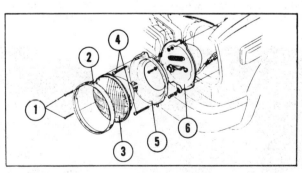

Fig 10.23 Headlight mounting components (Sec 26)

1 Retaining screw	*4 Adjusting screw*
2 Retaining ring	*5 Mounting ring*
3 Headlight	*6 Headlight housing*

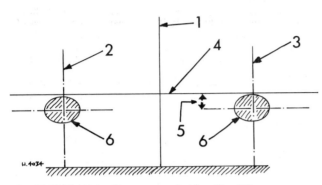

Fig 10.24 Headlight alignment - main beam (Sec 27)

1 *Centre line of vehicle*
2 *Centre line of left headlight*
3 *Centre line of right headlight*
4 *Line of adjustment and horizontal centre line of headlight*
5 *4 inches*
6 *Centre of main beam illumination*

6 The main/dipped lights are sealed and prefocused, therefore once the main beams are correctly aligned, the dipped beams will also be correctly aligned.

28 Front side/turn lights

1 The front lens can be removed after the two retaining screws have been undone. (photo)
2 The bulb may be removed and replaced once the lens is off.
3 If it is necessary to remove the light housing, the two retaining nuts accessed through the inspection holes beneath the bumper, need to be removed.
4 Lift the light unit from the bumper and separate the electrical connector which serves the light.
5 Installation follows the reversal of removal, but as always ensure that the electrical connections are clean and secure. Also ensure that the water seals are in good order and properly positioned.

29 Turn repeater lights

1 The front side repeater lights are retained by two nuts on the inside of the wheelarch. Once the nuts have been undone, remove the light assembly. (photo)
2 The lens and reflector can be removed once their retaining screws have been undone from the rear side of the light. Another two screws hold the reflector and lens together, once these have been removed, the bulb can be extracted.
3 Refitting follows the reversal of removal, but as usual ensure that all electrical connections are clean and secure. Also ensure that the interior of the light is clean and that seals are in good order and properly positioned on reassembly.
4 The rear side repeater lights are retained by two nuts on the inside of the bodyshell, but access to them depends on the model. On two door Civics the nuts are accessible from inside the luggage compartment. The three door (hatchback) Civics, the rear combination light will need to be completely removed, and the side repeater light nuts can be reached through the aperture which contains the rear combination lights. The dismantling and reassembly of the rear repeater light is the same as the front.

30 Rear combination lights

1 *2 door Civic:* Open the lid of the luggage compartment, then

28.1 Lens removal from front combination light

29.1 Lens removal from side turn repeater light

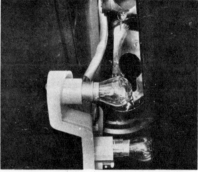

30.1A Rear combination light bulb holder removal

30.1B Rear combination light lens removal

31.1 Rear License number plate light dismantled

33.4 The main fuse revealed

remove the small access covers which reveal the rear of the combination lights. Then remove the two screws which retain the light socket assembly. Extract the socket and bulb. Inspect the bulb and renew if necessary. (photo) If it is desired to remove the light assembly from the car, the upper and lower retaining nuts will need to be undone. It should be noted that the lens and reflector cannot be separated. (photo)

3 door (Hatchback) Civic: Open the hatchback door and remove the rubber plugs immediately behind the rear lights. Then proceed as per the 2 door Civic.

31 License plate and reversing lights

1 The license number light assembly is secured by two nuts accessed from inside the luggage compartment. Once the light assembly has been removed, the cover, lens and base can be separated to expose the bulb. (photo)
  Inspect the bulb and replace if necessary. As usual ensure that all connections and parts are clean and in good order on reassembly.
2 The reversing light is secured to the rear bumper by a mounting nut. The lens can be removed separately for bulb replacement. As usual, ensure all parts are clean and serviceable on reassembly.

32 Interior lights

1 The lens pulls off the light base for bulb inspection and replacement.
2 The base is secured to the bodyshell by two nuts and there are electrical connectors behind the base.

33 Fuses

1 There is a fuse box fitted to the electrical system in the Civic, containing eight fuses.
2 Fuse failure can be identified by the simultaneous "failure" of several electrical systems in the car. The particular fuse can be identified by the systems it protects.
3 Never replace a fuse without finding the cause of the failure - and **never** fit a fuse of higher current capacity than specified for that position.
4 The main current (45 amp) supply fuse is located beside the battery, it is intended to give protection to the main power distribution cables. If this fuse fails, the task of checking the battery/alternator system must be entrusted to your nearest Honda agent. (photo)

34 Warning lights

1 *Oil pressure light:* If the oil pressure light remains on when the engine is running, check the pressure of the engine lubrication system. If the pressure is not to specification the engine will need dismantling to find the reason. If the pressure is to specification, the transducer and warning light circuit should be checked. If the light fails to come on when the ignition is switched on, the continuity of the oil pressure warning system circuit should be checked, and the bulb suspected.
2 *Battery charge light:* Refer to Section 8, of this Chapter which details the checks and tests on the battery warning system. This light should come on immediately the ignition is switched on; if it does not, check the bulb and the continuity of the warning circuit.
3 *Brake failure warning:* Again this light should come on immediately the ignition is switched on, but go off when the engine has started. If the light fails to come on, with the ignition, check the bulb and warning circuit continuity. If the bulb comes on when the engine is running, check the brake system first and then the sensor.
4 *Seat belt warning (where fitted):* Again this light should come on immediately the ignition is switched on, and go off when the seat belts are put on, or when the emergency (parking) brake is applied. On Hondamatic transmission cars the 'P' lock position can be selected instead of the parking brake. If the bulb fails to come on, when the ignition is switched on, or fails to go off when the seat belts are used, or the parking brake is applied, the continuity of the warning circuit, and the bulb and operation of the micro-switches should be checked.

35 Safety systems

  These circuits are straightforward and are included in this Chapter. The sensor switches and lights are arranged in simple logical arrangements, so that the warning lights only go out when the passengers are accommodated properly and the essential systems such as brakes are operational.
  Some sensors are therefore 'in parallel' and some 'in series' and complete the warning light circuit to earth.
  Examine the circuit diagrams given and check the continuity of the circuit wires, connections and devices, with the equipment and techniques described in Section 3, of this Chapter.

36 Radio installation

1 One fuse is available for a radio installation. On cars fitted with a radio when new, a 15 amp fuse is fitted with a 1 amp fuse adjacent to the radio.
2 The ignition system does have interference suppression devices fitted.
3 Again if a car is fitted with a radio when new, the aerial is accommodated in the front windscreen pillar.
4 The front facia panel is designed to accommodate a radio, and therefore it is worthwhile buying a radio to fit rather than alter the apertures.
5 The usual cause of trouble with radios is inadequate interference suppression.
6 Ensure that all HT leads are suppressed, and that the engine is properly earthed with a broad braid strap.
7 Extra interference may be identified by its frequency and accurance. Sometime the windscreen wiper motor needs to be suppressed.
8 It is also worthwhile ensuring that the vehicle is adequately earthed to prevent the build up of static over the bodyshell. A wire strand brush, fixed underneath the car to contact the road surface should earth the bodyshell.
9 A radio fitted to a vehicle which is not adequately earthed as a whole, will pick up random static noise from the vehicle.

37 Rear screen wiper and washer

1 Apply the same test procedures and checks as detailed in Section 16, of this Chapter.
2 The installation and design of the wiper and washer system is also similar to the front screen systems, and therefore the same dismantling and inspection procedures apply.

38 Rear window defroster

1 The rear window defroster uses the same fuse as the radio, and the circuit comprises a switch and warning light.
2 If the defroster is inoperative, check the continuity of the circuit wires and components using the equipment and techniques described in Section 3, of this Chapter.

39 Cigar lighter

This device uses the same fuse as the interior lights, and is operated by pressure on the lighter device.

If the lighter is inoperative, check the continuity of the circuit and device with the equipment and techniques described in Section 3, of this Chapter.

40 Hazard warning system

1   The system comprises a main switch and a heavy duty flasher unit. The switch de-activates the direction indicator system and stop light system, and couples the heavy duty flasher when operated.

2   The system can be used to simultaneously test all the bulbs and fixtures in the direction indicator and stop light system.

3   As usual the circuit is straightforward and the testing involves continuity checks of the wires and switches using the equipment and techniques described in Section 3, of this Chapter. The Specification at the beginning of this Chapter includes continuity details for the hazard warning switch.

41 Petrol level and engine temperature gauges

1   The gauges are essentially ammeters measuring the current flowing through the sender units. Each gauge incorporates its own voltage regulator so that it is immune for supply voltage variations.

2   If either gauge is suspected of giving incorrect readings, disconnect the connection to the appropriate sender unit and substitute a know resistance in its place.

3   A resistance of 30 ohms should give a 'normal' reading (95° to 100° C) on the temperature gauge, and the same resistance placed in the petrol gauge circuit should give a reading of 'half full'. See the Specification at the beginning of this Chapter.

4   The Specification at the beginning of this Chapter gives details of the sender unit characteristics.

5   Replace the gauges if they fail to give the correct readings appropriate to the resistances substituted.

6   Replace the sender units if the gauges give correct readings.

7   If the gauges fail to read at all, or read full scale, check the continuity of the circuits and devices using the equipment and techniques described in Section 3, of this Chapter.

Full scale readings are typical of a short to earth between the gauge and sender unit. No reading at all is typical of a break in the circuit.

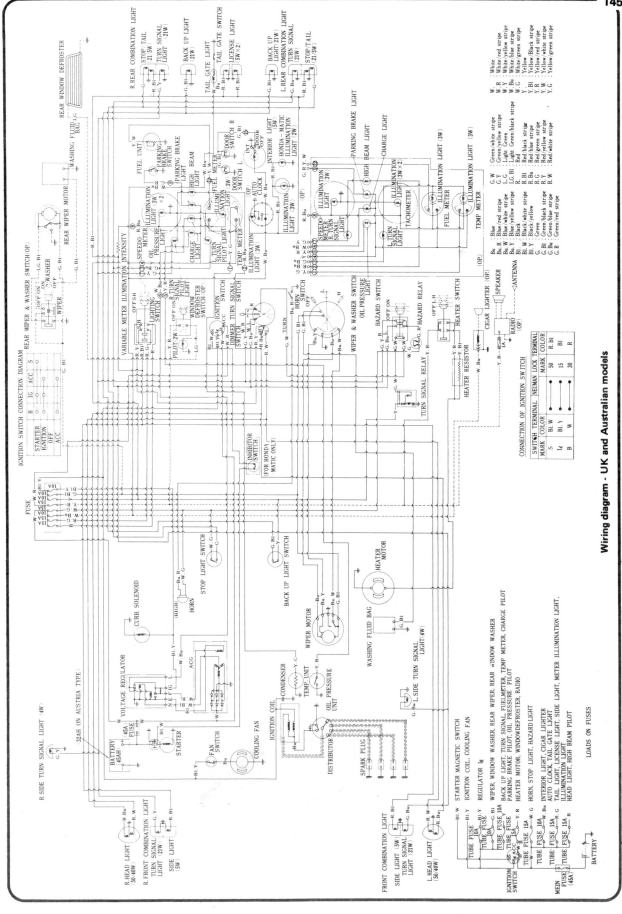

Wiring diagram - UK and Australian models

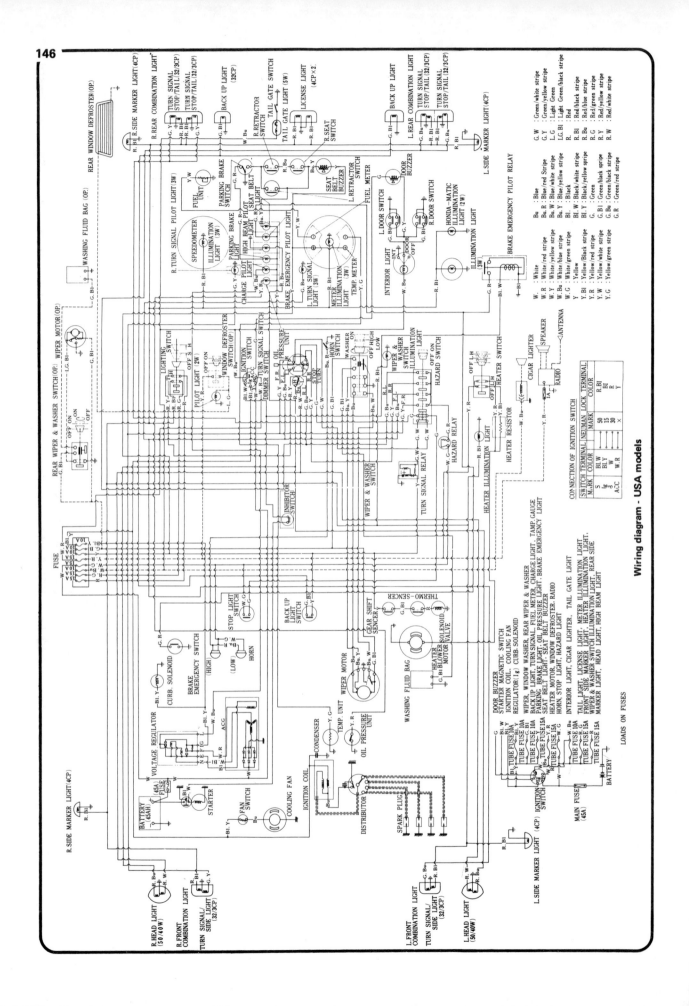

Wiring diagram - USA models

Chapter 11 Bodywork and fittings

Contents

Specifications

Torque wrench settings								kg f m	lb ft
Door striker ...	...	...	...	...	...	...	...	1.5 - 2.0	11 - 14
Door lock ...	...	...	...	...	...	...	...	0.4 - 0.7	3 - 5
Door inside cable ...	...	...	...	...	...	...	...	0.4 - 0.7	3 - 5
Front seat ...	...	...	...	...	...	...	...	1.9 - 2.5	14 - 18
Front seat belt ...	...	...	...	...	...	...	...	3.0 - 4.5	22 - 33
Seat belt anchor bolt ...	...	...	...	...	...	...		3.0 - 4.5	22 - 33
Front and rear bumpers ...	...	...	...	...	...	...		1.8 - 2.6	13 - 19
Heater assembly ...	...	...	...	...	...	...		1.8 - 2.6	13 - 19

1 General description

The vehicle structure for the Civic is a welded fabrication of many individual shaped panels to form a 'monocoque' bodyshell. Certain areas are strengthened locally to provide location for the suspension subframes and jacking points. The resultant structure is strong and rigid.

It is as well to remember that monocoque structures have no discreet load paths and all metal is stressed to an extent. It is essential therefore to maintain the whole bodyshell both top and underside, inside and outside, clean and corrosion free. Every effort should be made to keep the underside of the car as clear of mud and dirt accumulation as possible. If you were fortunate enough to acquire a new car, then it is advisable to have it rust proofed and undersealed at one of the specialist workshops who guarantee their work.

This Chapter describes the 'everyday' measures that can be taken to ensure that your car will look good and be structually safe to ride in for many years. It does not attempt to describe the methods of structural repair, such tasks have always and will remain, outside the scope of the average owner.

2 Maintenance - exterior

1 The general condition of a car's bodywork is the one thing that significantly affects its value. Maintenance is easy but needs to be regular and particular. Neglect - particularly after minor damage - can quickly lead to further deterioration and costly repair bills. It is important to keep watch on those parts of the bodywork not immediately visible, for example the underside, inside all the wheel arches and the lower part of the engine compartment.

2 The basic maintenance routine for the bodywork is washing; preferably with a lot of water from a hose. This will remove all the loose solids which may have stuck to the car. It is important to flush these off in such a way as to prevent grit from scratching the finish. The wheel arches and underbody need washing in the same way, to remove any accumulated mud which will retain moisture and tend to encourage rust. Paradoxically enough, the best time to clean the underbody and wheel arches is in the wet weather when the mud is thoroughly wet and soft. In very wet weather the underbody is usually cleaned of large accumulations automatically and this is a good time for inspection.

3 Periodically, it is a good idea to have the whole of the underside of the car steam cleaned, engine compartment included, so that a thorough inspection can be carried out to see what minor repairs and renovations are necessary. Steam cleaning is available at some garages and is necessary for removal of accumulation of oil grime which sometimes collects thickly in areas near the engine and gearbox. If steam facilities are not available there are one or two excellent grease solvents available which can be brush applied. The dirt can then be simply hosed off. Any sign of rust on the underside panels and chassis members must be attended to immediately. Thorough wire brushing followed by treatment with an anti-rust compound and underbody sealer will prevent continued deterioration. If not dealt with the car could eventually become structurally unsound and therefore unsafe.

4 After washing the paintwork wipe it off with a chamois leather to give a clear unspotted finish. A coat of clear wax polish will give added protection against chemical pollutants in

the air and will survive several subsequent washings. If the paint-work sheen has dulled or oxidised use a cleaner/polisher combination to restore the brilliance of the shine. This requires a little more effort but it is usually because regular washing has been neglected! Always check that door and drain holes and pipes are completely clear so that water can drain out. Brightwork should be treated the same way as paintwork. Windscreens and windows can be kept clear of smeary film which often appears if a little ammonia is added to the water. If glass work is scratched, a good rub with a proprietary metal polish will often clean it. Never use any form of wax or other paint/chromium polish on glass.

3 Maintenance - interior

The flooring cover (usually carpet) should be brushed or vacuum cleaned regularly to keep it free from grit. If badly stained, remove it from the car for scrubbing and sponging and make quite sure that it is dry before replacement. Seat and interior trim panels can be kept clean with a wipe over with a damp cloth. If they do become stained (which can be more apparent on light coloured upholstery), use a little liquid detergent and a soft nailbrush to scour the grime out of the grain of the material. Do not forget to keep the headlining clean in the same way as the upholstery. When using liquid cleaners inside the car do not over-wet the surface being cleaned. Excessive damp could get into the upholstery seams and padded interior, causing stains, offensive odours or even rot. If the inside of the car gets wet accidentally, it is worthwhile taking some trouble to dry it out properly. **Do not** leave oil or electric heaters inside the car for this purpose. If, when removing mats for cleaning, there are signs of damp underneath, all the interior of the car floor should be uncovered and the point of water entry found. It may only be a missing grommet, but it could be a rusted through floor panel and this demands immediate attention as described in the previous Section. More often than not, both sides of the panel will require treatment.

On cars fitted with the factory sunroof, avoid touching the interior canvas. Keep it clean and rectify all tears immediately. Consult your local Honda agent as to the most suitable type of repair depending on the material used. Keep the stays and fixings very lightly but frequently oiled, particularly at the front of the roof, and periodically release and roll back the roof so that it does not become too stiff and weak.

4 Minor bodywork damage - repair

The photograph sequences on pages 149, 150 and 151, illustrate the operations detailed in the following Sections.

Repair of minor scratches in the car's bodywork

If the scratch is very superficial, and does not penetrate to the metal of the bodywork, repair is very simple. Lightly rub the area of the scratch with a paintwork renovator (eg. T-Cut), or a very fine cutting paste, to remove loose paint from the scratch and to clear the surrounding bodywork of wax polish. Rinse the area with clean water.

Apply touch-up paint to the scratch using a thin paint brush, continue to apply thin layers of paint until the surface of the paint in the scratch is level with the surrounding paintwork. Allow the new paint at least two weeks to harden; then, blend it into the surrounding paintwork by rubbing the paintwork, in the scratch area with a paintwork renovator (eg. T-Cut), or a very fine cutting paste. Finally apply wax polish.

An alternative to painting over the scratch is to use Holts "Scratch-Patch". Use the same preparation for the affected area; then simply pick a patch of a suitable size to cover the scratch completely. Hold the patch against the scratch and burnish its backing paper; the patch will adhere to the paintwork, freeing itself from the backing paper at the same time. Polish the affected area to blend the patch into the surrounding paintwork. Where the scratch has penetrated right through to the metal of

the bodywork, causing the metal to rust, a different repair technique is required. Remove any loose rust from the bottom of the scratch with a penknife, then apply rust inhibiting paint (eg. Kurust) to prevent the formation of rust in the future. Using a rubber nylon applicator fill the scratch with bodystopper paste. If required, this paste can be mixed with cellulose thinners to provide a very thin paste which is ideal for filling narrow scratches. Before filling the stopper-paste in the scratch, wrap a piece of smooth cotton rag around the top of a finger. Dip the finger in cellulose thinners and then quickly sweep it across the surface of the stopper-paste in the scratch; this will ensure that the surface of the stopper-paste is slightly hollowed. The scratch can now be painted over as described earlier in this Section.

Repair of dents in the car's bodywork

When deep denting of the car's bodywork has taken place, the first task is to pull the dent out, until the affected bodywork almost attains its original shape. There is little point in trying to restore the original shape completely, as the metal in the damaged area will have stretched on impact and cannot be re-shaped fully to its original contour. It is better to bring the level of the dent up to a point which is about 1/8 inch (3 mm) below the level of the surrounding bodywork. In cases where the dent is very shallow anyway, it is not worth trying to pull it out at all.

If the underside of the dent is accessible, it can be hammered out gently from behind, using a mallet with a wooden or plastic head. Whilst doing this, hold a suitable block of wood firmly against the impact from the hammer blows and thus prevent a large area of bodywork from being 'belled-out'.

Should the dent be in a section of the bodywork which has a double skin or some other factor making it inaccessible from behind, a different technique is called for. Drill several small holes through the metal inside the dent area - particularly in the deeper sections. Then screw long self-tapping screws into the holes just sufficiently for them to gain a good purchase in the metal. Now the dent can be pulled out by pulling on the pro-truding heads of the screws with a pair of pliers.

The next stage of the repair is the removal of the paint from the damaged area, and from an inch or so of the surrounding 'sound' bodywork. This is accomplished more easily by using a wire brush or abrasive pad on a power drill, although it can be done just as effectively by hand using sheets of abrasive paper. To complete the preparations for filling, score the surface of the bare metal with a screwdriver or the tang of a file, or alternatively, drill small holes in the affected area. This will provide a really good 'key' for the filler paste.

To complete the repair see the Section on filling and re-spraying.

Repair of rust holes or gashes in the car's bodywork

Remove all paint from the affected area and from an inch or so of the surrounding 'sound' bodywork, using an abrasive pad or a wire brush on a power drill. If these are not available a few sheets of abrasive paper will do the job just as effectively. With the paint removed you will be able to gauge the severity of the corrosion and therefore decide whether to replace the whole panel (if this is possible) or to repair the affected area. Replacement body panels are not as expensive as most people think and it is often quicker and more satisfactory to fit a new panel than to attempt to repair large areas of corrosion.

Remove all fittings from the affected area except those which will act as a guide to the original shape of the damaged body-work (eg. headlamp shells etc.,). Then, using tin snips or a hack-saw blade, remove all loose metal and any other metal badly affected by corrosion. Hammer the edges of the hole inwards in order to create a slight depression for the filler paste.

Wire brush the affected area to remove the powdery rust from the surface of the remaining metal. Paint the affected area with rust inhibiting paint (eg. Kurust); if the back of the rusted area is accessible treat this also.

Before filling can take place it will be necessary to block the hole in some way. This can be achieved by the use of one of the

Typical example of rust damage to a body panel. Before starting ensure that you have all of the materials required to hand. The first task is to ...

... remove body fittings from the affected area, except those which can act as a guide to the original shape of the damaged bodywork - the headlamp shell in this case.

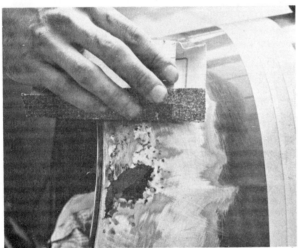

Remove all paint from the rusted area and from an inch or so of the adjoining 'sound' bodywork - use coarse abrasive paper or a power drill fitted with a wire brush or abrasive pad. Gently hammer in the edges of the hole to provide a hollow for the filler.

Before filling, the larger holes must be blocked off. Adhesive aluminium tape is one method; cut the tape to the required shape and size, peel off the backing strip (where used), position the tape over the hole and burnish to ensure adhesion.

Alternatively, zinc gauze can be used. Cut a piece of the gauze to the required shape and size; position it in the hole below the level of the surrounding bodywork; then ...

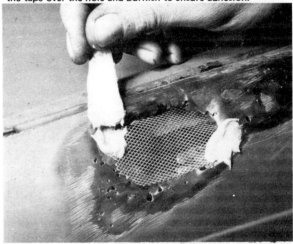

... secure in position by placing a few blobs of filler paste around its periphery. Alternatively, pop rivets or self-tapping screws can be used. Preparation for filling is now complete.

Mix filler and hardener according to manufacturer's instructions - avoid using too much hardener otherwise the filler will harden before you have a chance to work it

Apply the filler to the affected area with a flexible applicator - this will ensure a smooth finish. Apply thin layers of filler at 20 minute intervals, until the surface of the filler is just 'proud' of the surrounding bodywork. Then ...

... remove excess filler and start shaping with a Surform plane or a dreadnought file. Once an approximate contour has been obtained and the surface is relatively smooth, start using ...

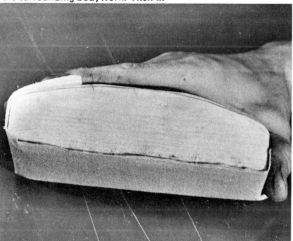

... abrasive paper. The paper should be wrapped around a flat wood, cork or rubber block - this will ensure that it imparts a smooth surface to the filler.

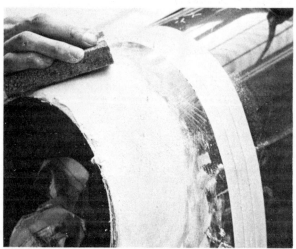

40 grit production paper is best to start with, then use progressively finer abrasive paper, finishing with 400 grade 'wet-and-dry'. When using 'wet-and-dry' paper, periodically rinse it in water ensuring also, that the work area is kept wet continuously.

Rubbing-down is complete when the surface of the filler is really smooth and flat, and the edges of the surrounding paintwork are finely 'feathered'. Wash the area thoroughly with clean water and allow to dry before commencing re-spray.

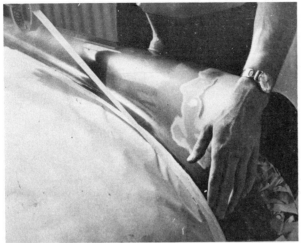

Firstly, mask off all adjoining panels and the fittings in the spray area. Ensure that the area to be sprayed is completely free of dust. Practice using an aerosol on a piece of waste metal sheet until the technique is mastered

Spray the affected area with primer - apply several thin coats rather than one thick one. Start spraying in the centre of the repair area and then work outwards using a circular motion - in this way the paint will be evenly distributed.

When the primer has dried inspect its surface for imperfections. Holes can be filled with filler paste or body-stopper, and lumps can be sanded smooth. Apply a further coat of primer, then 'flat' its surface with 400 grade 'wet-and-dry' paper.

Spray on the top coat, again building up the thickness with several thin coats of paint. Overspray onto the surrounding original paintwork to a depth of about five inches, applying a very thin coat at the outer edges.

Allow the new paint two weeks, at least, to harden fully, then blend it into the surrounding original paintwork with a paint restorative compound or very fine cutting paste. Use wax polish to finish off.

The finished job should look like this. Remember, the quality of the completed work is directly proportional to the amount of time and effort expended at each stage of the preparation.

following materials: Zinc gauze, Aluminium tape or Polyurethane foam.

Zinc gauze is probably the best material to use for a large hole. Cut a piece to the approximate size and shape of the hole to be filled, then position it in the hole so that its edges are below the level of the surrounding bodywork. It can be retained in position by several blobs of filler paste around its periphery.

Aluminium tape should be used for small or very narrow holes. Pull a piece off the roll and trim it to the approximate size and shape required, then pull off the backing paper (if used) and stick the tape over the hole; it can be overlapped if the thickness of one piece is insufficient. Burnish down the edges of the tape with the handle of a screwdriver or similar, to ensure that the tape is securely attached to the metal underneath.

Polyurethane foam is best used where the hole is situated in a section of bodywork of complex shape, backed by a small box section (eg; where the sill panel meets the rear wheel arch - most cars). The unusual mixing procedure for this foam is as follows: Put equal amounts of fluid from each of the two cans provided in the kit, into one container. Stir until the mixture begins to thicken, then quickly pour this mixture into the hole, and hold a piece of cardboard over the larger apertures. Almost immediately the polyurethane will begin to expand, gushing frantically out of any small holes left unblocked. When the foam hardens it can be cut back to just below the level of the surrounding bodywork with a hacksaw blade.

Bodywork repairs - filling and re-spraying

Before using this Section, see the Sections on dent, deep scratch, rust hole, and gash repairs.

Many types of bodyfiller are available, but generally speaking those proprietary kits which contain a tin of filler paste and a tube of resin hardener (eg. Holts Cataloy) are best for this type of repair. A wide, flexible plastic or nylon applicator will be found invaluable for imparting a smooth and well contoured finish to the surface of the filler.

Mix up a little filler on a clean piece of card or board - use the hardener sparingly (follow the maker's instructions on the packet) otherwise the filler will set very rapidly.

Using the applicator, apply the filler paste to the prepared area; draw the applicator across the surface of the filler to achieve the correct contour and to level the filler surface. As soon as a contour that approximates the correct one is achieved, stop working the paste - if you carry on too long the paste will become sticky and begin to 'pick-up' on the applicator. Continue to add thin layers of filler paste at twenty-minute intervals until the level of the filler is just 'proud' of the surrounding bodywork.

Once the filler has hardened, excess can be removed using a Surform plane or Dreadnought file. From then on, progressively finer grades of abrasive paper should be used, starting with a 40 grade production paper and finishing with 400 grade 'wet-and-dry' paper. Always wrap the abrasive paper around a flat rubber, fork, or wooden block - otherwise the surface of the filler will not be completely flat. During the smoothing of the filler surface the 'wet-and-dry' paper should be periodically rinsed in water. This will ensure that a very smooth finish is imparted to the filler at the final stage.

At this stage the 'dent' should be surrounded by a ring of bare metal, which in turn should be encircled by the finely 'feathered' edge of the good paintwork. Rinse the repair area with clean water, until all of the dust produced by the rubbing-down operation is gone.

Spray the whole repair area with a light coat of grey primer - this will show up any imperfections with fresh filler paste or bodystopper, and once more smooth the surface with abrasive paper. If bodystopper is used, it can be mixed with cellulose thinners to form a really thin paste which is ideal for filling small holes. Repeat this spray and repair procedure until you are satisfied that the surface of the filler, and the feathered edge of the paintwork are perfect. Clean the repair area with clean water and allow to dry fully.

The repair area is now ready for spraying. Paint spraying

must be carried out in a warm, dry, windless and dust free atmosphere. This condition can be created artificially if you have access to a large indoor working area, but if you are forced to work in the open, you will have to pick your day very carefully. If you are working indoors, dousing the floor in the work area with water will 'lay' the dust which would otherwise be in the atmosphere. If the repair area is confined to one body panel, mask off the surrounding panels; this will help to minimise the effects of a slight mis-match in paint colours. Bodywork fittings (eg; chrome strips, door handles etc.,) will also need to be masked off. Use genuine masking tape and several thicknesses of newspaper for the masking operation.

Before commencing to spray, agitate the aerosol can thoroughly, then spray a test area (an old tin, or similar) until the technique is mastered. Cover the repair area with a thick coat of primer; the thickness should be built up using several thin layers of paint rather than one thick one. Using 400 grade 'wet-and-dry' paper, rub down the surface of the primer until it is really smooth. While doing this, the work area should be thoroughly doused with water, and the 'wet-and-dry' paper periodically rinsed in water. Allow to dry before spraying on more paint.

Spray on the top coat, again building up the thickness by using several thin layers of paint. Start spraying in the centre of the repair area and then, using a circular motion, work outwards until the whole repair area and about 2 inches of the surrounding original paintwork is covered. Remove all masking material 10 to 15 minutes after spraying on the final coat of paint.

Allow the new paint at least 2 weeks to harden fully; then, using a paintwork renovator (eg. T-Cut), or a very fine cutting paste, blend the edges of the new paint into the existing paintwork. Finally, apply wax polish.

5 Major body damage - repair

1 Because the body is built on the monocoque principle, major damage must be repaired by a competent body repairer with the necessary jigs and equipment.
2 In the event of a crash that resulted in buckling of body panels, or damage to the roadwheels, the car must be taken to a Honda dealer or body repairer where the bodyshell and suspension alignment may be checked.
3 Bodyshell and/or suspension mis-alignment will cause excessive wear of the tyres, steering system and possibly transmission. The handling of the car also will be affected adversely.

6 Doors - tracing and silencing rattles

1 The most common cause of door rattles is a misaligned, loose or worn striker, but other causes may be:

a) Loose door handles, window winder handles and door hinges
b) Loose, worn or misaligned door lock components
c) Loose or worn remote control mechanism

2 It is quite possible for door rattles to be the result of a combination of these faults, so careful examination must be made to determine the cause of the noise.
3 If the leading edge of the striker loop is worn, and as a result the door rattles, renew it and adjust its position.
4 If the leading edge of the lock pawl is worn, and as a result the door rattles, fit a new door latch assembly.
5 Examine the hinge; it is quite possible that it has worn and causes rattles. Replace the hinge if necessary.

7 Interior handles and trim panel - removal and replacement

1 The doors are the usual pressed steel panel construction specially strengthened to resist sideways impact into the car.

They are retained to the bodyshell by two hinges which are bolted to the pillar. The exterior fittings are secured from the door interior; the interior handles clip onto the spindles which project through the trim from the respective mechanisms bolted to the door interior structure.

2 In order to gain access to any component attached to the door, it will be necessary to begin by removing the interior facing fittings and trim.

3 Make a note of the positions of the various handles on the interior face, so that they can be refitted in their original positions.

4 Depress the bezel around the window wind handle, then pull the wire clip retaining the handle on the splined end of the spindle, out of its slot. Use a length of piano wire fashioned to a hook at one end to pull out the clip. (photos)

5 The door pull handle is retained by two screws; the handle can be detached once the screws have been undone.

6 The door latch and lock handle trim is secured by another two screws. The handle assembly is attached to the door shell, and cannot be removed until the door trim has been detached from the shell. (photo)

7 To remove the trim panel, use a wide bladed screwdriver or similar, and insert it between the door and trim. Lever the trim away very carefully, to release the retaining clips from the door panel. (photo)

8 Refitting follows the reversal of the removal procedure.

8 Door exterior fittings - removal and refitting

1 All exterior fittings are secured in position by either nuts or clips. Remove the interior trim panel as detailed in the previous Section in order to gain access to the exterior handle and lock fasteners (Fig. 11.1).

2 The exterior door handle is secured by two nuts to the door shell. Undo and remove the nuts and recover the locking washers and facing washers. The handle is connected to the latch mechanism by a small link. Remove the clip which retains the link to the handle, and then remove the handle from the door.

3 The door lock is retained by a single spring steel clip. The clip registers in the door and in the lock case. The lock is connected to the latch by another link rod. A small circlip secures the rod to the lever on the end of the lock.

4 Replacement of those components follows the reversal of the removal procedure.

7.4A Removal of window wind handle clip

7.4B Window wind handle, clip and bezel

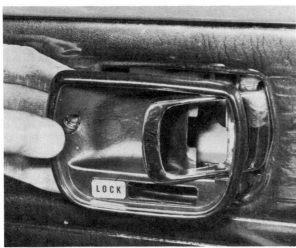
7.6 Door latch relay handle trim

7.7 Door trim panel removal

9 Door latches, door locks and window wind mechanism - removal and refitting

1 The interior trim and handles will need to be removed, as detailed in Section 7, in order to gain access to the interior mechanisms (Fig. 11.1).

2 *The door latch and lock relay handle* and linkage are retained to the door panel by two screws. Once the screws have been removed, undo and remove the relay cable clamps so that the handle mechanism can be lifted away from the door and the cables detached. (photo)

3 *The door latch and lock mechanism:* The latch mechanism is retained to the edge of the door by three screws. In order to gain full access to the mechanism, raise the door window fully and remove the bolt which secures the lower end of the rear window

guide; then raise the guide so that it lies beneath the raised window (Fig. 11.2). Finally remove the three screws which secure the mechanism to the door shell and lift the mechanism to enable its four operating links to be detached. It will be necessary to remove the link cable clamps to give enough freedom of movement to detach those links from the mechanism. (photo) The lock is retained by a single forked spring clip.

4 *Window wind mechanism and window glass:* (Fig. 11.3) Having already removed interior handles and trim panel proceed as follows to remove the wind mechanism and glass. Remove the weatherstrips which seal the gap between window and door interior. Both strips, inner and outer, are retained to the door panels by steel spring clips. Prise the clips upwards with a screwdriver to free the strip from the door. Take care not to damage the strip. Raise/lower the window so that the two bolts which secure the door glass regulator to the door glass holder strip

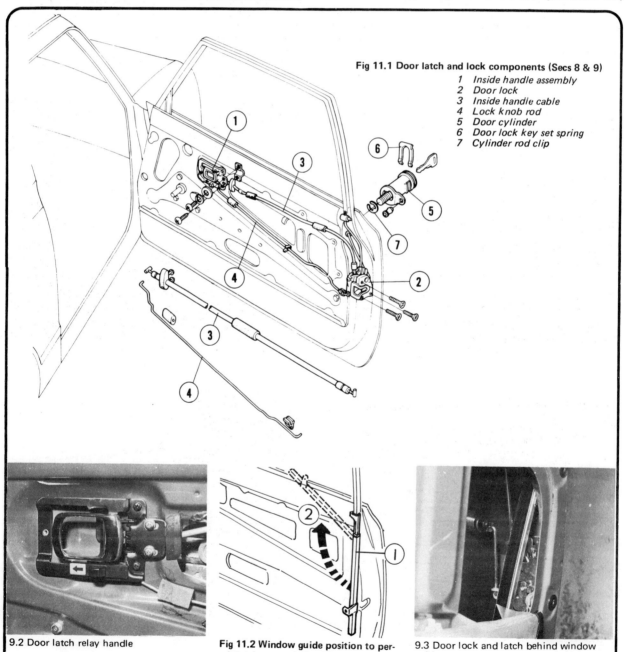

Fig 11.1 Door latch and lock components (Secs 8 & 9)

1 Inside handle assembly
2 Door lock
3 Inside handle cable
4 Lock knob rod
5 Door cylinder
6 Door lock key set spring
7 Cylinder rod clip

9.2 Door latch relay handle

Fig 11.2 Window guide position to permit latch removal (Sec 9)

9.3 Door lock and latch behind window guide

along the base of the glass, can be located. Undo and remove the two bolts. Lift the glass from the door. Once the glass has been removed, undo and remove the four bolts fastening the glass height regulator unit to the door frame. Then extract the regulator unit through the large central opening in the door panel.

5   As usual the replacement of the glass height regulator and window glass follows the reversal of the removal procedure. The following tasks are in addition:

i)   *Smear grease on the moving parts of the glass height regulator mechanism*

ii)   *Do not tighten the regulator/holder bolts fully, until the movement and alignment of the glass has been checked*

iii)   *As when the weatherstrips were being removed, take care not to damage the strips as they are installed.*

10 Doors - removal and replacement

1   The doors are bolted to the hinges mounted to the front pillar. Shims are fitted between the door and hinge to ensure proper positioning of the door in the door aperture.

2   To remove the door, support it on a jack when open, and undo the hinge bolts, beginning at the bottom.

3   When refitting the door, refit the old shims and check the alignment of the door in the aperture and relative to the striker.

4   Use the shims to carry out basic adjustments to the door's position.

5   Adjust the striker position finally to ensure smooth movement of the door and engagement of the latch.

11 Door striker plate and latch - positioning, removal and replacement

1   The door catch is retained by countersunk screws to the door aperture pillar. The latch should engage the striker so that the outer door surface is flush with the exterior surface of the car, and there is no in/out movement of the door.

2   If any movement or sloppiness is felt in the latch/striker engagement, inspect both latch and striker. Replace either if wear is seen.

3   Removal and refitting of the latch mechanism has been described in Section 9. The striker is retained by screws and removal/refitting is quite straightforward.

4   The latch position is not adjustable, but the striker can be moved when its retaining screws are loosened (Fig. 11.4).

5   The door latch and striker operate in a hrash environment, and the lubricants used should withstand water and high surface impact loads. A number of water repellent oil sprays are available and are well suited for this task.

12 Front grille, engine hood and latch - removal and replacement

1   The hood hinges are bolted to the frame across the front of the engine compartment. It is necessary to remove the grille trim to gain access to the hinge bolts and the turn/side light housings to permit removal of the grille. The grille is removed by undoing the two screws retaining the bottom strip of trim; remove the strip. Then undo and remove the screws which secure the centre section of the grille to the bodyshell. There is one screw midway along the base of the grille, and three screws along the

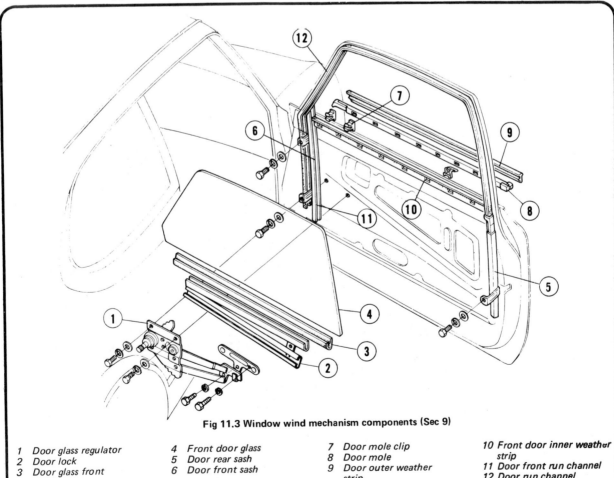

Fig 11.3 Window wind mechanism components (Sec 9)

1 *Door glass regulator*	4 *Front door glass*	7 *Door mole clip*	10 *Front door inner weather strip*
2 *Door lock*	5 *Door rear sash*	8 *Door mole*	11 *Door front run channel*
3 *Door glass front cushion*	6 *Door front sash*	9 *Door outer weather strip*	12 *Door run channel*

top of the grille. Finally remove the two screws which retain the headlight trims in position. Remove the trims (Fig. 11.5).

2 Once the grille has been removed, undo and remove the hinge bolts and prepare to lift the hood.

3 It is preferable to lift the hood with the aid of at least one person; it is large and can easily be damaged.

4 Remember to detach the windscreen wash jet pipe.

Hood latch

5 The latch is retained to the rear engine compartment bulkhead by three screws. A cable assembly connects the latch to the release lever in the car. Grease should be smeared into the latch fairly regularly (Fig. 11.6).

6 Refitting the hood follows the reversal of the removal procedure. The striker position is adjustable if it is necessary to alter the engagement of striker and latch. The hood should be secure and there should be no up/down or side/side movement of the rear of the hood.

13 Luggage compartment - bonnet and latch (2 door Civic)

1 Separate the vehicle number plate light connection, and then undo and remove the screws which secure the bonnet hinges to the bodyshell.

2 Finally separate the bonnet stay from the bonnet before

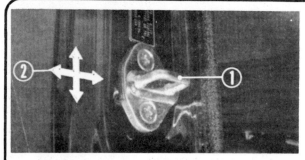

Fig 11.4 Door striker adjustment (Sec 11)

1   Striker   2   Adjustments

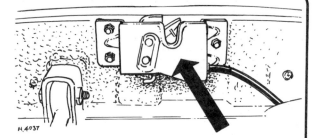

Fig 11.6 Engine compartment latch (Sec 12)

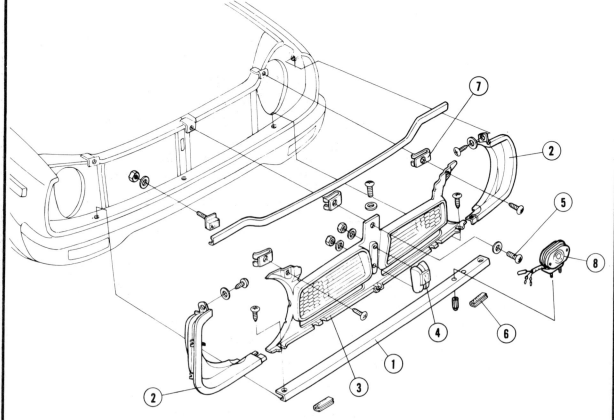

Fig 11.5 Front grille components (Sec 12)

1 Front grille lower moulding	3 Front grille	5 Front grille attaching screw	7 Clip nut
2 Head light garnishes	4 Front grille emblem	6 Rubber patch	8 Turn signal light

lifting the bonnet clear.

3   Inspect the seal rubbers and replace as necessary.

4   The latch lock is retained by a spring plate, and the latch by screws to the bonnet frame. The striker position is adjustable, to allow the engagement of the latch and striker to be connected (as per Hatchback door).

5   As with the door latch and striker, use water repellent spray lubricant on the latch and striker members.

14 Hatchback door (3 door Civic)

1   With the hatchback door open, remove the lining from near the door aperture to reveal hinge bolts to the body (Fig. 11.7).

2   Then detach both door stays from the door. It is wise from this point on to enlist the aid of at least one person. The door can easily be damaged.

3   Finally undo and remove the bolts securing the door hinges to the bodyshell, and then straighten the clips which retain the electrical harness to the door. Remove the harness and separate the connectors so that the hatchback door can be lifted from the car.

4   Refitting follows the reversal of the removal procedure. The door position can be altered when the hinge bolts are loosened. The engagement of latch and striker can be adjusted when their mounting bolts are slackened.

5   As with the two door Civic bonnet the lock cylinder is retained by a single spring plate, and the latch is a separate assembly bolted to the hatchback frame.

15 Windscreens - removal and refitting

1   The windscreens are held in rubber mouldings which are 'locked' by the trim moulding in the outer side of the rubber (Fig. 11.8).

2   Removal of the windscreens proceeds as follows: begin by carefully extracting the bright trim moulding from the windscreen seal. The ends of the trim can be exposed by moving the moulding joint covers to one side.

3   Once the 'locking trim' has been removed, enlist the help of at least one person, then with one person inside the car and one outside, very carefully push the windscreen outwards from its aperture beginning at either top corner of the screen.

4   The rubber moulding around the screen should deform to allow the screen to move outwards once the 'locking trim' has been removed.

5   Refitting - Check that the rubber moulding is in good condition, and that no cracks or surface deterioration can be found.

6   Fit the rubber moulding around the screen, and then insert a length of string 3 to 4 mm diameter, into the major slot on the periphery of the seal. Pass it totally around the seal, and exit it with about 5 inches of overlap and 8 inches hanging near one of the bottom corners.

7   Position the glass and seal into the window aperture from the outside with the string hanging into the car interior. Again enlist the help of at least one person and press the screen into the aperture.

8   Press the screen at the point where the strings exit the moulding, then pull the strings to bring the lip of the moulding around the edge of the window aperture. Continue to apply pressure to the screen near to the moving exit of the strip as it is pulled slowly and smoothly from the seal.

9   Once the string has been pulled out of the seal, check that the seal is properly fitted on both sides of the window aperture.

10 Now that the rubber seal and screen glass are in place, 'lock' the seal by pressing the bright trim moulding into the outside of the seal. Lubricate the seal with soap solution to ease the insertion of the trim. A special tool, which can be improvised is necessary to lift the seal rubber lips over each side of the bright trim.

16 Roof lining, facia and central console - removal and refitting

The trim fitted both internally and externally is a very simple construction. Its removal is obvious in each case, and if a screw is not visible the trim is push on.

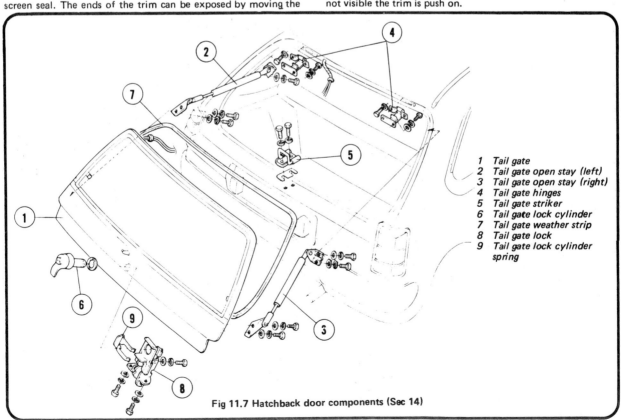

1   Tail gate
2   Tail gate open stay (left)
3   Tail gate open stay (right)
4   Tail gate hinges
5   Tail gate striker
6   Tail gate lock cylinder
7   Tail gate weather strip
8   Tail gate lock
9   Tail gate lock cylinder spring

Fig 11.7 Hatchback door components (Sec 14)

The roof lining is retained by clips and the interior light screws.

Facia: the removal of the instrument panel and facia has been detailed in Chapter 10 of this manual in connection with repair tasks on switches and electrical systems mounted on the facia.

Central console: the removal of the central console has been detailed in Chapter 6 in connection with repair tasks associated with the gear shift mechanisms.

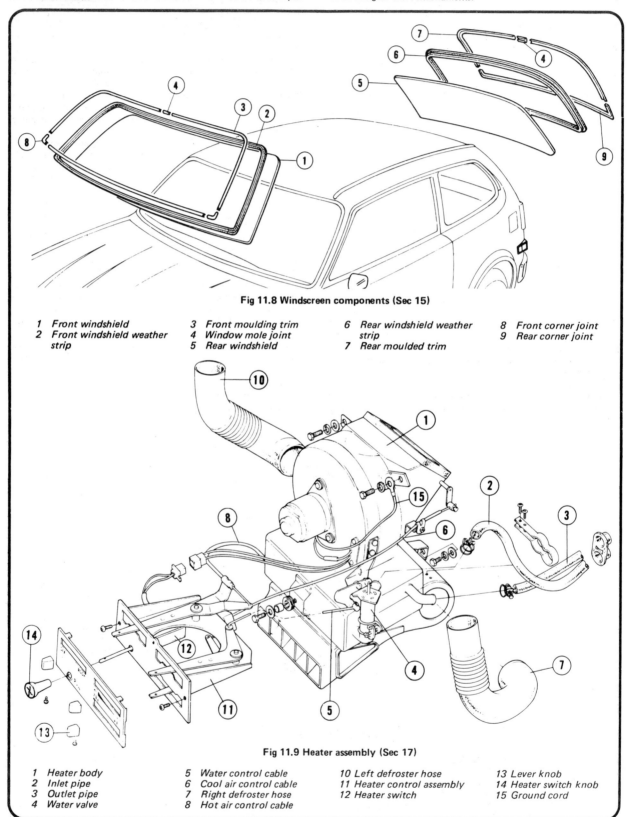

Fig 11.8 Windscreen components (Sec 15)

1 Front windshield	3 Front moulding trim	6 Rear windshield weather strip	8 Front corner joint
2 Front windshield weather strip	4 Window mole joint	7 Rear moulded trim	9 Rear corner joint
	5 Rear windshield		

Fig 11.9 Heater assembly (Sec 17)

1 Heater body	5 Water control cable	10 Left defroster hose	13 Lever knob
2 Inlet pipe	6 Cool air control cable	11 Heater control assembly	14 Heater switch knob
3 Outlet pipe	7 Right defroster hose	12 Heater switch	15 Ground cord
4 Water valve	8 Hot air control cable		

Fig 11.10 Front jacking point (Sec 18)

1   Jack   3   Front skirt
2   Jack point

Fig 11.11 Rear jacking point (Sec 18)

1   Jack point   2   Jack

Fig 11.12 Front chassis stand point (Sec 18)

1   Chassis stand
2   Front sill - strengthened point

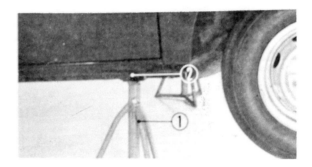

Fig 11.13 Rear chassis stand point (Sec 18)

1   Chassis stand
2   Rear sill - strengthened point

17 Heater - removal and refitting

1   The heater motor is not repairable and forms part of the
heater/fan assembly. If the motor is inoperative refer to Chapter
10 and the electrical circuit diagrams, and carry out continuity
checks on the electrical circuit associated with the heater motor.
If the motor is reckoned to be at fault the heater assembly will
need to be removed to gain access to the motor (Fig. 11.9).
2   If the motor works but only a small amount of air seems to
be moving, check the mechanical control systems on the heater
assembly and again it is preferable to remove the heater in order
to complete a thorough examination.
3   Removal of the heater assembly proceeds as follows:
4   Drain the coolant as detailed in Chapter 2. It will give more
space for work if the facia panel is temporarily removed as
detailed in Chapter 10.
5   Detach the screen defroster hoses from the heater.
6   Pull the carpets away and put dry rags beneath the heater to
catch coolant when the inlet and outlet hoses are detached from
the heater. The coolant will corrode paintwork and stain carpet.
7   Detach the Fre-Rec control cable from the heater, then the
temperature control rod, room/def. control cable, and fan motor
switch connector.
8   All that remains now is the removal of the upper and lower
attachment bolts and the lower support bracket.
9   Remove the heater assembly.
10 Check the availability of spares before attempting any repair
work on the assembly. It is normally replaced as a whole unit if
any part is faulty.
11 The heater control panel comprises a legend plate, and a
control lever and switch assembly mounted directly on the facia.

12 Undo the lever and switch knob retaining screws and pull off
the knobs. Then gently prise the legend plate off the facia with a
broad screwdriver.
13 The lever and switch assembly is retained on the facia by four
screws, and once they have been undone, the control assembly
can be removed.
14 Refitting heater assembly: This task follows the reversal of
the removal procedure, but add the following work:
15 Remember to connect the motor earth wire to the right-hand
side mounting bolt.
16 Check that all connections are secure and that the hoses are
positioned correctly and not strained and distorted.
17 Check the operation of the mechanical air and coolant flow
controls.
18 After refilling the cooling system, bleed the engine cooling
system as directed in Chapter 3, Section 4, of this manual.

18 Vehicle strong points - jacking and support

The bodyshell has been strengthened locally to provide
points for jacking and support whilst work is being carried out
beneath the car.
Be sure to use the correct and appropriate support points for
jacks and chassis stands or else your safety beneath the car will
be endangered. See the following illustrations:

Front jacking point (Fig. 11.10).
Rear jacking point (Fig. 11.11).
Front chassis stand position (Fig. 11.12).
Rear chassis stand position (Fig. 11.13).

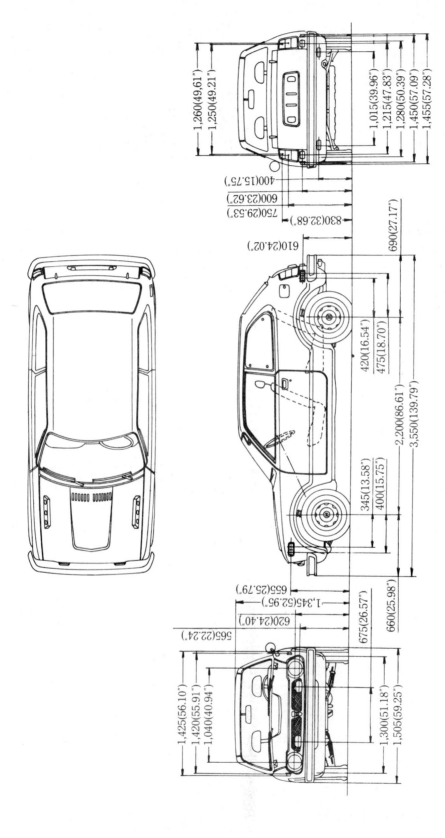

Fig 11.14 Major dimensions of the HONDA CIVIC

Metric conversion tables

Inches	Decimals	Millimetres	Millimetres to Inches		Inches to Millimetres	
			mm	Inches	Inches	mm
1/64	0.015625	0.3969	0.01	0.00039	0.001	0.0254
1/32	0.03125	0.7937	0.02	0.00079	0.002	0.0508
3/64	0.046875	1.1906	0.03	0.00118	0.003	0.0762
1/16	0.0625	1.5875	0.04	0.00157	0.004	0.1016
5/64	0.078125	1.9844	0.05	0.00197	0.005	0.1270
3/32	0.09375	2.3812	0.06	0.00236	0.006	0.1524
7/64	0.109375	2.7781	0.07	0.00276	0.007	0.1778
1/8	0.125	3.1750	0.08	0.00315	0.008	0.2032
9/64	0.140625	3.5719	0.09	0.00354	0.009	0.2286
5/32	0.15625	3.9687	0.1	0.00394	0.01	0.254
11/64	0.171875	4.3656	0.2	0.00787	0.02	0.508
3/16	0.1875	4.7625	0.3	0.01181	0.03	0.762
13/64	0.203125	5.1594	0.4	0.01575	0.04	1.016
7/32	0.21875	5.5562	0.5	0.01969	0.05	1.270
15/64	0.234375	5.9531	0.6	0.02362	0.06	1.524
1/4	0.25	6.3500	0.7	0.02756	0.07	1.778
17/64	0.265625	6.7469	0.8	0.03150	0.08	2.032
9/32	0.28125	7.1437	0.9	0.03543	0.09	2.286
19/64	0.296875	7.5406	1	0.03937	0.1	2.54
5, 16	0.3125	7.9375	2	0.07874	0.2	5.08
21/64	0.328125	8.3344	3	0.11811	0.3	7.62
11/32	0.34375	8.7312	4	0.15748	0.4	10.16
23/64	0.359375	9.1281	5	0.19685	0.5	12.70
3/8	0.375	9.5250	6	0.23622	0.6	15.24
25/64	0.390625	9.9219	7	0.27559	0.7	17.78
13/32	0.40625	10.3187	8	0.31496	0.8	20.32
27/64	0.421875	10.7156	9	0.35433	0.9	22.86
7/16	0.4375	11.1125	10	0.39370	1	25.4
29/64	0.453125	11.5094	11	0.43307	2	50.8
15/32	.46875	11.9062	12	0.47244	3	76.2
31/64	0.484375	12.3031	13	0.51181	4	101.6
1/2	0.5	12.7000	14	0.55118	5	127.0
33/64	0.515625	13.0969	15	0.59055	6	152.4
17/32	0.53125	13.4937	16	0.62992	7	177.8
35/64	0.546875	13.8906	17	0.66929	8	203.2
9/16	0.5625	14.2875	18	0.70866	9	228.6
37/64	0.578125	14.6844	19	0.74803	10	254.0
19/32	0.59375	15.0812	20	0.78740	11	279.4
39/64	0.609375	15.4781	21	0.82677	12	304.8
5/8	0.625	15.8750	22	0.86614	13	330.2
41/64	0.640625	16.2719	23	0.90551	14	355.6
21/32	0.65625	16.6687	24	0.94488	15	381.0
43/64	0.671875	17.0656	25	0.98425	16	406.4
11/16	0.6875	17.4625	26	1.02362	17	431.8
45/64	0.703125	17.8594	27	1.06299	18	457.2
23/32	0.71875	18.2562	28	1.10236	19	482.6
47/64	0.734375	18.6531	29	1.14173	20	508.0
3/4	0.75	19.0500	30	1.18110	21	533.4
49/64	0.765625	19.4469	31	1.22047	22	558.8
25/32	0.78125	19.8437	32	1.25984	23	584.2
51/64	0.796875	20.2406	33	1.29921	24	609.6
13/16	0.8125	20.6375	34	1.33858	25	635.0
53/64	0.828125	21.0344	35	1.37795	26	660.4
27/32	0.84375	21.4312	36	1.41732	27	685.8
55/64	0.859375	21.8281	37	1.4567	28	711.2
7/8	0.875	22.2250	38	1.4961	29	736.6
57/64	0.890625	22.6219	39	1.5354	30	762.0
29/32	0.90625	23.0187	40	1.5748	31	787.4
59/64	0.921875	23.4156	41	1.6142	32	812.8
15/16	0.9375	23.8125	42	1.6535	33	838.2
61/64	0.953125	24.2094	43	1.6929	34	863.6
31/32	0.96875	24.6062	44	1.7323	35	889.0
63/64	0.984375	25.0031	45	1.7717	36	914.4

1   Imperial gallon = 8 Imp pints = 1.16 US gallons = 277.42 cu in = 4.5459 litres

1   US gallon = 4 US quarts = 0.862 Imp gallon = 231 cu in = 3.785 litres

1   Litre = 0.2199 Imp gallon = 0.2642 US gallon = 61.0253 cu in = 1000 cc

Miles to Kilometres		Kilometres to Miles	
1	1.61	1	0.62
2	3.22	2	1.24
3	4.83	3	1.86
4	6.44	4	2.49
5	8.05	5	3.11
6	9.66	6	3.73
7	11.27	7	4.35
8	12.88	8	4.97
9	14.48	9	5.59
10	16.09	10	6.21
20	32.19	20	12.43
30	48.28	30	18.64
40	64.37	40	24.85
50	80.47	50	31.07
60	96.56	60	37.28
70	112.65	70	43.50
80	128.75	80	49.71
90	144.84	90	55.92
100	160.93	100	62.14

lb f ft to Kg f m		Kg f m to lb f ft		lb f/in^2 : Kg f/cm^2		Kg f/cm^2 : lb f/in^2	
1	0.138	1	7.233	1	0.07	1	14.22
2	0.276	2	14.466	2	0.14	2	28.50
3	0.414	3	21.699	3	0.21	3	42.67
4	0.553	4	28.932	4	0.28	4	56.89
5	0.691	5	36.165	5	0.35	5	71.12
6	0.829	6	43.398	6	0.42	6	85.34
7	0.967	7	50.631	7	0.49	7	99.56
8	1.106	8	57.864	8	0.56	8	113.79
9	1.244	9	65.097	9	0.63	9	128.00
10	1.382	10	72.330	10	0.70	10	142.23
20	2.765	20	144.660	20	1.41	20	284.47
30	4.147	30	216.990	30	2.11	30	426.70

List of illustrations

Index

Printed by
J. H. HAYNES & Co. Ltd
Sparkford Yeovil Somerset
ENGLAND